Barriers and Belonging

BARRIERS
AND BELONGING

Personal Narratives of Disability

Edited by

Michelle Jarman, Leila Monaghan,

and Alison Quaggin Harkin

TEMPLE UNIVERSITY PRESS
Philadelphia • *Rome* • *Tokyo*

TEMPLE UNIVERSITY PRESS
Philadelphia, Pennsylvania 19122
www.temple.edu/tempress

*DISCLAIMER: The views and opinions expressed herein are those of the authors
and do not necessarily reflect the views of Temple University Press or Temple
University.*

Library of Congress Cataloging-in-Publication Data

Names: Jarman, Michelle, 1966– editor. | Monaghan, Leila Frances, 1960–
    editor. | Quaggin Harkin, Alison, 1958– editor.
Title: Barriers and belonging : personal narratives of disability / edited by
    Michelle Jarman, Leila Monaghan, and Alison Quaggin Harkin
Description: Philadelphia : Temple University Press, [2016] | Includes
    bibliographical references and index.
Identifiers: LCCN 2016018611| ISBN 9781439913871 (cloth : alk. paper) |
    ISBN 9781439913888 (paper : alk. paper) | ISBN 9781439913895 (e-book)
Subjects: LCSH: Sociology of disability. | People with disabilities. | Disabilities.
Classification: LCC HV1568 .B36 2016 | DDC 305.9/080922—dc23 LC record
    available at https://lccn.loc.gov/2016018611

9 8 7 6 5 4 3 2 1

Contents

       / Michael T. Salter   163

IV.6   Brother and Sister in Arms / Rachel Anderson   169

PART V   IDENTITY, RESISTANCE, AND COMMUNITY

 V.1   Disability, Belonging, Pride / Allegra Heath-Stout   179

 V.2   Deconstructing "Accessible" Education in Academia
       / Nancy La Monica   185

 V.3   Fake It until You Make It (or until You Find Your Place)
       / Megan L. Coggins   195

 V.4   My Anxiety / Susan Macri   201

 V.5   Disability, the Lure of Escapism, and Making
       the Invisible Visible / Suzanne Walker   208

 V.6   Discovering My Deaf Identity / Denton Mallas   214

PART VI   THEORIES AND LIVES

VI.1   Taking Great Pains with Disability Theory
       / Adena Rottenstein   225

VI.2   Medicating My Socially Constructed Disability
       / Cindee Calton   229

VI.3   Flourishing with Polio: A Spiritual, Transformational,
       and Disability Studies Perspective
       / Rodney B. Hume-Dawson   237

VI.4   Learning to See Myself in the Mirror / Adam P. Newman   245

VI.5   Writing Myself into Madness and Disability Studies
       / Rebekah Moras   252

VI.6   Autism Isn't Speaking: Autistic Subversion in Media
       and Public Policy / Lydia X. Z. Brown   258

       Afterword: Negotiating the Future / Leila Monaghan   275

       Index   279

Acknowledgments

We thank all the *Barriers and Belonging* authors for their creative and insightful contributions and for so generously sharing their experiences with us and with readers. We have enjoyed working together and acknowledge the diligent and collaborative effort that brought this collection to fruition. In addition, Michelle Jarman thanks her disability activist friends and committed colleagues who have taught her so much about the field of disability studies and living creatively. She deeply appreciates the love and support of her entire extended family, with special thanks to her spouse, Paul Bergstraesser, for always being in her camp, and to their son, William, for his compassionate heart and for reminding her to play. Leila Monaghan thanks her Deaf friends and colleagues, who introduced her to the rich world of Deaf culture; all the medical staff, family, and friends who helped her survive 2015; and particularly her partner, Bob McGovern, who has created a home with her in beautiful Wyoming. Alison Quaggin Harkin thanks her children, Caroline Harkin, a University of Wyoming disability studies graduate, for her commitment to disability issues and advocacy; James Harkin, for his understanding of social justice; and William Harkin, who helped her find her way to disability studies and continues to make scholarly work meaningful.

Introduction

Entering the Field

MICHELLE JARMAN AND
LEILA MONAGHAN

I want to express my heartfelt gratitude to all of the people who have fought to construct a campus and community that are physically and socially accessible to people with all types of disabilities, even in the face of statewide budget cuts. My deepest appreciation goes to the [University of California at Berkeley] students who were at the helm of the Disability Rights Movement in the 1960s. They sparked a campus mentality of inclusion and equal rights for all, based on the premise that a university ought to value all of its students.

As this quotation from Chapter I.1, by Alyse Ritvo, reflects, over the last fifty years, people with disabilities have sparked a revolution, fighting for and winning rights to education and access in the United States and around the world. In tandem with the success of disability rights movements and activism, the international academic field of disability studies has grown and flourished. In North America, almost forty postsecondary institutions have formal disability studies undergraduate and graduate programs.[1] These numbers, while impressive, do not adequately represent the increasing importance of disability studies in postsecondary education. The field focuses on social, cultural, and political aspects of disability and contributes to and draws from a wide range of disciplines, including anthropology, social sciences, social work, psychology, international studies, gender studies, cultural theory, ethnic studies, literature, education, law and policy studies, and the arts. Despite the breadth of the field, there are few introductory works available. We hope this collection of narratives, many of them from students, will fill some of this gap.

As an umbrella term, **disability** is meant to encompass a broad range of physical, sensory, psychological, and cognitive capacities and variations. Its parameters are fluid, changing, and expanding. Disability has become, for many, a category of personal identity; for others, the term is fraught—identification with disability is partial, contingent, and even contested. In popular usage and through legal, policy, and biomedical definitions, disability links individuals and groups with differing and conflicting ideas about what disability means, both individually and within larger structures. The differences between competing approaches to disability correspond in many ways to the distinctions between deafness and Deaf culture; in this rubric, deafness refers to a hearing impairment and diagnostic category, whereas Deaf culture designates a cultural-linguistic affiliation and identity. Culturally Deaf people often distinguish between their own social position as a linguistic minority and that of other people with disabilities. Notably, in this context, Deaf does not equal disability. While Deaf and deaf activists worked alongside disabled activists in support of the Americans with Disabilities Act in the United States, and while they benefit from its protections, for many in Deaf communities, disability does not describe their collective experience or personal self-concept. At the same time, these are not hard and fast divisions. In recent years, rich scholarship bridging and clarifying distinctions between disability and Deaf studies has emerged (Brueggemann 2009; Burch and Kafer 2010; Krentz 2007). In fact, Deaf culture has provided a powerful context for imagining disability in distinctly cultural frameworks. As Denton Mallas puts it in Chapter V.6, "I've learned to announce my identity as Deaf, not in a pathological way but in a cultural-linguistic way. I am no longer afraid to say, 'Yes, I'm Deaf, and I sign.'"

Disabilities and the Classroom

The twenty-fifth anniversary of the Americans with Disabilities Act (ADA) in the United States was marked in 2015 with celebration and frustration, and the narratives included in this book reflect both the changing landscape of possibility as well as the enduring limited perceptions about disability. These tensions are reflected within college classrooms: while many students begin college with an ethic of respect for people with disabilities and some familiarity with disability rights and inclusion, few have critical tools for understanding the sociopolitical dimensions of disability. As Joshua St. Pierre points out in Chapter III.1, deficit-based medical and rehabilitation approaches prevail and often produce the unintended consequences of instilling negative self-perceptions in people: "Studying disability theory was revolutionary for me, as it helped me understand that disability as an individual, biological 'malfunction'—the medical model—is only one reading of disability, and a poor one at that." St. Pierre's disability, stuttering, had been addressed by doctors and speech therapists as a problem to be fixed. In college, however, disability studies perspectives liberated him to think of it as something beyond "malfunction." Many students echo St. Pierre's sentiment—that disability studies provides a revolutionary reorientation to disability that is personally empowering and intellectually invigorating.

In our undergraduate classrooms and others across the United States and Canada, students demonstrate an interesting and fairly consistent range of perspectives about disability. In a representative introductory course, as students begin discussing what they think about disability, a few students may immediately situate disability in a sociocultural context, articulating advocacy or activist perspectives. These students usually have disabilities or have important relationships with disabled people. Other students, many of them preprofessionals planning to work in special education, rehabilitation, or the health or service fields, talk about wanting to "help" people with disabilities—an approach that is advocacy-minded but commonly informed by pity or ableist assumptions that situate disability as dependency or deficit. Many such students, sincere and self-reflective, can be quick to reorient their thinking toward disability, rights, and access. Still another group of students are skeptical of the social context of disability; they expect biomedical "facts" about disability and expert knowledge about treatments, interventions, and cures. While this research is important, disability studies is focused on the personal, cultural, and political context of medical and rehabilitation approaches and encourages students to engage with the relations and tensions across these domains. On occasion, a few students articulate acutely negative perceptions of disability, sometimes grounded in personal experience. Upon further reflection, such individuals often offer painful insights about material hardship, lack of opportunity, and multiple intersectional oppressions. Finally, some students admit that they really do not know much about disability; they do not have a family member or friend with a disability and have not really given the subject much thought. As these students probe more deeply, they often realize that students with disabilities were not actively integrated in their schools—that their lack of familiarity is also a product of able-bodied and able-minded privilege.

We open with this glimpse into the classroom because this book has emerged out of ongoing conversations among the coeditors about pedagogical practices and our collective desire for an introductory narrative collection that would speak to this wide range of experiences. We found that few disability studies anthologies were specifically designed for undergraduates or introductory courses. While disability studies scholarship is rich, multidisciplinary, and rapidly growing, we wanted a narrative anthology that would include reflections on a range of impairments, material experiences, and sociopolitical perspectives in relation to important issues in the field. One of the tasks we have set to our own students is short **autoethnographic** writing assignments that ask them to apply a critical disability studies lens to self-reflect about specific incidents and contexts of their own lives. The student voices emerging from our own classrooms made us realize that selected essays from our own students, combined with those of other disabled students formally working in the field, would provide a rich array of material—especially for college students new to disability studies. In effect, this collection of narratives features disabled students grappling with disability studies frames—from students newly acquainted with sociocultural dimensions of disability to activists deeply familiar with political issues and theory.

Autoethnography is closely connected to two other forms of writing frequently used within disability studies, **critical self-reflection** and **disability life writing**. New genres of disability life writing focus on the rich insight that emerges from disability experience. Further, as students are exposed to disabled people's unique knowledge as well as discussions of their experiences with environmental and social barriers, they are encouraged to reflect about able-bodied and able-minded privilege. As disability studies scholars in the humanities and social sciences have demonstrated, disability has shaped cultural understandings of personhood, citizenship, gender, sexuality, ethnicity, class, and nation (Baynton 2001; Garland-Thomson 1996; Linton 1998). When students are asked to probe and reflect on their own beliefs and perceptions about disability, they begin to notice and discuss dominant cultural (mis)perceptions about disability. For example, they become aware of how fears proliferate in media representations of mental illness or are engendered by the rhetoric of autism as an "epidemic"; they witness how "inspirational" stories featuring disability erase important social or political inequities. In one exercise, we ask students to reflect on the first time they recall being conscious of disability as a notable difference, an exercise that inevitably reveals internalized beliefs and structures of **ableism**, alive and well. As Fiona Kumari Campbell explains, "'Ableism' refers to the ideological hypervaluation of ableness and the ways in which such norms of abled and disabled identity are given force in law, social policy, and cultural values" (2015, 13). Disability studies endeavors to expose and critique ableist norms, practices, and structures within a larger project of justice and inclusivity.

Disability life writing often provides students with more complex understandings of the social dimensions of disability. In *Signifying Bodies*, G. Thomas Couser identifies the "new disability memoir" (2009, 164) as a distinct genre, one grounded in disability studies, where authors use their

autobiographies to articulate complex sociopolitical dimensions of disabil-
ity. Memoirs cited by Couser are well known in the field: Stephen Kuusisto's
Planet of the Blind (1997), Georgina Kleege's *Sight Unseen* (1999), Harriet
McBryde Johnson's *Too Late to Die Young* (2005), and Simi Linton's *My Body
Politic* (2007), to name a few. All of these writers contextualize disability as
personal, familial, social, and political and use narrative to explore their
evolution into what Couser calls "disability consciousness" (2009, 165).
Linton, whose *Reclaiming Disability* (1998) has been a foundational text in
defining the parameters of the field in the United States, invites readers into
an intimate political history in *My Body Politic* (2007). In this memoir, she
recounts emerging from a spinal-cord injury into a dramatically inaccessible world as well as into the excitement of the burgeoning disability rights
movement. Although covering similar analytical territory in both books,
Linton's life writing invites readers into an embodied, epistemological journey. Disability memoirs allow readers to inhabit bodies, minds, and histories
different from their own and to reorient, through authors' reflections, their
critical thinking about disability. Linton's story resonates with readers across
diverse backgrounds and disabilities, including several contributors to this
book. Mycie Lubin recalls in Chapter II.1:

> Just like Linton, I could not accept my changes at first. I cried,
> blamed my family for not informing me of medical issues we have,
> and became angry, depressed, and resigned. . . . I am an immigrant
> with a very thick accent. English is my fourth language. I am black
> and a woman. I thought, *No way am I going to add disability to the
> list.* I already had too many obstacles in a country as racialized as
> America. . . . [B]ut I found out soon that I was using the wrong
> method to fight the disease. The best approach was to face it, accept
> it, and keep going.

Another disability-conscious memoir, *The Shape of the Eye* (2011), written by George Estreich, whose daughter Laura has Down syndrome, positions narrative as a necessary humanizing force in relation to the potentially
reductive qualities of science. Thinking of his daughter's future in a world
both *accepting of* and *correcting for* Down syndrome, he offers this reflection:

> We live in a world where Down syndrome is described both as an
> element of a diverse humanity and as a defect to be eliminated. . . .
> If our technologies are to benefit people with Down syndrome, then
> their lives need to become more real to us. Science can illuminate
> one part of that reality, and technology can affect it. But only story
> can convey it. (207–208)

Complex disability narratives work against reductive ideas about abilities and future potential; in addition, such stories challenge hollow stereotypes and presumed limitations attached to diagnostic labels. The narratives in this book resonate strongly with the ideas expressed in new disability memoirs. Some writers are deeply engaged with disability theory, while others powerfully recount processes of discovery; across this range, all these writers actively make meaning and produce knowledge from personal experiences of disability.

Barriers and Belonging

> All . . . changed when I found disability studies. I began to see myself in the mirror. I didn't have to be a lone "sick kid" trapped in his room; I could be a member of a community—a community of those who had been excluded and overlooked due to their various physical and mental disabilities but who still had something important to contribute to the world.

As this quotation from Adam P. Newman's chapter (VI.4) illustrates, the title for this book emerged organically from the included narratives and reflects intrinsic political goals of disability studies: to expose and dismantle attitudinal and structural **barriers** and to promote and create meaningful sociopolitical **belonging** for disabled people. From the beginning of modern disability rights movements, activists have articulated their concerns and demands around identifying physical and attitudinal barriers. While many architectural barriers in public spaces have been removed, as these narratives demonstrate, disabled people continue to face significant obstacles, many of which are exacerbated by ableist attitudes that situate disability as an individual issue. As Newman also mentions, experiences of exclusion and isolation among people with disabilities are far too common, and finding community can be a transformative experience. These narratives promote complex knowledge of disability as a valued element of human diversity, and they provide glimpses into spaces of what we call **radical belonging**—within families and communities, and across the lifespan. By radical belonging, we wish to underscore the idea that integrating people with disabilities into the broad social fabric—from family units to social networks, communities, employment, and larger institutional structures—is a shared responsibility.

The chapters in *Barriers and Belonging* speak to this communal labor and conceptual shift. Central to actively engaging in this shared perspective is adopting a critical and relational approach to **access**. Tanya Titchkosky provides indispensable tools for this process in *The Question of Access* (2011).

Titchkosky sees access as a form of perception and invites disabled and nondisabled people alike to engage in a "politics of wonder," an open-ended questioning, and a "restless reflexive return" (15) to what access means and how it shapes relationships:

> Exploring the meanings of access is, fundamentally, the exploration of the meaning of our lives together—who is together with whom, how, where, when, and why? Once we recognize this, we can begin to regard disability as a valuable interpretive space for denaturalizing our existence and complicating singular or totalizing ways of making meaning as bodied beings. Denaturalizing existence does not require us to deny the materiality of the body, nor that of social space, but it certainly does make the relation between people and places a significant, historical, material fact, worthy of concerted critical reflection. (6)

Many of the narratives in this book address access from this perspective of relationship, reflexivity, and wonder. All the chapters engage with disability as a significant "interpretive space," and many contributors recount experiencing a personal paradigm shift when they first considered disability as valuable or as a source of insight worth sharing. Zachary A. Richter, for example, describes in Chapter I.6 how the concept of ableism utterly transformed his internalized shame about disability into pride and activism. Garrett R. Cruzan, in Chapter IV.4, grapples more with how disability reshapes the meaning of our lives together. He traces an intellectual journey of embracing his spinal-cord injury as liberating him into newfound knowledge while also reframing his personal relationships with family and activist networks. He also articulates a larger responsibility: "I am learning to embrace my place in spreading awareness, and I know how important that is."

Like the new disability memoirs described by Couser, the autoethnographic narratives in this collection focus (to varying degrees) on the complex interactions between an individual's physical, mental, and sensory experience of impairment and the person's social context. As Carolyn Ellis, a pioneer in autoethnographic theory, methodology, and writing, explains, autoethnography begins with one's personal life and requires "attention to . . . physical feelings, thoughts, and emotions" (2004, xvii). Further, it involves what Ellis refers to as "'systematic sociological introspection' and 'emotional recall' to try to understand an experience" (xvii); in her case, she has used autoethnography to explore a variety of issues such as marriage, aging, teaching, and her experience with cancer. This approach, reflected by the narratives included here, invites readers to engage with the writer's experiences and gain sociocultural understanding on a profoundly personal, empathic level.

In line with the field's foundational practice of focusing on the perspectives of disabled people, this collection brings together a wide range of disability experiences from contemporary students in the United States and Canada. The contributors provide insight into distinct disability experiences, from sensory impairments, chronic pain, cognitive and learning disabilities, mental illness diagnoses, and autism, to stuttering, spinal-cord injuries, memory loss, and post-traumatic stress. The narratives also reflect diverse ethnic, religious, class, cultural, and regional backgrounds as the authors reflect on experiences from childhood, from adolescence, and into adulthood.

As contributors grapple with barriers and belonging, they are also negotiating the interplay between the biological and the cultural. As disability studies scholars Lennard Davis and David Morris have pointed out, "The biological without the cultural, or the cultural without the biological, is doomed to be reductionist at best and inaccurate at worst" (2007, 411). While Davis and Morris focus largely on bridging humanities and science scholarship, their **biocultural** model provides a useful framework for situating the narratives in this collection. Biomedical conditions—whether sensory, physical, emotional, or cognitive—are constantly shaped by the cultural, and the writers of the chapters in this book capture crucial elements in the self-knowledge that results from this interaction.

This collection is designed to capture this process of disability knowledge formation. Through an autoethnographic lens, these chapters address a number of questions, including:

- How do people currently contextualize their experience of disability?
- How does disability studies matter—especially to disabled students? How does it shape or transform students' understanding of able-bodied and able-minded privilege and material relations of power?
- What work does disability theory perform to enhance biocultural understandings of disability?
- How can nondisabled peers better understand and critically analyze disablement as well as engage in confronting barriers and cocreating environments of belonging?

Social Approaches

Social approaches to disability are foundational to disability studies. Disability rights movements in many nations, in which groups demanded greater access to education, employment, housing, public spaces and services, and the support necessary to live independently, also articulated new frameworks for understanding disability. In coalition with disability activists, academic advocates—primarily from the social sciences—challenged the dominance of medical and rehabilitation fields as the key producers of disability knowledge. The **social model**, first introduced in the United Kingdom by physically disabled activists and scholars in the 1970s, has powerfully influenced disability studies (Oliver 1990; Shakespeare 2006). The model strictly distinguishes between **impairment** (the biological embodied difference) and **disability** (the social, structural, and attitudinal barriers that limit a person's participation and access to opportunities available to nondisabled citizens). The simplicity of this early model, often referred to as the **strong social model**, has been the source of its success but also of its weaknesses (Shakespeare 2006). The impact of the social model has been profound. Tom Shakespeare distills the strengths into three key areas: political effectiveness of building a social movement, instrumental effectiveness in supporting the passage of rights legislation, and psychological effectiveness in supporting positive self-esteem and a sense of collective identity for disabled people (2006, 30). At the same time, as feminist scholars pointed out early on (Crow 1996; Wendell 1996), the artificial separation of impairment and its disabling effects prevented discussions of the complications of illness, pain, chronic conditions, dependency, and care relations, as well as of the interconnected issues of gender, sexuality, ethnicity, and other social positions.

In the United States, social frameworks have been more aligned with a **minority group model** and coalitional rights approach. Activists in the 1960s and 1970s, such as Judith Heumann and Ed Roberts, worked in collaboration with people with a wide range of impairments, and disabled people came together to demand changes in built environments, social attitudes, and policy (Shapiro 1994). Disability rights leaders also learned strategies from civil rights activists, war protesters, and women's rights leaders, among other social justice groups. These social and theoretical histories are important to the field, but recent disability studies scholarship has integrated more interactional approaches that are mindful of the complex interconnectedness and contextual nature of impairment and disability. This is reflected in *Keywords for Disability Studies* (2015), in the editors' description of disability: "Although the social model predominates, in much recent scholarship, disability refers to a subjective state, the condition not only of identifying as disabled but also of perceiving a world through a particular kind of lens" (Adams, Reiss, and Serlin 2015, 8). In other words, disability experience, in relation to contextual and larger structural forces, functions as a core site of theoretical knowledge. As Michael T. Salter puts it in Chapter IV.5, "I changed my view of my PTSD [post-traumatic stress disorder]. . . . I refuse to be the victim, and I embrace this change."

Sharon Snyder and David Mitchell have powerfully formulated the interactional nature of impairment and disability through a **cultural model** framework, which insists that the meaning and experience of impairment and disability are intensely contextual and bound by social and cultural beliefs. In the cultural model, impairment is not simply a biological reality but a site of critical engagement: "Impairment is both human variation encountering environmental obstacles and socially mediated difference that lends group identity and phenomenological perspective." They suggest, further, that this more complex understanding of impairment is encompassed in the "*politicized* term disability" (Snyder and Mitchell 2006, 10; emphasis in original). This broader cultural definition allows disability to operate "both as a referent for a process of social exposé and as a productive locus for identification" (10). Individual experiences of impairment and disability produce important knowledge, which is always mediated by social meanings, personal context, and multiple other factors such as class, gender, sexuality, ethnicity, and citizenship.

Interactional social frameworks of disability, those informed by a combination of elements described above, are now well established and have shaped national and global approaches. In the United States, the passage in 1990 of the Americans with Disabilities Act (ADA), which codified a social dimension of disability by protecting people "regarded as" having an impairment, was seen as landmark legislation for acknowledging social biases against disability within the definitional prongs (it was amended in 2008; see Americans with Disabilities Act of 1990 2009). International definitions of disability, such as that of the World Health Organization (WHO), are even more specific in highlighting interactional social dimensions of disability:

> Disability is not an attribute of an individual, but rather a complex collection of conditions, many of which are created by the social environment. Hence, the management of the problem requires social action, and it is the collective responsibility of society at large to make the changes necessary for full participation of people with disabilities in all areas of social life. (2001, 20)

As this brief history demonstrates, social approaches to disability have shaped laws, policy, and international definitions. Notably, the shift in thinking from the individual and medical to the sociopolitical remains counterintuitive to people outside disability fields, but as many contributors make clear, it is also deeply transformational.

Prevailing Themes

Across this collection, several key terms and themes in disability studies recur. We note these here to provide context, and we encourage readers to consider tensions and interconnections between these concepts. Because cultural meanings of disability are deeply bound up with medicine, rehabilitation, psychiatry, special education, and other professions, diagnostic categories have exerted a great deal of influence not only on medical and rehabilitation understandings of disability but also on individual and social perceptions. Disability studies has called attention to the power dynamics of this **naming process** and takes seriously activist and advocacy efforts to articulate, name, and "reassign meaning" (Linton 1998, 9) from personal and collective experiences. Within current health-care, education, and economic systems, diagnostic categories are crucial to claim coverage, gain access to appropriate services, and qualify for financial support. At the same time, individuals and subgroups often experience varying forms of **stigma** associated with specific disability diagnoses. Erving Goffman (1963) defined "stigma" as a socially discrediting attribute, one that results in a form of **spoiled identity**, which he saw as a process of being classified, stereotyped, and socially excluded based on one negative attribute. Tracing the enduring relevance of stigma in relation to disability, Lerita Coleman Brown (2013) sees the unequal relationship between the **stigmatized as inferior** and the **nonstigmatized as superior** as crucial to understanding how stigma continues to function. In this power dynamic, nonstigmatized people assert their privilege by conveying the social inferiority of stigmatized individuals and groups through "social rejection," especially "social isolation and lowered expectations" (Brown 2013, 154).

Several contributors address personal experiences of stigma, describing feelings of inferiority, social rejection, internalized shame, or fears of social isolation. For example, Megan L. Coggins, who lives with schizoaffective disorder, shares in Chapter V.3, "I still struggle with prejudices and issues of stigma. I often hear, when I share my story, that I do not 'look sick.'" Each response to stigma is unique, and every narrative reframes disability on its own terms; part of this process is critical engagement with naming. Some people resist stigma by proudly self-disclosing or claiming a diagnosis, while others resist labels or assert the power to rename, reclaim, or resignify their condition.

The social rejection of disabled people and the use of disability rhetoric to mark specific groups as inferior have long histories. Documenting and resisting historical and contemporary stigmatizing uses of disability, as well as rescripting disability as positive, integral, or generative—or further, as transgressive, edgy, or sexy—is at the heart of disability studies. New terms, introduced by disability activists and scholars, have been central to resisting the stigma that is still associated with disability. The term **non-disabled**, for example, is used in disability studies to decenter and mark the social privilege embedded in the terms "able-bodied" or "able-minded" (Linton 1998). Contrasting **disabled people** with **nondisabled people** calls attention to the constructed nature of both positions. Similarly, Rosemarie Garland-Thomson (1996) introduced the term **normate** to signify a category of multiple privileged positions, in which able-bodied privilege becomes interlinked with white privilege and heterosexual, gender, class, religious, and other forms of privilege. As Rodney B. Hume-Dawson, in Chapter VI.3, keenly recalls of his childhood in Sierra Leone, "Most of the people who loved me wanted me to walk the 'normal' way. For some of them, the implications of what that meant did not matter. As long as I walked like them, that was what was important." Blake Culley (Chapter III.3) embraced such normative pressures as well; as a deaf child, she wanted to be "normal" and worked to convince her hearing classmates that she was not like the other deaf students, who were seen as being "behind in their education."

Even with tools to expose such privilege, **normative pressures** on disabled people are often intense. Indeed, in order to resist internally damaging emotions or internalized shame, many disabled people assert some form of positive **disability identity**, which, while its meaning varies for different people, has come to reflect political orientation with disability rights and justice; to many, it has become an assertion that disability is integral to, not separate from, one's sense of self and understanding of the world—that disability shapes and informs one's membership and participation in communities and groups. Identity claims also work to gain recognition for an impairment that, while unseen, shapes one's political affiliation and activism. Allegra Heath-Stout cites such a moment in Chapter V.1:

> "But you're not disabled!"
> I stare at my friend from just inside his front door on our college campus, watching as he takes in the sight of my bright purple T-shirt emblazoned with "Disabled and Proud." I am taken aback by his declaration. Finally I respond, "Yes, I am. I have learning disabilities."

While some writers assert strong disability-pride identities, others resist identity claims as political strategy toward social change. Building on Robert McRuer's influential *Crip Theory*, many disability studies scholars have reclaimed the term "crip" to signal an orientation toward disability and a resistance to compulsory able-bodied and able-mindedness, as well as to challenge the stability and coherence of identity (McRuer 2006; Kafer

2013). The narratives in this book engage with these tensions—with the importance of identity to an affirmative self-concept as well as to its fluidity and instability.

Connected to this, in addressing the unique and heightened **stigma of psychiatric disability**, some contributors with mental illness diagnoses reclaim the term **madness** to openly reject assumptions of incompetence and to challenge false binaries between sanity and insanity. Shayda Kafai explains in Chapter I.2, "I became aware of the power inherent in claiming this aspect of my identity, of reframing it in a context distinct from the stereotypes that had for so long dominated my understanding of madness." Further, Rebekah Moras explicitly traces important overlaps between madness and disability studies. As Moras describes in Chapter VI.5:

> Through disability studies, I am accepted and nurtured, as much in times of active madness as in those of relative balance. . . . I have been able to work with feminist and disability-positive practitioners who have supported me in framing my experiences within social and institutional contexts and who have not solely individualized my madness.

Historically, one of the gaps in disability studies has been a predominance of focus on physical disability. In recent years, however, there has been a surge of scholarship in the field focused on disabilities of the mind—from cognitive, intellectual, and developmental disabilities to trauma, autism, and psychiatric disabilities. Margaret Price coined the term "**mental disability**" (2011, 9) to link these broad categories and to analyze their sociocultural connections. However, while this proves useful in some instances, it runs the danger of drawing too sharp a line between the physical and the mental. Price has grappled with this issue herself and has recently suggested the term "**bodymind**" (2015, 269) to signal the impossible separation between bodies and minds, and as a more accurate container for the complex interaction between mental and physical processes. This term is a useful placeholder in a field that has been more focused on corporeal and visible markers of difference than on cognitive impairments and mental diversity.

In fact, the complicated difference between **visible** and **invisible disability** is another recurring theme, and the boundaries between them, like those between mental and physical disabilities, are often porous. Having an invisible disability—like chronic pain, migraines, illnesses, and, for some, autism—brings up questions of **self-disclosure**, **passing** as able-bodied or able-minded, or having to assert one's disability status against others' visual assumptions. Strictly speaking, most disabilities encompass a range of (in)visibility, much of which is situational. People with chronic pain, for example, may be perceived as more or less disabled depending on whether they are using a cane or a scooter, but their experience of pain may be much the same. As Catherine Graves writes in Chapter III.2, "The natural tendency is to associate disability with physical appearance. If you don't look sick, you must not be sick. I often wish I changed colors to reflect my pain and fatigue levels, so I could say, 'See, I told you I don't feel well.'" Price suggests that many disabilities are neither visible nor invisible "but *intermittently* apparent." Further, she suggests, "A better metaphor than vision for some kinds of disability might be *apparition*. Consider the act of stimming, a repetitive behavior such as snapping a rubber band against one's wrist, or tapping one's fingers" (2015, 272; emphasis in original). Indeed, many disabilities might be better described as **apparent** and **nonapparent**, depending on the context of the encounter. These terms push against sight as perceptual norm; moreover, they are meant to call attention to the transitory and situational nature of individual disability experience and expression.

Overview of Parts

> Gone are the days when the focus of telling one's disability story was about overcoming one's challenge. For me and many others whose work I have been privileged to read, our focus is not so much on the triumphant aspects of our lives but on telling the story from a social perspective.
> —RODNEY B. HUME-DAWSON, CHAPTER VI.3

In an effort to revisit key concerns and highlight commonalities across disability experience, we have organized the chapters in this book into six parts, often grouping together work by authors with quite different **impairment effects**—the individual complications and adaptations to specific conditions—but united by similar sociocultural concerns and perspectives. This structure is meant to circle back to foundational concepts and themes, deepening complexity and insight for readers as they move through the collection. At the opening of each part, we provide brief introductions to the chapters included as well as questions to frame readings and promote discussion. In these introductions, we have made key terms and phrases boldface. Most of these concepts are defined explicitly, but others are meant to serve as critical reflection prompts for readers to investigate on their own. We encourage students to use the boldface terms as themes to focus on while reading and as elements for discussion. At the end of each part, we offer suggestions for additional pairings and linkages across the collection as an invitation to broader conversations about the diverse perspectives included.

The chapters in Part I, "Laying the Groundwork," introduce foundational themes in disability studies—themes that echo throughout the collection.

Authors explore key sociocultural issues that shape what disability has come to mean in their lives. These issues include the personal impact of (in)accessible environments, the complexity of mental illness diagnosis and its relationship to disability rights, and the distinctions between apparent and nonapparent disability. Most importantly, these chapters provide a glimpse into the range of experience—from ableist discrimination and cross-cultural diversity to internalized shame and the creative adaptations of everyday living.

Part II, "Families, Adaptive Living, and Reorienting Expectations," is grounded in the ways family systems shape and transform ideas about disability. Children come to understand their impairments and develop a sense of self through their parents' and family members' orientation toward—or away from—disability. In addition, as a few narratives demonstrate, parents who have disabilities often develop adaptive strategies centered on physical, sensory, or cognitive differences; inevitably, children and partners participate in these processes. In the best situations, families are involved in fostering inclusion and promoting environments of radical belonging, but family dynamics are often complicated by normative pressures and dominant negative assumptions about disability.

The chapters in Part III, "Disability and Communication," consider multiple layers of interpersonal exchange, including hearing and speech acts, artificial but persistent social demands for disclosure, and the (im)possibility of accurately communicating hidden and variable disabilities. This section links the following broad questions: What are the complications of communicating about disability? What constitutes "aberrant" communication, and how do disabled people navigate normative expectations and pressures to conform? Building on the potential embedded in difficult conversations, Part IV, "Mapping Complex Relations," explores aspects by which disability informs, challenges, and enlivens relationships and mutual communication. Authors disclose vulnerabilities and adjustments to disability, focusing on how disability has affected or changed friendships, families, and broader social relations, including (dis)connections with civilian and military contexts. Further, these narratives encourage readers to reexamine their own relations to disability, to disabled people, and to the beliefs and practices that shape their personal perceptions of diverse bodyminds.

Part V, "Identity, Resistance, and Community," explores myriad ways in which disability informs personal identity, social relationships, community affiliations, and political commitments. Several contributors describe how disability studies has contributed to personal empowerment and philosophical reorientation toward disability. These chapters reveal intricate connections among integrating disability into a positive self-concept, resistance to ableism, and participating in communities that are both sustaining and sustainable. Finally, in Part VI, "Theories and Lives," narratives focus on ways in which disability studies theories have both influenced and transformed authors' self-perceptions, political concerns, and professional goals. Included are chapters by student activists and graduate students pursuing scholarly research in disability studies. These narratives critically examine the enduring effects of structural ableism, the ongoing necessity of expanding sociocultural knowledge of disability, and the ever-present need for disability activism.

While themes reverberate and overlap across the book as a whole, these narratives underscore the incredible diversity of **bodymind experience.** In disability studies, the blurring boundaries of disability are constantly in motion, and the field opens itself to a capacious understanding of the term itself—in which anxiety speaks to blindness, Deaf identity opens to mad pride, neurodiversity bumps up against PTSD, and acquired impairments are juxtaposed with congenital conditions. As the narratives in this collection demonstrate, students welcome the critical lens of disability studies; at the same time, many, through their own experiences, engage in a process of stretching their own understanding—and in some cases of nudging the field—to make room for new, yet resonant, insights. These narratives, these stories, weave new threads into a vibrant, colorful, and diverse tapestry that celebrates—and struggles with—the messy richness of disability experience.

Orienting toward Relations

As these contributors critically reflect on experiences of disability, they capture over and over the relational nature of disability. At times, they describe how disability may complicate, trouble, or foreclose relationships, but just as often, and more importantly, these narratives illustrate new relational formations. Rosemarie Garland-Thomson's (2011) articulation of **fitting** and **misfitting** provides a useful framework for a relational reading. These terms provide theoretical flexibility for looking at interactions between bodyminds and environments. Garland-Thomson explains, "When we fit harmoniously and properly into the world, we forget the truth of contingency because the world sustains us. When we experience misfitting and recognize that disjuncture for its political potential, we expose the relational component and the fragility of fitting" (597). This dynamic process corresponds to this book's overarching framework of barriers and belonging. While much can be learned through identifying barriers and contexts that produce misfitting, new models for relationships and communities are brought to life as contributors recount fitting spaces—environments of belonging. Zachary A. Richter captures this juxtaposition in Chapter I.6: "In the case of my most dominant pathology, the symptoms at first separated me from other people . . . but they now unite me in solidarity with a wider community through my new self-identification as autistic."

Ultimately, as these autoethnographic narratives shed light on the nuances of environmental, attitudinal, and systemic barriers, they invite readers to think more expansively about relations of access, to consider privilege and subordination, and to work toward creating locations of belonging for everyone. Many writers reflect on family systems, mapping out what Rayna Rapp and Faye Ginsburg call a new "kinship imaginary," in which the presence of disability in a family "catalyzes new forms of activism that are reshaping . . . communities" (2011, 381). Parent advocates such as Joanne De Simone (Chapter II.3) and Tricia Black (Chapter II.4) participate in such kinship reframing, as do many family members and partners of the contributors. Beyond family systems, many narratives map out participation in politically active disability communities. Like Zachary A. Richter, other contributors, such as Allegra Heath-Stout (Chapter V.1), Denton Mallas (Chapter V.6), Adam P. Newman (Chapter VI.4), and Lydia X. Z. Brown (Chapter VI.6), experience belonging in activist, cultural, and academically rich disability communities. In such groups, they are engaged in what Alison Kafer calls the "political/relational model" (2013, 6) of disability, in which people come together through affinity and political affiliation. Through a relational orientation, everyone invested in integrating disability into the fabric of human variation has a role to play in the creation and establishment of new models of collaborative living. This collection invites readers to self-reflect upon and expand their own relationships to disability—to break down barriers and make possible a sense of radical belonging—not through blurring, diminishing, or transcending diversity in bodies and minds but through critical engagement across difference.

NOTE

1. The most accurate and up-to-date list of disability studies programs in the United States and Canada is maintained by the Disability Studies program at Syracuse University; see the list at http://disabilitystudies.syr.edu/programs-list.

REFERENCES

Adams, R., B. Reiss, and D. Serlin. 2015. *Keywords for Disability Studies*. New York: New York University Press.

Americans with Disabilities Act of 1990. 2009. Available at http://www.ada.gov/pubs/adastatute08.htm.

Baynton, D. C. 2001. "Disability and the Justification of Inequality in American History." In *The New Disability History: American Perspectives*, edited by P. Longmore and L. Umansky, 33–57. New York: New York University Press.

Brown, L. C. 2013. "Stigma: An Enigma Demystified." In *The Disability Studies Reader*, 4th ed., edited by Lennard J. Davis, 147–160. New York: Routledge.

Brueggemann, B. 2009. *Deaf Subjects: Between Identities and Places*. New York: New York University Press.

Burch, S., and A. Kafer. 2010. *Deaf and Disability Studies: Interdisciplinary Perspectives*. Washington, DC: Gallaudet University Press.

Campbell, F. K. 2015. "Ability." In *Keywords for Disability Studies*, edited by R. Adams, B. Reiss, and D. Serlin, 12–14. New York: New York University Press.

Couser, G. T. 2009. *Signifying Bodies: Disability in Contemporary Life Writing*. Ann Arbor: University of Michigan Press.

Crow, L. 1996. "Including All of Our Lives: Renewing the Social Model of Disability." In *Encounters with Strangers: Feminism and Disability*, edited by J. Morris, 206–226. London: Women's Press.

Davis, L. J., and D. B. Morris. 2007. "Biocultures Manifesto." *New Literary History* 38 (3): 411–418.

Ellis, C. 2004. *The Ethnographic I: A Methodological Novel about Autoethnography*. Walnut Creek, CA: AltaMira.

Estreich, G. 2011. *The Shape of the Eye: Down Syndrome, Family, and the Stories We Inherit*. Dallas, TX: Southern Methodist University Press.

Garland-Thomson, R. 1996. *Extraordinary Bodies: Figuring Physical Disability in American Culture and Literature*. New York: Columbia University Press.

———. 2011. "Misfits: A Feminist Materialist Disability Concept." *Hypatia* 26 (3): 591–609.

Goffman, E. 1963. *Stigma: Notes on the Management of Spoiled Identity*. New York: Simon and Schuster.

Johnson, H. M. 2005. *Too Late to Die Young: Nearly True Tales from a Life*. New York: Henry Holt and Company.

Kafer, A. 2013. *Feminist, Queer, Crip*. Bloomington: Indiana University Press.

Kleege, G. 1999. *Sight Unseen*. New Haven, CT: Yale University Press.

Krentz, C. 2007. *Writing Deafness: The Hearing Line in Nineteenth-Century American Literature*. Chapel Hill: University of North Carolina Press.

Kuusisto, S. 1997. *Planet of the Blind*. New York: Delta.

Linton, S. 1998. *Claiming Disability: Knowledge and Identity*. New York: New York University Press.

———. 2007. *My Body Politic: A Memoir*. Ann Arbor: University of Michigan Press.

McRuer, R. 2006. *Crip Theory: Cultural Signs of Queerness and Disability*. New York: New York University Press.

Oliver, M. 1990. *The Politics of Disablement: A Sociological Approach*. London: Palgrave Macmillan.

Price, M. 2011. *Mad at School: Rhetorics of Mental Disability and Academic Life*. Ann Arbor: University of Michigan Press.

———. 2015. "The Bodymind Problem and the Possibilities of Pain." *Hypatia* 30 (1): 268–284.

Rapp, R., and F. Ginsburg. 2011. "Reverberations: Disability and the New Kinship Imaginary." *Anthropological Quarterly* 84 (2): 379–410.

Shakespeare, T. 2006. *Disability Rights and Wrongs*. London: Routledge.

Shapiro, J. 1994. *No Pity: People with Disabilities Forging a New Civil Rights Movement*. New York: Three Rivers.

Snyder, S. L., and D. T. Mitchell. 2006. *Cultural Locations of Disability*. Chicago: University of Chicago Press.

Titchkosky, T. 2011. *The Question of Access: Disability, Space, Meaning*. Toronto: University of Toronto Press.

Wendell, S. 1996. *The Rejected Body: Feminist Philosophical Reflections on Disability*. New York: Routledge.

WHO (World Health Organization). 2001. *International Classification of Functioning, Disability, and Health*. Geneva, Switzerland: World Health Organization.

PART I

LAYING THE GROUNDWORK

THE CHAPTERS IN THIS PART introduce foundational concepts that resurface throughout the book. A few narratives touch on Tanya Titchkosky's idea of access as "a relation between people and places" (2011, 6), with particular attention to **accessible environments**: those in which people with disabilities can easily get what they need to function effectively within their communities and institutions. The use of wheelchair symbols to denote physically accessible spaces has been around since the Architectural Barriers Act of 1968, but the notion of accessible environments goes far beyond physical accessibility to provisions such as sign-language interpreters, real-time captioning, audio description, accessible technologies and instructional materials, universal design, and support for people with cognitive, emotional, or psychiatric disabilities. Alyse Ritvo's chapter (I.1) provides a classic example of enduring problems with built environments—and institutional commitments to access. Ritvo sustained a sports injury that caused her to use crutches for some time. In her first college, an elite private institution, she had trouble accessing the most basic elements of school life. She could not get to her dorm room without crutching up slick linoleum stairs, and she found shuttle services unreliable and elevators frequently broken. She compares this institution with the University of California, Berkeley, where she worked with a full-time counselor with a strong understanding of her needs and disability rights. Through this contrast, Ritvo vividly describes the personal impact that physical environments and institutional orientation have on students' sense of value and belonging in a community.

In Chapter I.2, Shayda Kafai shares a very personal story of living with bipolar disorder. While Ritvo's physical disability oscillates between being visible and invisible, depending on her use of crutches, Kafai's psychiatric disability is **nonapparent**, known only to those with whom she chooses to share her story. Like other narratives of mental illness or anxiety, Kafai recounts a deep sense of internalized stigma and devaluation. As she explains, her fear of disclosure is deeply wrapped up in stigmatized images and terms such as "abnormal," "dependent," "passive," "unruly," and "unstable." Margaret Price argues that questions of **naming** take on a "particular urgency" in the domain of psychiatry, "for often the very terms used to name persons with mental disabilities have explicitly foreclosed our status *as* persons" (2011, 9). Changing the description of someone with manic depression from "crazy" to "having a mental disability" is one way to assert control over this process, and for Kafai, renaming and reframing allows her to build bridges and validate her knowledge within the field.

How stigma functions has often been discussed through **models of disability**. Anmol Bhatia was born in India. There, as he notes in Chapter I.3, his blindness was considered "one of the worst things that can happen." He connects this perception with a Hindu **moral model** that interprets blindness as "a punishment from God; it is *karma* for a serious misdeed in a previous life." Diverse sociocultural milieus, including religious practices, will, of course, produce very different moral models. These may range from viewing disability as a sign of punishment to labeling a person with a disability "a gift from God." All moral models, however, share a belief that disabilities are part of a great supernatural schema. Bhatia also discusses two alternate models, the **medical model**, in which "disabilities are viewed as medical conditions that reduce the quality of life," and the **social model**, which emphasizes understanding disabilities as part of socially constructed environments.

While discussions of the sociopolitical dimensions of disability are richly dissected in the field of disability studies, within many institutions, disability is still situated and experienced as an individual problem. As is shown by Joshua Phelps's chapter (I.4), on growing up with ADHD, understanding disability as individual pathology—rather than as a shared social issue—still plagues the education system and can result in deeply punitive approaches to students with disabilities. Christopher Weingardt's chapter (I.5) illustrates a different aspect of the social construction of disability, the enduring notion of the **supercrip**, a trope, widely critiqued in disability studies, which positions attractive, talented, often athletic disabled people as inspirational role models. Weingardt resists such inspirational framings; he simply celebrates his adaptive participation in sports as a personally important yet ordinary aspect of his life.

The power of sociocultural theories and activist disability communities is evidenced in Chapter I.6, by Zachary A. Richter. Richter lives a life explicitly framed by understandings from disability studies, particularly the work of Fiona Kumari Campbell (2009). Campbell's notion of **ableism**, the prejudice against people based on disability and the unnoticed construction of an able-bodied, able-minded world, informs both Richter's activism and his scholarship. A self-identified autistic, Richter has found a home in radical disability communities that actively expand notions of accessibility and openness to diverse **bodyminds**. He explains, "My presence in such locations . . . has allowed me to position my unique experience as part of a larger project of reorganizing social machineries to make them more open to unusual experiences and standpoints." This project of reorganizing social machineries can be as radical as Richter recounts or as simple as the joy Suzi Vee describes in Chapter I.7, of sitting in her wheelchair in the kitchen and rediscovering her love of dancing.

Reference the boldface terms as themes for discussion, and consider the following questions as you read the chapters in Part I:

1. How does accessibility shape a sense of exclusion or belonging? Aside from physical access, what are some dimensions of belonging and integration that need to be considered? How should the responsibilities for access, community, and belonging be shared?
2. In what ways do perspectives on disability differ across cultures? How can an understanding of these differences enrich disability studies?
3. Several chapters describe a process of evolution from seeing disability as individual or medical toward understanding it as social and political. What factors contribute to these changes in perspective? How does disability studies, including an understanding of ableism, contribute to this sociopolitical awareness?

Suggestions for Related Readings

- Read Alyse Ritvo's chapter (I.1) with those by Allegra Heath-Stout (V.1) and Adena Rottenstein (VI.1) to discuss issues of campus access, peer dynamics, and disability identity.
- Shayda Kafai (in Chapter I.2) opens a conversation about imposed silences and mental illness, which could be linked to a number

of chapters, including those by Megan L. Coggins (V.3), Cindee Calton (VI.2), and Rebekah Moras (VI.5).

- Pair Anmol Bhatia's chapter (I.3) with those by Tasha Chemel (III.4) and Emily K. Michael (IV.3) to compare familial and cultural perceptions of blindness, or with Rodney P. Hume-Dawson's chapter (VI.3) to consider differing cross-cultural orientations of disability.
- Read Joshua Phelps's chapter (I.4) with that by Nancy La Monica (V.2) to discuss learning disabilities in academic environments: What insights do they offer to preservice teachers?
- Pair Zachary A. Richter's chapter (I.6) with Joshua St. Pierre's chapter (III.1) to discuss ableism in relation to speech and stuttering, and with Lydia X. Z. Brown's chapter (VI.6) to consider overlapping themes of autism and neurodiversity, political identity, and activism.

REFERENCES

Campbell, F. K. 2009. *Contours of Ableism: The Production of Disability and Abledness.* Houndmills, UK: Palgrave Macmillan.
Titchkosky, T. 2011. *The Question of Access: Disability, Space, Meaning.* Toronto: University of Toronto Press.

I.1

From Poison Ivy to Live Oak

*How Transferring Colleges Changed
My Perception of Disability*

ALYSE RITVO

In the twenty-first century, diversity is de rigueur for most institutions of higher education. Former all-male colleges boast that the incoming freshman class is the first to have more female than male students; internationally renowned universities emphasize that students hail from all fifty states and numerous other countries; Christian schools recruit Jews. All schools seek to obtain racial diversity. Implicit in this quest for diversity is a message that all students, regardless of gender, birthplace, religion, race, or other demographic factors, will be valued by and enrich the university community.

Disability disorders diversity. A human difference that is a source of pride for some and shame for others, and which demands that the external environment make accommodations, disability tests the sincerity of an institution's embrace of diversity. Each university has the power either to

Alyse Ritvo graduated summa cum laude from the University of California, Berkeley, in 2012. She won the Departmental Citation in Sociology, awarded by the faculty to the most accomplished student in the graduating class, for her academic achievement and honors thesis, "To See or Not to See: How UC Berkeley Undergraduates with Invisible Disabilities Manage Disability-Related Information and Selectively Pass." Ritvo attends the University of California, Berkeley, School of Law. She hopes to apply her legal training to advocate for underrepresented populations, especially children and people with disabilities. She continues to narrate the trials, tribulations, and triumphs of her own embodied experience as a young woman with an invisible physical disability.

genuinely accommodate disabled students, thereby showing them that they command the same respect and value as other students, or to pay lip service to accommodations, thereby treating disabled students as second-class students.

My social reality as a college student with a disability has taken two forms, a direct result of the distinctly different valuation of the Americans with Disabilities Act (ADA) of 1990 by the two schools I attended. Transferring from a university that was ill equipped—physically and socially—to deal with my disability to one that is accessible on multiple planes has allowed me to discover my identity as a disabled person.

In 2007, I called the dean's office at Chadwick University, an elite institution of higher learning on the East Coast, to notify the administrators that I had experienced a serious sports injury and would be arriving on campus for the start of freshman year with significant mobility limitations.[1] The next day, I picked up a voicemail from the freshman dean advising me to postpone matriculation a year so I could heal. Already having taken a "gap year" between high school and the start of college and unsure of how long my injury would last, I was determined to hit the quad, even if it would be the rubber tips of crutches rather than both my feet that would be grazing the grass. I set off across the country to join the Ivy League.

I explained to the housing dean that I had severed a ligament, torn others, burst a joint capsule, and suffered contusions to the talus and calcaneus bones in my right ankle and would be on crutches indefinitely. My prognosis was ambiguous but the doctors made it clear that I would be non-weight-bearing for at least a few months. The dean assured me that my dorm was ADA accessible. I didn't think to ask her about the dorm's proximity to the dining hall or my classrooms; I assumed that the school would have some sort of shuttle to transport me from my room to other key locations.

On move-in day, my parents and I arrived in front of my new home, a centuries-old brick building. There was a placard outside the entryway with the International Symbol of Access and a sign saying "Handicapped access in rear." At the back of the building was a cage with an elevator large enough to accommodate a wheelchair. The lift went to the basement of the building; however, it served no useful purpose, as the basement was closed off from the other five floors, and there was no interior elevator. The school had installed the elevator at great expense, meeting the letter but not the spirit of the ADA. The building was deemed ADA accessible thanks to its elevator to nowhere.

Thankfully, my room was on only the second floor, and that day I managed to crutch up the flight of steep, narrow stairs without a spill. I would not be so lucky when winter hit and the linoleum stairs became slick from foot traffic on snowy, icy days. By the end of the year, I was proud of myself for having tumbled down the stairs only three times—no small feat considering the many trips I made crutching up and down the dorm's stairs to my room. In hindsight, I find it appalling that my university—elite, world famous, and well endowed—housed me in a dangerous dorm with the pretense of ADA accessibility. When I later complained about the misleading "accessibility" of the building, the housing dean said that if I had indicated a physical disability on my housing application, I would have been placed in the building that houses "all of the students in wheelchairs, et cetera."

This statement galled me. If the dean had even mentioned the notion of having a specified dorm for all of the students receiving full financial aid or all of the students in one racial group, every member of campus would have been up in arms, and there would have been a piece about this separate-but-equal diversity on the front page of the *New York Times* the very next day. The school does not have an option for substance-free housing or single-gender housing, two housing designations that are common on campuses nationwide, but everyone with a physical disability is housed in the "disabled dorm." To add insult to injury (disability), students with psychiatric disabilities are relegated to two dorms, both removed from the freshman quad, which are infamous for having "psycho singles" (single rooms).

The inaccessibility of my dorm room ended up being the least of my concerns in navigating the campus. An unreliable shuttle service and broken elevators proved to be my day-to-day nemeses. I was shocked that a university with one of the largest endowments in the nation refused to fork out the money necessary for a reliable transportation system or fully functioning elevators. The demand for accessible services and the resources to provide them were there. What was missing were two key elements: (1) the recognition of disabled students as being equals of their able-bodied classmates and (2) heart—that human element that tells us that even though a built environment might meet legal standards, it does not fulfill the quotidian needs of every student and thus sends a message that some students are worth more than others.

The inaccessibility of the campus was consonant with a campus culture of boundless excelling that prized perfection and therefore could not metabolize any dose of disability or impairment. Students crammed their schedules with extracurricular activities that would enhance their curriculum vitae. Everything—from assignments in the academic arena to plays in performance halls and events at exclusive venues—was a competition. Walking to dinner at the pace of a girl on crutches meant fifteen fewer minutes to devote to something that would "count." Having heart didn't count at Chadwick.

As months passed and my foot continued to be painful and constrained by limited range of motion, I realized that my acute injury was turning into a chronic condition. I did not consider myself "disabled" and was somewhat optimistic about finding a cure to my ankle ailment; however, I was, for all intents and purposes, disabled and remained in a leg brace and on crutches or a cane for the entirety of the academic year.

The only way I was able to stay in school with my disability was with the assistance of my mother, who took family medical leave and moved across the country to become my chauffeur. To this day, people respond with incredulity when I recount that Chadwick's solution to my disability was to ship me back home on a leave of absence and hope that my condition would improve in time for the following academic year. Since my school was unwilling to support me, I turned to family. My mom spent the year driving me to classes, meals, and social events. The story presents all kinds of dissonance: I moved across the country at the brink of young adulthood to gain autonomy and grow up, but I was dependent on my mother for care; the university propounded the idea that it was ADA accessible, but barriers to accessibility included an elevator to the dining hall that repeatedly broke down, the closure of the handicapped access to the library sans the construction of an alternate accessible entrance, and inaccessible meeting rooms such as the one for an a cappella audition that was up six flights of stairs.

The dissonance that prevailed in the external social structure seeped into my internal world: I was at once injured, a temporary state, and disabled, a state that suggests more permanence. Furthermore, the implicit message of Chadwick's policies (for example, I could call a shuttle only to take me to class, not to extracurricular activities, orientation events, meals, or social engagements) was that the able-bodied me who had been accepted into the school was much more worthy than the disabled me who was actually attending.

When the academic year ended and I still had mobility limitations and pain, I reevaluated my priorities. Yes, Chadwick was world renowned, and a diploma with its seal could open doors. But the school was continuously closing doors on me. When push came to shove (or more like when crutch came to fall), it was inaccessible. I could have blamed the physical inaccessibility on the old buildings, which was what most school administrators did, but Chadwick had plenty of extra money to build ramps, elevators, and pathways. The reality was that Chadwick's philosophy left little room, or support, for disability.

Ironically, it would be by moving close to my childhood home that I would be afforded the opportunity to gain independence and enter adulthood—thanks to a university that genuinely embraces accommodations of disabilities. In turn, this newfound independence would foster the realization that I am indeed disabled and that disability need not hinder my education or development.

After spending a year at a California community college to gain eligibility as a junior transfer student, I transferred into the University of California at Berkeley (UCB or, more colloquially, Cal) in the fall of 2009. Friends and family who weren't familiar with UCB's Disabled Students' Program (the DSP) were perplexed that I was transferring to a huge campus that was on a slope.[2] The campus seemed to be the ultimate challenge for my arthritic ankle. But the true ADA accessibility of the campus, the DSP's services, and a campus mentality that takes pride in differences and diversity that include disability made for a smooth, ankle-friendly transition.

I have chosen to use UCB's real name because I want to express my heartfelt gratitude to all the people who have fought to construct a campus and community that are physically and socially accessible to people with all types of disabilities, even in the face of severe statewide budget cuts. My deepest appreciation goes to the UCB students who were at the helm of the Disability Rights Movement in the 1960s. They sparked a campus mentality of inclusion and equal rights for all, based on the premise that a university ought to value all of its students.

As part of the DSP, I had a counselor who was my liaison to the university. My counselor, who specialized in working with students with mobility impairments, wrote letters of accommodation for a reduced course load (which could be necessary in the event of an ankle flare-up) and arranged the location of courses to make them accessible to me. The spring semester of my first year at UCB, a required course for my major and another I needed to take in order to be eligible to write a senior honors thesis were back to back in buildings across campus from each other. With advance notice, my DSP counselor and her team of colleagues helped move the classes to the same room so that I was able to take both without missing class time or hurting my ankle. When one of my other lectures was, against DSP practice, moved to an inaccessible building, the DSP helped me get the class moved back to an accessible location.

It is remarkable that a university will relocate a three-hundred-person lecture mid-semester in order to accommodate one disabled student. I do not believe that my DSP counselor and her colleagues moved the class in fear that I would otherwise sue them (à la Chadwick). Rather, they were acting in accordance with a dedication to meeting the needs of disabled students and to overruling changes—such as the unannounced room change to an inaccessible location—that impinge on disabled students' right to equal access to education. I got no joy out of making three hundred students move rooms "for me"[3] (although thankfully, most of the students preferred the new room because of its central location); however, I do feel gratitude—and pride—that I attended a university that takes the core principles behind the ADA to heart, and to such an extent that it would go to the trouble of doing what it did for me. The accommodations extended beyond the academic realm: during sorority recruitment (yes, I did give the Greek system an initial go), a sorority sister ensured that there would be a parking spot reserved for me at each chapter and rode with me in my car as I visited each house. At all twelve houses, I was able to park in or near the driveway. The process of rushing, which would have been inaccessible to me without the parking spaces and the sister's guidance, was totally foot friendly. And to boot, everyone involved in making the accommodations was welcoming.

Granted, UCB's DSP has some flaws. For example, while its shuttle system is better than Chadwick's, it is still lacking:[4] the golf cart that serves as the on-campus shuttle for students with mobility impairments stops running at 5:00 P.M. and does not operate on weekends, making it difficult for students who rely on the shuttle to attend late classes or extracurricular activities that meet in the evening. But "The Loop," as the shuttle is nicknamed, is reliable, picking students up wherever they are on campus within twenty minutes of their phone call. Also, I was able to purchase an on-campus parking permit that, when paired with my California disabled parking placard, allowed me to park anywhere on campus (except for a Nobel Laureate's or department head's spot, which seemed fair enough to me!). With these parking accommodations, I could access most locations on campus during most times of the day and night.[5]

At UCB, disability is not only accepted; it is embraced. Students can minor in disability studies, and several courses are offered each semester that directly pertain to disability. Learning about disability in an academic context has deepened my understanding of what it means to be disabled. For my senior honors thesis in sociology, I interviewed twenty UCB undergraduates who identified as having an invisible disability—one that is not readily noticeable to the casual observer—in order to learn about how they decide to disclose or conceal disability-related information and thereby come out as disabled or pass as able-bodied.

My thesis was an intimate project, and I would be lying if I said that my research aims were purely selfless. (If my disability had not become invisible when I eventually switched from crutches to a restrictive brace, I don't think I would even know what "passing" is!) But the high number of responses I received from students who were interested in participating in my research, and the thoughtful ideas that the participants shared in their interviews, have led me to realize that many students are living with invisible disabilities or other stigmatized social "statuses" (such as homosexuality). I had to turn down more students than I interviewed.

The process of reading about disability and interviewing disabled students in a vibrant academic community that accommodates, accepts, and values its disabled members has led me to own my identity as a disabled student. I am not happy that my foot is often in pain; I still get frustrated that I can't participate in many activities and that I spend a lot of time tending to my ankle, and part of me wonders how my life would be if I had been sufficiently able-bodied to stay at Chadwick University.

While I will never know how things would have turned out had I stayed at Chadwick, I do know that at Chadwick I was viewed by most as a nuisance, a wrench thrown into a system that was supposed to function like clockwork. I was officially accepted when I was able-bodied and unofficially unaccepted when I was injured-turned-disabled upon matriculation. Perhaps the following year I would have proven a useful statistic in the admissions office's pamphlet for prospective students, a token of disability diversity next to the pie chart depicting the high percentage of students of color. At UCB, I was more than a nuisance or a number: I was a full, valued person who was always welcome—better yet, encouraged—to participate in every aspect of campus life. Yes, I felt the effects of budget cuts—from overenrolled lectures to shortened library hours to an ever-thinning list of course offerings. But I was never asked to take time off to heal; I was never trapped in an elevator; I was never excluded from an activity because I could not access it. I was never made to feel a second-class student.

NOTES

1. I use a pseudonym for the name of the school because my aim is not to denigrate a particular school but rather to demonstrate that, even post-ADA, there are elite universities with ample financial resources that fail to accommodate disabled students.

2. My disability makes walking on inclines particularly difficult.

3. I put this phrase in quotation marks because, while this anecdote is about a specific, personal incident, it is relevant to many disabled students and is therefore symbolic of a more general process.

4. Chadwick had no on-campus cart. Instead, there was a perimeter bus that ran every forty-five minutes, and drivers could not even be counted on to drive the full circuit. One evening in January, I was left in the snow far from my shuttle stop because the driver's shift was over. My complaint to Chadwick's disability services office elicited zero response.

5. I could afford the cost of the permit, but I know others can't. I hope that when the state's budget crisis is resolved, the DSP will be able to pay for parking permits for students who cannot currently afford them.

I.2

Speaking Madness

> Yet why not say what happened?
> —ROBERT LOWELL, "Epilogue"

I have thought many times of speaking this story, an acknowledgment of body and disability. Each time I have reached for pen and paper, I have reminded myself of the stigma attached to this silent knowledge, the potential harm that can come of revealing difference. Any one of us who discloses our disabilities engages in risk. In simply "claiming disability" (Linton 1998), especially an invisible one, we enter into the unfamiliar, uncertain of how we will be read or how we will be culturally and socially positioned. (Discomfort is something I negotiate now, even as I write this. Even now, I am wondering what to tell or even if I should tell anything; I am walking into that hidden place aware of my desire to censor this story at the root.)

I have decided to disclose as a woman with a psychiatric disability, manic depression, now because I believe that continuing to engage in the overwhelming battle of refusing to claim this identity would enact more harm than that caused by disclosure. Despite the potential academic and professional dangers of disclosing, I am sharing this because I believe that to *not* claim a psychiatric disability merely replicates the ableist perception that it is a defect, a sign of incompetence, a chaotic unraveling.

Shayda Kafai has received her Ph.D. in cultural studies from Claremont Graduate University since she wrote this narrative. She is a lecturer in the Ethnic and Women's Studies Department at California State Polytechnic University, Pomona, and lives in Los Angeles with her wife.

I had my first breakdown during the start of my freshman year in college. (This is a sentence I write and rewrite. What word other than *breakdown* can I use to describe the process of entering madness? I do not know how to talk about a psychiatric disability without speaking about the dissolve and loss, the collapse, the internal unraveling.) My depression was overpowering. I felt like my body was covered in weights, like I was in a room without a doorknob. Trying to read while depressed pushed me into a foreign, unfamiliar place. The lines in front of me would merge, and the words would render themselves unclear blocks of text. English was no longer English. I would read the same line of *Beowulf* over and over again, arriving each time at an unintelligible nothing. During states of mania, which were significantly briefer and fewer, my focus improved, and I was able to complete my assignments, unrestricted by time. The anxiety that came with this unraveling caused me to arrive on campus in the early mornings and park in an empty lot, only to drive home when I saw other students arriving. When group work was about to begin, I would leave the classroom, closing myself away in a bathroom stall. I was fearful that, with a racing mind, I could not contribute to the conversation and that, even worse, someone might read the signs of madness.

After my first hospitalization, I felt fragmented, ashamed, and unable to connect words to feelings. My family's support helped me move past an almost mechanical impulse to end my life, an eagerness to stop the repetitious cycles of moods. Because school grounded me, I decided to stay a full-time student. I felt anchored by my classes and assignments and the stability of the routine. When I could not drive, my mother would drive me to and from campus, watching me walk to class, my back heavy with mood. I would be hospitalized two more times before completing my bachelor's degree in English. (It is challenging for me to reveal these stories, the literalness of a psychiatric disability.) Although I graduated in four years, and although school became a grounding center, the intensity of my emotions and the speed at which they shifted from depression to mania were constant.

During this time, I deeply embedded the potential disclosure of my disability in fear. When I had to explain to a professor what manic depression was, I felt shame. I was terrified of uttering the word "hospitalization," worried about how this word—and yet is it not more than a word?—would position me. Disability had for so long been equivalent to the overwhelmingly stigmatic: abnormal, dependent, and passive. Having watched *One Flew over the Cuckoo's Nest* and *Girl, Interrupted*, it did not take long for me to assume that I, too, could be seen as unstable and unraveling. Those with unruly minds are, after all, relegated to contained places—to institutions, board-and-cares, and attics. We are bound in a narrative of forced hiding. Explaining why I could no longer stay in another professor's morning class because of the drowsiness caused by one of my medications carried a similar pressure. Most often, I simply did not disclose my disability or the fact that I was on medication, circumventing the conversation and the threat of stereotype altogether.

Along with this trepidation came the relief of being understood and heard. After my second hospitalization, I was able to tell one of my professors about what I was experiencing. Having shared with our class her stories of living with a chronic illness, she had demystified the process of *telling* for me. I soon saw the act of sharing and owning my narrative as distinct from an ableist social narrative that belittled and diminished individuals with psychiatric disabilities. Here, in this newly entered place, I was able to tell someone else about the hospitals, the stress and uncertainty that un-avoidably came with constant medication changes, the tension and chaotic randomness of highs and lows. I remember this moment as a time of exhales, of comfort that comes with confession. I learned that sharing my disability unlocked the pathways that shame had rendered inaccessible.

Those early years were grounded in my inability to rewrite the script about disability that I had grown up to believe. I had learned that what my mind holds must remain secret, that it was a truth best kept to the silent folds of my brain. Madness is, after all, the story a family never tells. (How devastating, how humiliating was this part of me that I was never supposed to speak it or give it a name?) Living in such an obligatory place of secrecy and restraint rendered my disability a voiceless mass that grew alongside me. When I no longer hushed my own stories of madness, I unsettled my bodily history from the stigmas that framed me in shame. The role of silence became clear to me. Shame was starved for silence, for the tight-lipped mouth. It required me to label myself as deviant, as aberrant. The shame of having a psychiatric disability was amplified by silence, just as silence was amplified by shame; it was a frenzied, cyclical feeding. Although it felt coun-terintuitive, the act of sharing my disability—this territory I had marked as shameful—allowed for the removal of that stigma. The experiences of speaking and sharing my body made me realize the transformative urgency that comes with verbalizing the secrets we are taught to keep silent. To use the tongue served as political protest; to speak a bodily story that I was told to hide was restorative.

Immediately after graduation, I began my master's degree in English with an emphasis in creative writing. I finally had found the most effective combination of medications, and my moods had stabilized. During these two years, I tutored students in writing and taught freshman composition. I joined the Students with Disabilities group on campus and organized poetry and art events aimed at bringing nondisabled and disabled communities together. This was the first time that I began to feel comfortable with the word *disability*. Even though I had not yet used it as a way to describe myself, I had begun to *see* myself as a person with a disability. I learned for the first time about the field of disability studies while I wrote my master's thesis, a collection of poetry about women, the body, and illness. Recalling the strength that comes with voicing one's disability rather than silencing it, my poetry began to embrace my own personal narrative and I began to directly engage with the politics of disclosure.

I was drawn into my Ph.D. work because of disability studies and the ways that disability activists and authors Simi Linton and Nancy Mairs gave bold voices to the their bodies. As I read their personal narratives, I began to identify with my own embodied experience of disability. My disability is embedded within my mind: prefrontal cortex and parietal cortex ablaze. Manic depression, however, is also a physical experience; exhaustion and distraction enclose my body or catapult it into agitation, the embodiment of chronically racing thoughts. These locations of psychiatric disability, though they may seem disjointed, are in fact aggressively linked within me—corpo-reality and mind are in constant dialogue. I am aware of how my thoughts affect my body, how my energy affects my moods.

The more I learned about disability studies, the more I learned to speak about my own psychiatric disability. I learned that saying I have a disability does not mean that I *am* my disability. I became aware of the power inherent in claiming this aspect of my identity, of reframing it in a context distinct from the stereotypes that had for so long dominated my understanding of madness. Ableism as a construction, a sedimented and ubiquitous force, came clearly into view. It is ingrained in our built environments (Siebers 2008) and in the language we use. With this new lens, I saw ableist principles ingrained in our movies and television shows. Visual culture uses disabilities as shorthand to reveal the moral weakness or evil nature of a character, while ability and health are used to demonstrate heroism and goodness (Longmore 2003). The more I understood about the formation of stigma, the more I questioned the validity of the stereotypes I had so feared. Madness is not abject; it is merely constructed as such. Once I became aware of this, I revised the ways I saw myself. I no longer considered my mind and body as defective, as staggering sources of shame that swallowed everything else.

As I moved from coursework into my qualifying exams, I began to speak my truth, wholly. I shared the experience of a hospitalization during my doctoral program with those closest to me, and I spoke of all the moments of growth and peacemaking that came with it. In this way, I returned power to my experiences. I no longer surrendered myself to fear and stigma, to that place where I had hidden madness in my body. I reclaimed my memory and experience. Not only did I adopt a disability studies perspective for my scholarly work, but also I adopted it as a way to view myself. I fully embodied this principle during a conference workshop I led toward the end of my program. I introduced myself as a woman with a psychiatric disability, something that came out of me with certainty rather than with unease. In that act, I realized the inherent power of *telling*. In the moments when we articulate ourselves, particularly the parts of us that we thought should be hidden, we disempower shame.

Although I am invested in the political pull that self-identifying as a woman with a psychiatric disability brings, this desire to share does not live within me without a tremendous sense of fear and risk. There is no guarantee of how this chapter will be received or how deeply it will carve itself onto me. Will I be viewed differently as an instructor and as a writer? How will this truth affect my chances of getting a secure, tenure-track job? As I move forward with this uncertainty, I am reminded of research professor and licensed mental health social worker Brené Brown's 2010 TED Talk on vulnerability and courage. Brown argued that courage was not bravery but rather the ability "to let ourselves be seen, deeply seen, vulnerably seen" (Brown 2010). Repositioning vulnerability as a site of courage resonates tremendously within me. I hold Brown's call for vulnerability as a compass as I write this chapter. (Perhaps this is why I am sharing these things, why I am not pressing delete. I am enacting vulnerability in these small, added spaces.) Having taken all things into balance—the ethics of writing, reading, and theorizing disability against the hiding of my disability—I have found this juxtaposition incongruent. There is now simply too much at stake.

REFERENCES

Brown, B. 2010. "The Power of Vulnerability." *TED Talks* lecture, June. Available at https://www.ted.com/talks/brene_brown_on_vulnerability?language=en.

Linton, S. 1998. *Claiming Disability: Knowledge and Identity.* New York: New York University Press.

Longmore, P. K. 2003. *Why I Burned My Book and Other Essays on Disability.* Philadelphia: Temple University Press.

Lowell, R. 1977. "Epilogue." In *Day by Day,* by R. Lowell, 127. New York: Farrar, Straus and Giroux. Available at https://www.poetryfoundation.org/poems-and-poets/poems/detail/47693.

Siebers, T. 2008. *Disability Theory.* Ann Arbor: University of Michigan Press.

I.3

Transitioning from One Culture to Another

ANMOL BHATIA

I was born on May 24, 1979, in what is now known as Mumbai, India. Upon my birth, it was discovered that my eyes were abnormally small. After consulting with doctors, my parents learned that I was born with an eye disorder called microphthalmia and that I would be blind for the rest of my life. This came as a total shock to them. They were not quite ready to accept this news. They, and the doctors they took me to, saw blindness from a medical model, in which disabilities are viewed as medical conditions that reduce the quality of life. Under these circumstances, accepting the news that your child will be blind for the rest of his life is not an option. My parents visited many doctors, hoping that my blindness could be cured through surgery or some other means. We even made a trip to Boston when I was five to consult with a specialist, but we received the same answer again and again.

Anmol Bhatia earned his master's degree in rehabilitation counseling from the University of Arkansas in December 2013. He has worked as a case-manager intern at the Lighthouse Center for Vision Loss in Duluth, Minnesota, and currently works as an employee support services manager at the Seattle Lighthouse for the Blind in Seattle, Washington. He is forever grateful for the many opportunities he has received in the last twenty-six and a half years, since coming to the United States at age ten, and he credits his success to the many American friends who helped him transition to American culture and overcome the internalized stigma of his disability.

In India, being blind is considered one of the worst things that can happen. From the perspective of the moral model of Hindu religious beliefs, blindness is a punishment from God; it is *karma* for a serious misdeed in a previous life. Since my parents had never been exposed to blindness, they did not understand how to handle this. There were few, if any, resources available to assist them. They also had to deal with the negative attitudes of our relatives. In India, the expectations for blind persons are that they will be helpless and live their life at the mercy of a protective family. They are not expected to receive a formal education, find a job, or have a family. As children, they are not expected to go out to play, go to a normal school, or do what every other child does. As Ved Mehta (2014) puts it, "In India, one of the poorest countries the world has ever known, the lot of the blind was to beg with a stick in one hand and an alms bowl in the other."

Like Mehta, I also had devoted parents who did all that was humanly possible—considering the resources available and social stigma—to ensure that I had a fair chance in life. However, in a country such as India, parents like my parents are rare. Many families themselves struggle, and, as a result, the disabled inevitably are sidelined.

The first decision my parents had to make was what to do about my education. Most of the schools for the blind in India were ill equipped and lacked many of the resources that schools in the Western world have. Teachers were not well trained. Most public schools were not willing to accept blind students. My parents visited most of the blind schools in India but were not pleased. And no public schools were ready to accept me. At one public school we visited in Gandhidham (a small town in the state of Gujarat), the principal asked my mom why we even came to visit her. She said, "You expect our teachers to teach your blind son?" Despite this, my parents decided that they would raise me as a normal child—or as normal as possible. They wanted me to receive a proper education and grow up to be an independent person who would one day work. Maybe I would marry if they could find a girl who would take care of me until I died. Their theory was that if they could not find a girl to take care of me, I would live with them until they died, and then my older brother, Dhiren, would take care of me.

My parents did allow me to go play with my brother and do things other children did. Every Thursday (equal to Friday in the United States, since Friday is the weekend in the Muslim world), my brother and I, along with our cousins, would go swimming or play in the tennis court at the Indian Club while the adults played bingo. However, my parents were also overprotective and felt pressure from others who thought that allowing me to do normal things meant that my parents did not care for me. When I was growing up, my parents would not allow me to go places by myself. My parents refused to teach me how to tie my own shoes, fearing that I would trip and fall on my own shoelaces. I did not learn how to tie my own shoes until I was fifteen years old.

At the age of three, I was enrolled in a special class for children with mental disabilities, not because I had a mental disability, but because that was the best my parents could do for me at the time. The teacher, Mrs. Patel, understood that I was not mentally disabled. She worked with me separately and taught me how the alphabet looks and what different colors and objects looked like. However, when Mrs. Patel's husband was transferred, she had to move away and leave her job as well. I was then enrolled in a normal kindergarten class for two years, but my progress was very limited. My parents again started looking for a school that would accept me, in both India and in the United Arab Emirates, where they lived at the time, but none of the schools were willing. At each school, staff feared that the teachers could not teach me, that other students would pick on me, and that the school would be responsible if I got hurt.

However, when visiting the Abu Dhabi Indian School, which my brother was attending, the principal recommended a school, Al Taouan. He said that he would talk with the principal there, Ms. George. Ms. George said that one of the teachers at Al Taouan had a sister who was blind and that this teacher could work with me. It was a Christian school, and Ms. George seemed to think that in a couple of years, the teachers could start talking with me about Christianity and, perhaps they hoped, convert me. However, my progress was very limited, and my parents could sense my unhappiness. The extent of my education was to sit in class and learn by listening to what was going on. My parents decided that I would not go back to that school the next year.

They eventually decided that I should attend a blind school in the United States. They wrote to many schools, only to be rejected by school after school. My uncle Rahm came across an article in *Reader's Digest* about the Arkansas School for the Blind (ASB). My parents wrote to ASB, and a phone call soon came: the board of directors had voted to accept me as a student. I arrived in Little Rock, Arkansas, with my mother in August 1989 at the age of ten to study at ASB. Before coming to ASB, I had never heard of braille or learned how to use a cane, and I never gave much thought to how the world perceived blindness. Within the first year, not only had I learned braille and how to use a cane, but I had caught up academically. At ASB, I felt like I was in my element, but I did not completely fit in, either.

ASB was a small school where everyone had one thing in common: all the students had vision impairments. The classrooms and the number of students in a class were smaller than I expected. In my first class, we had only four students, whereas in my previous school, my class had thirty or more students. I was surprised that I did not have to wear a uniform to school. When my braille teacher, Ms. McGraw, came to my class, I remember being surprised that a blind person was a teacher. I remember telling my mom that my teacher was blind. Although the environment was different, the people were friendly and very welcoming. At the end of my first year at ASB, I felt liberated that I could read and get around by myself, and I received many compliments on how well I was doing.

At the same time, I was struggling with stark cultural differences. One of the first decisions I had to make was whether or not to eat meat. Before arriving in the United States, I did not eat meat. After three days of eating just salads, my houseparent informed me that he talked to my mom and she told him to make me eat meat. I wondered what people back home would think about my eating meat. The next culture shock I had to deal with was how to handle the issue of having a girlfriend. At ASB, I would see my friends having girlfriends and boyfriends. I always seemed to be the odd one out (a guy without a girlfriend), and unlike back home, having a girlfriend in the United States was normal. I remember in braille class having a discussion about dating and how my family might perceive this. However, for me the challenge was the balance of two cultures: one where I was expected not to think about girls and focus on my studies, and the other where I was expected to have a girlfriend. I struggled with these issues throughout my time at ASB, and I still face difficulty managing such issues.

I also had to deal with misperceptions about blindness when I would visit my home in India every summer. In America, my teachers told me one thing, but when I returned home, my parents told me something totally different. My teachers told me to use my cane. My parents, however, were ashamed of what the cane represented and would not allow me to use it. Plus, my parents felt that if I used my cane, others would think they weren't caring for me. At home, I was not allowed to do much. In the United States, I was expected to do everything by myself: clean my own room, cook my own food, and do whatever my peers were doing. In India, my relatives were still hoping that my blindness could be cured, and they continued to suggest doctors who they thought could cure my blindness. In the United States, a social model of disability is prevalent. Being blind is considered something normal, one characteristic of what makes up an individual. In Indian culture, being independent means your parents do not care for you. In American culture, being independent is expected of all individuals, even those who are blind.

After graduating from ASB, I enrolled at Henderson State University, a small liberal arts college in Arkadelphia, Arkansas (one and a half hours from Little Rock), where I earned a bachelor's degree in public administration with minors in Spanish and communication in December 2004. At the university, I was on the debate team, served in the student government association, and was a member of the international student association. I represented international students in the student government association, participated on the student activities board, and worked as a peer adviser for three years. I then took some time off and did some minor work on various political campaigns before enrolling at Arkansas State University in Jonesboro, Arkansas, where I earned a master's degree in political science in August 2008. I then spent one and a half years doing odd jobs (working on local political campaigns) and, in January 2010, enrolled at the University of Arkansas at Little Rock, where I earned a graduate certificate in conflict mediation in December 2010.

I attended my first convention of the National Federation of the Blind (NFB) in July 2010. I got involved with the NFB when I relocated to Little Rock, and it has changed my life forever. When I attended the NFB convention, I saw how independent blind people live and what independence could do for me. Attending the convention, I learned some very important lessons—mostly that I have the right and deserve to be treated with dignity and respect. Blindness is only a small characteristic of who I am, like my nationality, my height, my weight, and everything else that makes me a person. I attended my first legislative seminar in January 2011, during which I had the opportunity to advocate with the United States delegation on behalf of the NFB and blind individuals.

I enrolled at the University of Arkansas in January 2011, where I earned my master of science in vocational rehabilitation counseling in December 2013. From August 2012 to January 2014, I worked as a case-manager intern with Lighthouse Center for Vision Loss in Duluth, Minnesota. In May 2015, I was hired at the Lighthouse for the Blind in Seattle, Washington.

I credit my success as a blind adult to my twenty-six and a half years of living in the United States, the many friends I have successfully made, and, above all, my ability to make the transition from Indian culture to American culture. Thanks to my association with the people of my host country, I was able to break down many barriers and stereotypes that are often associated with disability and often hold people back from having the quality of life that they so desire. Thanks to my professional and personal experience, I am able to serve my community and assist others living with a disability in making the adjustments necessary to have the quality of life they desire. However, many people with disabilities who come from a different culture are not able to make the transition. This is true even for those who are born in the United States to families who come from cultures other than the American culture. The struggle they face is an identity crisis. How can they deal with their disability? Which culture should they subscribe to? Should they view their disability from a medical model, a moral model, or a social model? These issues can affect anyone with a disability. We all have to make the transition from one culture to another.

REFERENCE

Mehta, V. 2014. "Deprivation Often Makes a Writer." Available at http://vedmehta.com/about.

I.4

Growing Up with ADHD

JOSHUA PHELPS

The Centers for Disease Control and Prevention report that 7.8 percent of school-age children have been diagnosed with attention-deficit/hyperactivity disorder (ADHD) (Mackelprang and Salsgiver 2009, 333). I was diagnosed with ADHD and began taking the medication Ritalin (methylphenidate) when I was seven years old. I was diagnosed because there were times in the classroom when I would get so distracted that it would frustrate me. For me, Ritalin worked for four hours and then wore off. I also had an issue with actually taking the medication. First, I took the medication at home before I went to school. Then there was a month when all my grades dropped, and there were many complaints from both my teacher and the recess supervisor. They eventually found out that I had not taken the medicine for the last month. That was when I had to start taking the medicine at school. I struggled with distractions from sights and sounds, paying attention to detail, making careless mistakes, and losing or forgetting items necessary for tasks. The slightest movement or noise could distract me, and I would get up and investigate what it was. I can also remember days in

Joshua Phelps completed his bachelor's degree from the University of Wyoming in 2013. As a person with ADHD, he knows his own strengths and has integrated strategies for living successfully with ADHD. He has worked nine different jobs in the past ten years, and all of them have been either late in the evening or overnight. He is in the final phase of a graduate program in professional counseling at Grand Canyon University.

class when I had my hand up for every question that the teacher asked. Even if I did not have an answer, I had my hand up. If I did answer the question, I usually made up a silly answer that made little sense. For this I was usually sent to the "refocus room." I spent most of my elementary-school years in the refocus room.

I was talented in some areas but very weak in others. I was exceptionally good at English but not good at math. In sixth grade, I placed at the highest level in a spelling bee and prepared night and day to go to the Wyoming state bee. However, my math skills were very low, and it was like pulling teeth to get me to do math work. The teacher would hold me in from recess so I could study math problems. She did not let me take breaks and was always pushing me as hard as she could to increase my math skills.

Because I grew up in a small community, every teacher knew that I had problems in the classroom. None of them looked forward to working with me. When I was in the third grade, I was always a problem student. The teacher at that time did not believe that I needed to go to the refocus room. He believed that what I was doing was an attention issue. The way he treated my behavior was to place me out in the hallway or in a second classroom so he could continue teaching. Several times that year, he placed me in in-school suspension. During suspension, I was able to use the refocus room all day and get assignments done.

At the end of the semester, the teacher and I got into a battle of wills. I could predict the point at which he would lose his temper and send me to the adjacent classroom. One day, when he lost his patience and sent me to the other room, I was already past the point of being able to control myself, so I started tapping and banging my hands on my desk. The teacher came out and slammed the door shut between the two rooms. That was a mistake: I began knocking and yelling through the door to the regular classroom. At that point, he came out with a roll of duct tape and taped my hands to my desk. He then placed a piece of duct tape over my mouth. He said that I could not move or talk until he told me I could.

So many things went wrong with this event. The teacher had accepted the fact that I came with a label, that I had ADHD and was a problem. By the time I was in third grade, I had already been given an individualized education plan (IEP). However, the teacher did not follow through with the IEP. The teacher had two different classrooms that he could have used while teaching, but he used the second room only as a punishment area for those students who acted out. There was a refocus room as well, but he did not utilize it.

Maltreatment for children with learning disabilities is not uncommon and can cause severe physical and psychological trauma. In recent years, children with learning disabilities have been locked in closets, tied up in duffle bags, and even killed while being restrained by professional staff. Parents who pursue legal action against schools are also met with much resistance. The schools usually just claim that all of the treatment plans were followed and that the child was too disruptive for the classroom.

Some methods, however, were truly helpful for me. One teacher used carrels—desks with small walls. These carrels were very effective for keeping me on track for a more extended period. When I was in the fourth and fifth grades, I would raise my hand, and the teacher would acknowledge that he saw my hand. This recognition from the teacher was beneficial to me. The other thing that worked well was a touch prompt on my desk to stay on task. At this point, I already knew that I was different from the other kids with my ability level. I was able to tell my teacher that I did not like being called out in front of the class to be asked if I wanted to go to the refocus room. Instead, when I felt like I was getting out of control, I would raise my hand and ask if I could be excused. I would go down to the refocus room for twenty or thirty minutes, and then I would come back.

I have lived with ADHD for most of my life. While at times it is easy to deal with, there are other times when it is very difficult. At times, ADHD can make life chaotic and challenging. As I live a very busy life, working two to three jobs at a time and going to graduate school, my biggest coping mechanism is developing a schedule and asking those I work with to be very flexible with me. I have found what I am good at in life, and I work within that area. The second coping mechanism that I have developed is doing everything within a routine. Everything in life that is important to me has its place. For example, I work the overnight shift on the weekends, and when I get home around eight or nine in the morning, I make sure to place my keys in the same place every time. If I do not put the keys in the same place, I freak out later when I cannot find them. The entire house gets torn apart as I search for them. The third coping mechanism is that I know what times of the day or night I am at my best. I do not function well from eight in the morning until about three in the afternoon. I plan my day around those times, because I know that by working during my optimal times, I can be successful.

REFERENCE

Mackelprang, R. W., and R. O. Salsgiver. 2009. *Disability: A Diversity Model Approach in Human Service Practice*. 2nd ed. Chicago: Lyceum.

I.5

Disability and Sports

CHRISTOPHER WEINGARDT

W hen disabled athletes are portrayed in movies, TV shows, and other media, they are usually shown in two camps. The first is that of the supercrip, the young, attractive (except, of course, for his or her disability), disabled protagonist who has to persevere and overcome his or her physical shortcomings to become the absolute best in the league while simultaneously becoming a figure of inspiration. The other camp is that of the ridiculed, in which the Special Olympics or Paralympics are used as jokes.

I was born with severe blood clotting in my right leg, causing my leg to be dying and infected by the time I took my first breath. It had to be amputated immediately, just below my waist, to prevent the clotting from migrating up into my torso, causing damage to my major organs. I have never known what it is like to walk on two legs; my entire life I have traveled on crutches.

Chris Weingardt is a graduate student of economics who does economic consulting work on the side. His clients have included the state of Wyoming. His research interests include improving forecast models, behavioral economics, and public finance, with an emphasis on curbing gambling spending. He is a lifelong amputee who believes disability should not be an inhibiting factor in anyone's life. His current hobbies include swing dancing, playing volleyball, and hiking in his "backyard" of Wyoming. He hopes one day to publish a best seller on economic research.

I love sports. I love watching them, and I love playing them. But, as you might imagine, playing most sports with a physical disability such as my own brings some challenges. For instance, as a child I played soccer and street hockey. While playing soccer, I was able to run and kick in much the same way the other kids did. However, in street hockey, I found it too burdensome to carry the stick while maneuvering on crutches. The other kids and I came to an agreement. I was allowed to use my crutches to strike the puck or ball, so long as I followed all the other rules. It worked beautifully. It is small changes like this that can make a big difference in whether or not a person with a disability can play a sport. However, attitudes, both of the person with the disability and of the nondisabled teammates and competitors, also play a big role.

During the summers when I was growing up, I was often a member of a local swim team. When I first started swimming, I was not as fast as the other kids, because I did not have the same leg strength. It was discouraging, of course, but my teammates and coaches encouraged me to keep practicing. After a lot of training, I made up for my lack of leg strength by working on my upper body strength. Pretty soon, I was as fast in the water as my teammates and competitors, and it was a confidence booster to be able to compete with my nondisabled peers. It helped me learn from a young age that a disability does not necessarily mean one is unable to do something; it just means that, with the right mind-set, one is able to do anything in his or her own way. Participating in sports, particularly swimming, gave me great opportunities as a kid. It gave me chances to connect with other kids, laugh with them, compete with them, and form friendships. It also presented a challenge for me to overcome, that of my lacking leg strength. Kids with disabilities should not miss out on these kinds of experiences.

Most athletes with disabilities are average people who may play a sport in a minor league or even just casually. These days, I play volleyball twice a week casually among friends. In that regard, I am an athlete with a disability. Just as I had to learn how to adapt myself when learning to swim competitively, I had to learn how to adapt the game of volleyball to fit my ability. My crutches are too restrictive for me to play normally, so I've learned to ditch them long enough for a game of volleyball. This frees my arms up to hit the ball, and I can hop around the field. It is little tweaks like these that make a disability a nonproblem. It also means that I am neither a supercrip nor a subject of scorn. I am just an average player, having fun.

I.6

Contours of Ableism and Transforming a Disabled Life

ZACHARY A. RICHTER

I start this chapter with my point of reference. My name is Zach Richter, and I have always been disabled. But for quite some time, disability was not an identity; rather, it was a series of symptoms or gaps between me and other people. In the case of my most dominant pathology, the symptoms at first separated me from other people, confining me within the diagnostic term "nonverbal learning disability" (NVLD), but they now unite me in solidarity with a wider community through my new self-identification as autistic. In the case of my lesser pathologies, dysfluency and phobia, the struggle to actualize those experiences and render them more coherent within a disabled identity has been ceaseless.

The turning point in my self-knowledge occurred when I first read Fiona Kumari Campbell's *Contours of Ableism* (2009). While I had long felt that the isolation and jeering in my childhood were different from those experienced by other children, I was incapable of putting into words the kind of trauma

Zachary A. Richter holds a master of science degree in disability studies and recently completed a master of arts degree in communication at the University of California, San Diego. He comanages the anti–speech disability discrimination website *Did I Stutter?*, at http://www.didistutter.org, and occasionally blogs at http://www.zachrichter .weebly.com. His current research focuses on questions of nationality in disability studies' accounts of the freak show. His other research interests include queer disability studies, critical animal studies, and media theory. In his spare time, he enjoys biking, Magic the Gathering, and board gaming.

I felt and the basis of my exclusion. What Campbell gave me was a language by which to articulate my experiences. The implication was jarring. While many middle-class suburbanites like myself find it so easy to fall into a nihilism that absolves them from questioning the unkind interactions that go on between institutions and minority groups, finding the words to name my traumas forced a recognition of the realities of power and inequity. To find that the words in my mouth and the movements of my body had been marked permanently by an uneasy relationship with hallowed ideals meant a final absolution for the inner struggles that had characterized my childhood. Campbell's explanatory prowess allowed me to begin my life as a disability activist and ended my attempts at blending in with an ableist ideal.

For many years, disability was a ghost that haunted various aspects of my life but could not be spoken. This haunting is similar to the haunting of alternative sexuality: while I described myself with words like "weird" and "strange," I was never comfortable letting others know about my diagnosis. This effort was, of course, in vain. My classmates could tell I was different, most obviously because every October I would miss school or melt down to various degrees due to my phobia of Halloween masks. There were other signs, too. I would be escorted out of class, sometimes early, by special education teachers. I would be given extra time on tests and essays, and my peers likely noticed. But I never wanted to think about myself as disabled in public. I never thought that identifying with disability could be useful or empowering. All the while, I had experiences in which I would stare at myself in the mirror and—even though I do not have a physical disability—regard my body as foreign and despicable. Worse than that are the moments that still happen but seemed worse back then: the moments in which I would make a mistake, lose a possession, trip over my feet, or stutter and instantly relate that particular moment to my overall status as disabled, despairing deeply about the limits that would forever bind me.

Sometimes this despair would fill me so heavily that the emotions would expand from minutes and hours into days and weeks. Days and weeks in which my tongue felt as if it was made of lead, because I knew that when I lifted it, it would move differently than those of people around me. Those longer moments of despair came to define who I was as a young person, as I walked around angry and in shame over who I was. I probably could have been, and still could be, diagnosed with depression because of the way these things commonly make me feel. But with much determination, I intentionally avoid such further diagnoses and falling once more into the medical or therapeutic gaze. This brings me back to my past of moving from therapist to therapist, distraught over missed social cues and mistakes in conversations. While the shame of my occasional misunderstanding in socializing due to noncomprehension of nonverbal communication was bad, even worse was getting more diagnoses and more reasons to see myself as an accumulation of flaws rather than as a valuable person capable of making a significant contribution to the world. My view of these experiences has evolved, but before I explain how, it is crucial to make some mention of how the specters of both disability and activism have haunted my life, even prior to my involvement with the disability studies community.

I attribute much of my thinking regarding disability to my relationship with my father. My dad, a fellow stutterer, could always be observed to have a strange passivity in his way of interacting with the world. As an angry teenager, I often lambasted him for this, stating that he let the world walk all over him. He passed stories on to me at a young age, stories about his struggle with stigma over the blips in his speech, social reactions that apparently altered him so much. He told me that his parents repeatedly made fun of him and that his peers at school did the same. While people around me have been much less cruel, his account has always made me determined to pursue a better life and be less ashamed of my impairments. I have never suffered as much over my speech difficulties because of the presence of other elements of difference (my NVLD). But other stories from my father have also played an important role in my understanding of disability; he informed me of his work and involvement in groups of stutterers, both local to his former home in Florida and affiliated nationally. My father's struggle and solidarity as a person with a speech disability, even during a time when disability studies did not exist, resonated with me and was one of the many factors that pushed me to become involved in activism early—in high school. I felt a subtle injustice that I could not describe with words. I knew that I had suffered in a way I could never describe to anyone and carried that burden; however, because of that suffering I felt compassion for many and became involved in the antiwar movement in my senior year of high school. For good reason, activism was something that I believed needed to be done. The suffering that I experienced but could not put into words was undoubtedly experienced by many others, and a part of me hoped to confront it. My experience as a debater in college would offer me just such a chance.

While involved in collegiate debate, I witnessed rhetorics of liberation being used by various groups within the intercollegiate debate community. Most successful among those rhetorical styles was an extremely successful indictment of white bias within the debate community. While witnessing various forms of philosophical and critical movements of liberation being born in debate, I learned how to research, and one of the first topics I chose to research was my own struggle for liberation. In this process, I discovered Campbell's *Contours of Ableism* (2009), which immediately changed both the way I approached debate and my own career as a scholar. *Contours of*

Ableism altered the way I understood both my own experiences with disability and those of my father.

Thinking about disability as a place of experience from which to network and build community implies a tremendous transformation of its former status as a shameful trait that should be hidden. Approaching disability as an injustice offers me membership in a new culture and allows me to think of my experiences of suffering in school and elsewhere as a unique form of knowledge, one not known by other people. After realizing my new identity as one of many oppressed for their stigmatized bodies and minds, I found a community waiting for me that offered greater support and belonging than I had found almost anywhere else. What is most important about this community is that it is one of few that did not require me to pretend to be something I was not. I am allowed and encouraged when I stim or act autistic, when I offer unique viewpoints, or when I express my frustrations with an overly normalized society. While this alternative, radical disability community first began to exist on Facebook through my communications with various important theorists, it also appeared among the social circles that I find myself in merely because of how vocal and militant I have become in my constant critique of ableism and discrimination against people with disabilities, whether it be in the form of inaccessible institutions or comments and words that make us feel abnormal. As other, more radically oriented friends of mine began to understand that if they were struggling against racism or misogyny, they also had to respect my movement against ableism, I have produced tiny spaces where the purity of discrimination against people like me is reduced and people are aware of what ableism is, even if they do practice it on occasion. Indeed, my professors and friends are aware of the importance of the concept and endeavor to fight ableism and be allies with me.

The best moments, however, happen when I am surrounded by my fellow radicals at places such as the Society for Disability Studies national conference. At such conferences, I find myself around a large number of people whose experiences are similar to mine but often manifested uniquely. The Society for Disability Studies is a group in which I am much less scared to be who I am and to express myself. At such radical disability events, access occurs in a number of different ways, from people switching seats to allow people forced to stand in an overly crowded session to sit down, to people working to speak slower so their words can be projected on a screen to assist hearing-impaired individuals in the audience. The radical disability community opens its doors to a wide range of different types of voices, bodies, and means of expression. This degree of openness is essential in creating a community in which ideas can be exchanged and new ideas can be generated. The recoding of social and educational spaces such that access becomes a priority invites new entryways into social spaces that were previously inaccessible for many disabled people. My presence in such locations has restored my faith in the basic claim of the social model of disability, that more affirming spaces can exist if we, as a society, work for them. This same confidence has spread generally to my social life and has allowed me to position my unique experience as part of a larger project of reorganizing social machineries to make them more open to unusual experiences and standpoints. This view has allowed me to experience a lesser degree of shame during those moments when my actions or words represent traits previously aligned with my disability. While the struggle does continue, how it began is important and corresponds deeply to the greater process of political awareness and thinking. Here, I am brought back to a consideration of the pervasiveness of ableism and to how, even when we are awakened to the exteriority of the compulsion of able-bodiedness, it inflects the ways that we communicate with ourselves. The struggle is far from over, but I am brought to a more apt place from which to struggle, and this is the most pressing transformation recorded here.

REFERENCE

Campbell, F. K. 2009. *Contours of Ableism: The Production of Disability and Abledness.* Houndmills, UK: Palgrave Macmillan.

I.7

I Can Dance!

I took ballet lessons for seventeen years. I loved the grace and elegance of floating through the air as the music entered my mind and spirit and exited through my body in beautiful movements. I can still remember the feeling, although I have not danced for a very long time. My legs will no longer lift me high into the air. Nor are they strong enough to balance me or support my weight as I try to thrust one leg high above my head. I now need assistance to walk, and this thought and the recurrent vision of dancing and walking unassisted have saddened me for years. I was encouraged, though, when I read about Simi and Glenn and Homer in Simi Linton's 2007 memoir, *My Body Politic*. They all danced!

I read about how Glenn moved in his wheelchair and how Homer experienced an amputation yet danced as the "one-legged man." In fact, Homer danced until just before his death. Moreover, he danced with enthusiasm and passion. Simi speaks of an experience in which she and others moved their arms and upper bodies while in their wheelchairs as others fluttered their legs about them. I thought of that image, and it seemed so beautiful and complete. The thought of dancing had left my world, but Simi brought it back.

Suzi Vee lives on the East Coast with her family.

I stood in the kitchen last evening. My legs and hips struggled to keep me upright as I adjusted my WalkAide devices, functional electrical stimulators that send responses to my lower legs and help me walk short to moderate distances. I began to move my arms up above my head in graceful ballet-like moves. I bent at my waist and swooped down and then up again. I fully extended my arms and felt that I was once again flying as I did when I flew through the air in ballet performances. I heard the background music of a soft song to which I had once danced. I *felt* the music.

My daughter, Abigail, was visiting and was upstairs bathing her daughter. I did not realize that she and my baby granddaughter, Megan, had come downstairs and were standing, immobilized, watching me. I looked up and smiled as Abigail smiled back and cried. She said, "Mom, you are dancing! I have not seen you dance in so many years. You are so elegant and so beautiful." I then asked if she would dance with me by fluttering her legs as I moved my arms and upper body. She did. Baby Megan squealed with joy and also fluttered her little legs and feet. I have never danced such a beautiful or joyful dance.

When I first began to read *My Body Politic*, I could not relate to Simi. Now, I realize that although so many of her experiences were unlike mine, she has motivated me, and I admire her. I am planning to dance with my sweet Abigail and little Megan at our Thanksgiving celebration. I cannot wait. I am grateful. And, yes, I can dance!

REFERENCE

Linton, S. 2007. *My Body Politic: A Memoir.* Ann Arbor: University of Michigan Press.

PART II

FAMILIES, ADAPTIVE LIVING, AND REORIENTING EXPECTATIONS

P ERSPECTIVES ABOUT DISABILITY are inevitably wrapped up in familial relations. Nondisabled parents shape early meanings for disabled children and their siblings—their acceptance, struggle, love, and advocacy inform how children understand their impairments as well as their value and place in the world. Parents with disabilities, in organizing around physical, sensory, or cognitive differences, often develop adaptive processes in which children and partners participate. In the best cases, families are involved in the alchemy of inclusion and promote a sense of self-worth, pride, and genuine belonging. However, family dynamics can also be damaging, especially when informed by **ableist scripts** that focus on deficits and limitations or situate disability as tragedy, misfortune, or incapacity.

The narratives in this section capture how interwoven these perspectives can be—how pain curtails and then reshapes futures, how struggle, depression, and anger intensify love, insight, and action. These chapters also highlight the broader social and material forces that shape familial responses to disability, such as economics, ethnicity, and gender. The authors offer insight into creatively adapting to disability. In mapping this process, several authors describe emotions connected with loss. Disability studies has rightly critiqued the dominance of loss rhetoric in professional and personal descriptions of disability. Too often, such narratives perpetuate the misconception of disability as primarily personal and familial rather than deeply shaped by social and political factors. At the same time, pain and loss, especially in the case of acquired disability, constitute part of the process of adaptation; these chapters provide insight into engaging honestly and creatively with disability, with reorienting expectations, and with the transformation—through familial relations—of physical and emotional pain into knowledge and insight.

The first two chapters, by Mycie Lubin (II.1) and Elizabeth Allyn Campbell (II.2), explore the pleasures and complications of mothering with disabilities—Lubin with memory loss brought on by strokes and Campbell with lupus, Sjögren's syndrome, and fibromyalgia. Both illustrate how disabilities have led to creative models of kinship and expanded methods of living and parenting. Joanne De Simone and Tricia Black became intimately acquainted with disability through their children: both have sons who were born with or diagnosed in early infancy with cognitive or neurodevelopmental disabilities. De Simone describes in Chapter II.3 the emotional intensity of parenting a child with multiple medical complications, but she also recounts remarkable resilience, familial adaptability, and the powerful bond she shares with her son Benjamin. The conversation in Chapter II.4 among Tricia Black, her son Michael, and Leila Monaghan shows the very different perspectives of a parent and someone who lives with disabilities: while Tricia fears for her son, Michael accepts his disability.

Christina Spence, in Chapter II.5, and Douglas Kidd, in Chapter II.6, reflect on acquiring impairments as young adults and the unique importance of familial relationships in their personal growth and emotional processes. Spence provides a glimpse into her own struggle after a spinal-cord injury. She shares the importance of being exposed in one of her classes to a version of Elisabeth Kübler-Ross's (1997) well-known **stages of grief**. While Spence's rehabilitation professionals were very attentive to her physical recovery, they offered little support for the intensity of new emotions, including fear, anxiety, and denial. While the stages of grief accurately describe many people's emotional processes, we note that disability studies scholars Carol J. Gill, Donald G. Kewman, and Ruth W. Brannon (2003) have critiqued the *imposition* of stage models as the only process for a person adjusting to disability. For Spence, understanding her emotions as common to other people helped her forge a path of adaptation through family support, faith, and community networks. Her narrative reminds readers that people dealing with acute injury need individualized psychological and emotional support in equal measure to physical rehabilitation.

Douglas Kidd's experience with traumatic brain injury (TBI) is deeply shaped by his familial experience with his brother Richard's TBI in the late 1980s, which left him in a coma for months and has resulted—due in some part to limited resources—in his confinement to an institutional care facility.

When Kidd experienced his own brain injury in 2005, he began to question how he had removed himself over the years from his brother's life and, in his chapter, poignantly reconsiders his ideas about disability through this significant sibling relationship. Taken together, these chapters uncover some of the internal and external pressures family members face, but the authors also compellingly explore the unique insights and creative support that emerge within family systems.

Reference the boldface terms as themes for discussion, and consider the following questions as you read the chapters in Part II:

1. What sociocultural and structural issues of disability do these authors identify, and how do these issues shape their emotional and practical responses to disability?
2. How can disability studies productively engage with narratives of struggle, loss, and grief while still holding people accountable for reproducing ableist beliefs and practices?
3. All of these authors describe the onset or arrival of disability— through injury or the birth of a child—and the intense transition they experienced in the process of living with and making meaning of disability. How do medical professionals, rehabilitation providers, other systems of support, and family members inform and influence this process?
4. All of these chapters address kinship and disability. What similar themes arise? How do their concerns differ? What gaps or tensions emerge between these narratives? What examples of reimagining kinship can you pull from these narratives?

Suggestions for Related Readings

- Mycie Lubin (Chapter II.1) and Elizabeth Allyn Campbell (Chapter II.2) have nonapparent disabilities. How do their experiences and adaptive strategies differ from or overlap with those described by Catherine Graves in Chapter III.2 or Leslie Johnson Elliott in Chapter III.6?
- Compare the interchange between Tricia Black and her son Michael in Chapter II.4 with narratives of other complex conversations, such as those described by Tasha Chemel in Chapter III.4 or Leigh A. Neithardt in Chapter III.5.
- Pair Christina Spence's chapter (II.5) with Garrett R. Cruzan's chapter (IV.4) to compare their adjustment to spinal-cord

injury—especially in terms of family, self-perception, identity, and the political dimensions of disability.

REFERENCES

Gill, C., D. G. Kewman, and R. W. Brannon. 2003. "Transforming Psychological Practice and Society: Policies That Reflect the New Paradigm." *American Psychologist* 58 (4): 305–312.

Kübler-Ross, E. 1997. *Death: The Final Stage of Growth*. New York: Scribner.

II.1

Life Given and Memory Lost

MYCIE LUBIN

G iving birth is a gift of life. My story began in the process of giving life to my third child. I am an immigrant woman who takes pride in following all the rules of society, but I did not know that even after following the rules of my doctor, I would suffer a terrible loss at the age of twenty-eight. I lost my ability to process language without difficulty, to understand and retain information. I may not be able to share the future of my children, as I am a prime candidate for Alzheimer's disease. Cerebral arteriosclerosis, or little strokes, is the disability that has robbed me of part of my memory. A few years ago, my husband and I decided to try for a third child, the little girl we so wanted to complete our family after our two sons. We followed all the rules, and I attended all of my prenatal appointments. Nine months later, I gave birth to a healthy, seven-and-a-half-pound boy, and my life changed on the delivery table.

Mycie Lubin has been diagnosed with many other health issues since she wrote this piece, but none of them is taking away her *joie de vivre*. She has graduated from college and works in a field she loves, providing services to formerly homeless individuals. She lives her days to the fullest, appreciating family and community and taking care of herself as she remains a servant to others. She has come across many who have made a difference in her life, but her spiritual connection and belief that love, kindness, courage, compassion, and acceptance are the keys to happiness are what keep her going day after day.

I had multiple strokes immediately after delivering my son. I had never drunk alcohol, even wine. I do not smoke or do anything that is considered deviant in my native culture or in the American culture into which I have assimilated. My family history, my past medical problems, and the environment I was subjected to as a child led to this life-changing disease. Nonetheless, brain injury can be dealt with if resources are made available for individuals in need. With the help of my family, primary care physician, neurologist, and network of close friends, I have been winning the fight against memory loss. I am now considered disabled, but I have used all resources made available to me. I have never regretted my babies, and they always remind me why I am thankful for each one of them. Giving new life exposed the hidden medical problem I had, but it has allowed me to learn how to take care of myself and live longer.

Memory loss has been, for many years, a tragically neglected condition. In my native home of Haiti, we do not know as much about it as we do about diabetes or high blood pressure. For most of us, except for those annoying moments when memory fails or when someone we know struggles with memory loss, we live comfortably unaware that just about everything we do or say depends on the smooth and efficient operation of our memory systems.

Prior to this event, I never knew that my family had a long history of mini-strokes, which resulted in memory loss, Alzheimer's, and other forms of dementia, passed down from my grandmother to my biological mother and father. During my early twenties, I experienced problems retaining information, and twice I lost consciousness and couldn't remember the previous day. I visited a number of doctors and had some tests run, but I was told that everything was fine, that I needed to relax since I was going to school, had two children, and was working two jobs. But everything was not fine, I later came to find out. Now, after experiencing several strokes, I am in an everyday battle to remember, speak, and fight other diseases in order to be able to participate in all areas of my own and my children's lives.

I have learned that memory is one of the most important processes in our brain (Katz and Rubin 1999). It helps us learn new skills and habits, to recognize everyday objects, to retain conceptual information, and to recollect specific events in everyday life. Memory involves more than just remembrance of things past; it is the glue that holds everything in our lives together (Restak 1995).

The amnesia that has resulted from my brain damage has provided me with an opportunity to make great improvements in my life. I woke up in the hospital and found out that I had damaged brain cells. I was told that I would not be able to complete my education, have a career, or experience being part of the lives of my children as I got older. I decided to fight.

In college, we were assigned Simi Linton's 2007 memoir, *My Body Politic*, which tells of how she adjusted to life after a major car accident. Just like Linton, whose work I first read in my beginning disability studies class, I could not accept my changes at first. I cried, blamed my family for not informing me of medical issues we have, and became angry, depressed, and resigned. One day, after my neurological appointment, I met a social worker named Lorna. We became friends, and she opened my mind to a new world of possibilities. Meeting Lorna and reading Linton gave me hope that life has much more to offer if I am willing to fight for it. Linton described how her whole world changed when she lost the use of her legs. She recognized then that society was made for nondisabled people. She had problems going places, and people saw her differently.

Linton's disability can be seen, and people usually react to what they can see. My disability, on the other hand, is hidden. For a few years, I tried to ignore facts and act as if everything was going well. I was miserable at work, in school, and at home. I made the lives of my children and my husband a nightmare because I refused to accept my disability. I am an immigrant with a very thick accent. English is my fourth language. I am black and a woman. I thought, *No way am I going to add disability to the list.* I already had too many obstacles in a country as racialized as America.

My friend Lorna became aware that something was wrong with me. She asked me to volunteer at the Developmentally Disabled Section of the Department of Social and Health Services in Tacoma, Washington, where she worked; there, she introduced me to groups of professionals with all sorts of disabilities. I learned that Lorna herself was diagnosed with bipolar disorder, but I never told her of my memory loss. I was offered a job and worked hard at hiding my difficulties. I was going to school, taking one class at a time, and using a tape recorder in all our course meetings. At home, I had sticky notes and message boards in every room, and I expected everyone to write down anything they wanted from me. It worked, for a while.

Because I assumed that my disability would make my coworkers treat me differently, I lived a lie. Because of this lie, I shut myself off from the resources available to me and from the strong network of family and friends I had. Finally, my husband, my family, and Lorna got together with my neurologist and decided they were going to help me deal with my depression, loss of memory, and the onset of Alzheimer's. Needless to say, I was unhappy with the fact that they were meddling in my affairs, but I found out soon that I was using the wrong method to fight the disease. The best approach was to face it, accept it, and keep going.

After months of family therapy, I learned to accept myself and rebuild a relationship with everyone in my life. I was bombarded with resources, from brain exercises to books on how to improve my memory. At school, I never informed my professors of my disability because I was afraid they would think I was looking for special accommodations and preferential treatment. My employer informed me of online classes; I enrolled, and it became the best environment for me. My three boys have been wonderful in helping with my education. They have been my cheerleaders for the past six years. They will also tease me, testing me to see if I can remember absurd things they have done that have made me angry. They call it "Mom's Jeopardy time," and, of course, I must "pay" (by walking an extra thirty minutes) every time I can't remember something. They will also encourage me to go for a long walk or to eat healthy food, which is often not my choice.

Often, memory loss is not the most serious part of my disability. Rather, it is the distress I suffer. There are days when I feel like giving up. This is where my "hourglass" becomes a major part of my life. My family made me a room filled with all the things I like—books, movies, and mirrors. We call it my hourglass. This is my sanctuary. Every time the struggle gets too hard to handle, which is often, I go into the hourglass and read the notes that my children, my family, my friends, and I have written. Often, I will write out my feelings, shed tears, and move on to the next day. I take different prescribed drugs to help me fight depression, but my physician likes to tell me, "You are not depressed; you have too much zest for life, Mycie. Everyone has downtime, and this is your downtime." I like to hear that, because it makes me feel, somehow, that I will be fine.

After doing a lot of research about memory loss, I have learned to manage my disease. In my workplace, I take "brain breaks." Half of my lunch hour is dedicated to exercising; I do low-impact workouts. I learn a new word every day and try to remember the meaning of it the next day. I take my prescribed medication daily, and I try to keep everything the same in my life. I have a routine that I follow every day, and so does every member of my family. When things change, it can be very chaotic for me, but with the help of my husband and my children, this does not happen often. (I can recall my husband trying to surprise me for my thirtieth birthday. He gave me a party, but I spent most of the time crying because there were so many details of my life that I did not remember.) At home, my disability is often forgotten, unless, of course, the children forget to do something and blame it on me. At work, I use devices to help me perform my job, from tape recorders to voice-recognition systems, which help me remember what and where each program is supposed to be.

People with disabilities have long faced discrimination, but our interactions with nondisabled people have improved. Once I learned to accept my disability, I stopped expecting people to discriminate against me. I have learned from books and the classroom so much more about the Americans with Disabilities Act (ADA). I now have a fulfilling life. I belong to People

First, an organization that advocates for the differences in people's lives and for acceptance. I stopped labeling myself, since all it did was present me with obstacles. My fight with the onset of Alzheimer's is a constant struggle, but I am preparing myself. Because of the memory loss, I have a form of learning disability. I cannot focus for an extended amount of time. When I forget the topic of conversation or my mind wanders into a world of old memories, it is difficult in school and at work. I can remember my childhood in Haiti and Canada, but I cannot remember what I ate yesterday or the day before. My neurologist gives me many types of exercises to complete daily, and I tell stories to my boys every night about the events of the day, especially if it is their birthday. I will pick out one special event from that day and teach myself to remember it. There are some medications I am taking to help keep my brain cells alive.

It is nice to read literature about disability. People are becoming aware that disability is part of everyday life. In a matter of a few hours, my life changed from that of a vibrant, intelligent twenty-eight-year-old woman to an individual with memory and speech problems. It has taken me a while to accept the fact and move on. Nonetheless, with the help of my family, friends, and outside resources, my daily journey continues. It has taken me six years to complete my bachelor's degree, and I do not know how long it will take to complete a master's, but it will be done. I have no intention of stopping my studies until I am diagnosed with full-blown Alzheimer's. The research and my interactions with professors, students, and librarians help me stay alert in trying to find new knowledge about the brain. I remain busy in order to stimulate my mind and stay vibrant. Learning of the upcoming possibilities in science for people diagnosed with Alzheimer's gives me hope. I am fulfilling my need to make a difference in the lives of everyone I meet. I teach my children resilience and tenacity. My disability has become a blessing because it allows me to be a better person and live a happier life.

REFERENCES

Katz, L. C., and M. Rubin. 1999. *Keep Your Brain Alive: 83 Neurobic Exercises to Help Prevent Memory Loss and Increase Mental Fitness.* New York: Workman.
Linton, S. 2007. *My Body Politic: A Memoir.* Ann Arbor: University of Michigan Press.
Restak, R. 1995. *Receptors: A Lively Exploration of the Ways Exploding New Knowledge about the Brain Is Making It Possible to Change the Very Nature of Who We Are.* New York: Bantam.

II.2

Beating the Odds

Life with an Invisible and Chronic Disability

ELIZABETH ALLYN CAMPBELL

Most people go through life believing that disability will never exist in their world. This utopian reality in which nothing can go wrong is suddenly nonexistent when a disability is acquired or diagnosed. My story begins when, at the age of nineteen, I was diagnosed with systemic lupus erythematosus (SLE). For years, I had experienced pain, skin rashes, multiple illnesses, and fatigue. After breaking out with a particularly bad facial rash that resembled welts, I made an appointment with a dermatologist. A couple of weeks after a skin biopsy was performed, I was informed over the phone that I had lupus. The nurse who gave me my test results didn't even know what lupus was and couldn't answer a single question I asked.

After my initial diagnosis, I went home to research the disease. In my research, I discovered that the prognosis for lupus was grim. Many people with lupus died within ten years, often from kidney failure. I had an overall

Elizabeth Allyn Campbell is a mother of five living with systemic lupus erythematosus, Sjögren's syndrome, and fibromyalgia. She was a military brat who has lived up and down the East Coast and currently calls Maryland her home. She graduated summa cum laude with a bachelor of science in social sciences from the University of Maryland, University College. She is currently earning her master's degree in school counseling at Liberty University, and her lupus has been relatively well controlled for three years. Her life has been touched by children with disabilities ranging from autism to Prader-Willi syndrome. Her love of these children, as well as her own, is the drive behind her vocation.

sinking feeling; I became preoccupied with my own mortality. It wasn't until I spoke with a rheumatologist that I realized that the statistics were skewed and that, with proper treatment, I could expect to have a normal life span. With continued research, I learned that lupus is an autoimmune disease that can affect almost every major organ in the body, including the heart, skin, lungs, brain, and, most notably, the kidneys. The antibodies that a body uses for protection against disease are unable to distinguish good tissue from bad tissue. When this happens, the individual's own antibodies begin to essentially attack and destroy healthy tissue. By my early twenties, my experience of fatigue, rashes, stiff joints, headaches, and chronic illness was commonplace. (Lupus symptoms include stiff joints, fatigue, rashes, headaches, and chronic illness, but connecting my symptoms to the disease took many years.)

After being referred to a rheumatologist for my care, I still didn't have all the answers. It took a few years and multiple symptoms to discern that I had systemic lupus rather than one of the less damaging varieties. During this time, I suffered from many common symptoms. I was a waitress and bartender and worked nearly every day. During some shifts, the bones in my feet would feel as if they were all broken. I would have horrible pains when I was on my feet rushing from table to table. I just dismissed this, thinking I was overworking myself. In addition, my muscle aches would keep me up at night.

Unfortunately, muscle aches and joint pain were only the beginning of my experience with lupus. One morning, I woke up alone in my apartment, terrified because I thought I was having a heart attack. I was unable to move or even breathe properly. I tried to sit up and was immediately seized with a sharp, shooting, horrendous pain that rendered me unable to move. Every breath I took was short and shallow. I could not catch my breath because every movement caused excruciating pain. It felt as if someone were stabbing me in the heart. The left side of my body was useless because pain made it unbearable to move. At twenty-two years old, I thought I was dying alone in my bed with no one to save me. Fortunately, this episode only lasted a few terrifying minutes. I still had pain afterward, but nothing compared to the initial intense episode. I went to see my rheumatologist and was told that I had pericarditis, a swelling of the tissue that surrounds the heart. These episodes are usually quick but at times can endure. The symptoms of pain near the heart, pain on the left side of the trunk, and shortness of breath are unmistakable.

After my pericarditis episode, I felt fine for a while, so I thought the occurrence was a fluke. However, I soon realized that it was only the beginning of my progression into lupus. I started having chest pain, tenderness, difficulty lifting my arms due to pain, difficulty breathing, and pain in my ribs. This pain affected me because it was long-lived and impacted my life in many ways. After an examination by my rheumatologist, I was diagnosed with pleurisy, which occurs when the tissue covering the chest wall and lungs becomes inflamed. Pleurisy is treatable, but some individuals develop scars that can cause lifelong problems with pain and shortness of breath. The pain, weakness, and fatigue from my bout with pleurisy lasted for quite a while. After several experiences with pleurisy, pneumonia, and bronchitis, X-rays revealed that my lungs are riddled with nodules and scar tissue. The damage is so severe that the doctor reviewing the X-rays listed tuberculosis as a possible factor in causing the destruction of my lungs.

On a regular visit with my rheumatologist, I was diagnosed with shingles. I had what appeared to be small, dark-purple bruises located on only the left side of my body—bruising I thought was caused by taking high-dose steroids. I had flu-like symptoms, including exhaustion, weakness, and headaches, but I attributed these to my long bout of pleurisy. Because I have had problems with migraines and cluster headaches since I was young, I dismissed the frequent headaches I was experiencing. All these symptoms were due to the shingles virus, which is the same virus that causes chicken pox. After a person contracts chicken pox, the virus remains dormant in the body and can wreak havoc when the immune system is compromised. I was lucky to catch my shingles while the rash was still purple bands, before it blistered. After a month's worth of antiviral medication, I was feeling much better.

When I finally had my lupus under control with myriad medicines, another disease I was unaware of crept up on me. Soon after the outbreak of shingles, I noticed that my skin was getting extremely dry. My skin hurt because of the dryness. It got so bad that I couldn't take showers very often because the water dried my skin out even more. I remember taking a shower in my apartment, and I couldn't even finish because my skin felt like it was burning. I tried applying a soothing cream to quell the pain, but it only made it worse. I got out of the bathroom quickly and jumped in bed, afraid to put any clothes on my skin. I couldn't help but cry as my skin continued to burn. My skin was not the only part of me that was dry. My mouth was so dry that I woke up choking because it felt as though my throat were closing. I usually woke up several times a night to get something to drink. To this day, I still keep a glass of water next to my bed every night. After consulting with my rheumatologist, I found out that I had Sjögren's antibodies. Sjögren's syndrome is another autoimmune disease that often accompanies lupus. People with Sjögren's can experience dryness in the eyes, mouth, and skin, as well as rashes and fatigue. After beginning to take the right medication, I was able to live a somewhat normal life again.

Within a few years, I discovered that I had two autoimmune diseases and found out the potential they had to harm my body. I was carting around a box of medicine with pills that I had to take between two and four times daily. I was taking Evoxac (cevimeline), Plaquenil (hydroxychloroquine), steroids, Ultracet (acetaminophen and tramadol), Celebrex (celecoxib), Topamax (topiramate), lorazepam, Zoloft (sertraline), Neurontin (gabapentin), ibuprofen, and painkillers for severe episodes. In addition, I was given Lidoderm (lidocaine) patches to use for chest pain. At this point in my life, I was attending the University of Maryland, College Park. I remember sitting in my car on campus and opening the box of medicine and thinking to myself, *What is all of this doing to me?* I wondered if I was destroying my body with medication. I already had mood issues and anxiety after being on these medicines for a while. How were they affecting my mood and behavior? I also began to wonder whether I would ever be able to have children. On my next appointment, I asked my rheumatologist about my fertility. He told me that I had an increased risk of miscarriage and premature delivery. He also said that I would need to be monitored and free of lupus flares for a year in order to have a successful pregnancy. At twenty-two years old, I was faced with the very real possibility that I might never have children.

However, in my case, during a period of intense illness, I got pregnant unexpectedly and had to immediately stop taking all drugs except Plaquenil and prednisone. During this pregnancy, I was completely full of nerves. No doctor knew how to deal with my lupus and a pregnancy, so I had to see my rheumatologist, an obstetrician/gynecologist, and another Johns Hopkins Medical Center rheumatologist who specialized in lupus and studied lupus pregnancies. In addition to this, I had blood tests performed every couple of weeks and sonograms to check the baby's heart and size every week. With the abundance of doctor appointments, I was exhausted. No one would treat me for any ailment, no matter how small. Having a primary diagnosis made most doctors apprehensive to treat me even for something benign, like a sinus infection. As a result, I was consistently pushed off to the next doctor until I exhausted all my referrals and begged the original source for help.

While under the care of a specialist at Johns Hopkins Medical Center, I was diagnosed with fibromyalgia. After a simple examination, I found that I had most of the eighteen positive tender points attributed to fibromyalgia. Pain, musculoskeletal pain in particular, is common with lupus. Further, other symptoms of fibromyalgia, like fatigue, sleep disturbances, and problems with cognition and mood, can also mimic lupus symptoms. People with fibromyalgia are more sensitive to pain sensations because of the way the brain processes the information. There isn't much that can be done to help with fibromyalgia, but doctors recommended that I exercise and try to sleep well.

I am now a mother of five smart, beautiful, funny, wonderful little children. Of my five successful pregnancies, three were uneventful, with few symptoms; this happens a lot with lupus mothers. I do not possess the antibodies that typically cause miscarriages, but I have had issues staying pregnant. I had one pregnancy that was extremely difficult; I was constantly in pain, struggling to breathe, and had to be hospitalized on a few occasions to receive high doses of steroids.

Through all this, I still cannot believe how blessed I am and how fortunate I am to have overcome the odds to have had successful pregnancies. Motherhood has changed my outlook on life and made my life worth living. My children have provided me with the best medicine available, love and laughter. But while motherhood has been central to the change in my outlook on life, as a person with a disability, I am limited in what I can do for my children, and this can be a source of tremendous guilt. After all my bouts of pneumonia and pleurisy, I have significant lung damage. The scar tissue and nodules indicative of years of disease have made it consistently difficult for me to breathe and made it painful for me to lift most things. Lifting my children is one of the things that I have to limit in order to minimize the pain. I used to take my children to gymnastics classes that required parental involvement. I was required to assist my children in getting on balance beams and to lift them onto bars while wearing the baby in a harness. I was able to do this with my first child with some limitations, but by the time I had my second child in gymnastics, I was unable to get through a class without taking painkillers for days afterward. I had to stop taking my two oldest children to the class they loved because my body could not handle it. The incident at gymnastics is not an isolated event. Any time my husband and I go out with the kids, I have a painful reminder for at least a couple of days. I have to seriously think about what will happen to my body every time I leave the house with my children. In order to go on vacation, I must get several cortisone shots, bring lidocaine patches, and bring emergency painkillers with me.

My limitations often leave me contemplating my effectiveness as a mother. I have moments of sheer guilt when I think about the things I cannot do for my children. To compensate for my disabilities, I try to provide my children with activities we can accomplish at home. For instance, my children and I cook together quite a bit, and we also do science experiments while cooking, like mixing oil and water together, and physics tricks with common kitchen items. We do not just cook; we look at the numbers on the recipe and discuss fractions while also counting each individual component to learn numbers. This gives me opportunities to interact with them while also providing an educational experience. I also coach my daughter's cheerleading squad, which has provided me with tremendous joy. Coaching is something that I am able to do because it requires no lifting and minimal strenuous activity. In addition to this, I have a great assistant coach who takes over when I cannot physically participate or when I am ill. Having this support system has meant the world to me because it allows me to continue to participate. I also have wonderful friends who understand what I am going through and go out of their way to help. My friends have helped by watching my kids or simply holding the little ones so that I can have a much-needed break. Also, my mother recently retired, and she has gone out of her way to help me with the kids. For years, I did everything on my own, but now I have a great support system that allows me to rest at times and to continue to participate in activities I enjoy.

While my situation has changed for the better, I cannot help but feel pangs of guilt when I am unable to do something with my kids. There are days when my chest pain is unbearable, making it painful to pick up my two babies. There are times when I cannot attend plays or sporting events because I am too ill. Early on in motherhood, I was told by several family members that I needed to stop having children because of my health. No one was excited when we announced each subsequent pregnancy after my second child. I spent years thinking I might not be able to have children and, indeed, I have not always had successful pregnancies. However, my family members do not realize that my children have given me all the happiness in the world. They do not understand that before I had children, there were days when I would question how long I could live through what seemed like endless pain. My outlook has changed dramatically simply because they exist. They give me the drive to push through the pain, and their smiles pull me out of the depression that chronic pain can bring. I can't make those family members understand how my children have changed my life for the better; all they see is my limitations. They see my raising children as a catalyst for lupus flares instead of the reason I continue to push on.

One of the ways that I have managed my disability is by acquiring a disability placard in order to park closer to buildings. This one allowance has provided me with an immeasurable amount of relief. Just a few weeks after picking up my placard, I noticed a difference in the amount of pain I was experiencing. Parking closer and carrying my children a shorter distance has dramatically reduced my daily pain. In addition to this, when I go to a store, I often find a shopping cart deserted in these spots, which is helpful because I can place my children in it right away. While the acquisition of a parking tag has proven extremely beneficial to my overall health, I often find that onlookers are assessing my disability status. (I have had people scream at me or demand to see my state-issued card that all placard holders must carry.) I look completely healthy and young. To onlookers, my appearance must go against preconceived notions of what it means to be disabled. The very nature of an invisible disability leaves me under direct scrutiny.

Living with a chronic and invisible illness does have its challenges, but I feel grateful for all the treasures I have in my life. Because my disease is invisible, I can decide whether or not to disclose this information. All I have to do is put on some makeup to cover my facial rash, and I blend right in. I do not feel as though my disability hinders my life; it just makes it different. I have come to realize that there are so many different types of disabilities, many of which are invisible. I no longer look for visual clues, like a wheelchair, to determine whether a person is disabled. For instance, a grocery-store clerk told me she was unable to lift a container of water the other day. I didn't question it or think she was lazy; I just thought that she may experience the same type of pain that I live with. Living with invisible disabilities has made me much more tolerant and aware of others like me. Instead of having the knee-jerk reaction to judge or criticize, I have empathy.

One thing I have learned throughout my years of living with a disability is to appreciate everything I have and can do instead of dwelling on what I cannot do. There are material realities that I face directly, however, such as the long-term repercussions of medications. For example, long-term steroid use causes bone destruction. Recently, I was diagnosed with osteopenia, which is the precursor to osteoporosis. To address this situation, my doctor has me weaning off steroids, which presents its own set of issues. Each taper is brutal, resulting in shakes, anxiety, mood swings, headaches, and fatigue. I'm hopeful that the combination of weight-bearing exercise and reduction in steroids is enough to avoid having to take another pharmaceutical. Such complications mean that there may be things that I cannot do, but I find other ways to make my life and my children's lives fulfilling. My five beautiful children are the greatest blessing I have ever received. I spent years questioning whether I would be able to have children, and I beat the odds and had five. I have a loving and understanding husband who picks up the slack when I am down and helps me accomplish the tasks I cannot do alone. My more understanding friends and family are able to see that I am a competent mother and worker. They don't let my disability overshadow my achievements. My husband and children have learned that just because they can't see a disability, it doesn't mean it doesn't exist. They are all so supportive and understanding. They are aware of my diseases and do not hold it against me when I am unable to go places or do certain things.

I have been without a flare for over a year, except for one recurrence of shingles that was short lived. I have my disease under control and have been proactively taking back control of my life. I have earned a bachelor of science degree in social sciences, graduating summa cum laude. I am looking forward to obtaining a master's degree in guidance counseling. I am able to do most anything I put my mind to and have proved that despite living with a disability, I am more than capable of achieving any goals I set forth and that I am a competent mother. My disability hasn't kept me from living a fulfilled and productive life; it has made me realize how precious every moment is. The unsupportive members of my family have only provided me with more motivation and drive to accomplish my goals. Proving everyone wrong and succeeding with my disability is becoming one of the most rewarding experiences in my life. I don't know what tomorrow may bring, so I relish every moment of today.

II.3

Benjamin Is Benjamin

JOANNE DE SIMONE

My ability to retain a sense of control was obliterated when my infant son Benjamin's neurologist unleashed a string of words a parent should never have to hear: "He'll probably never walk or talk or use his hands, but, more importantly, I have no idea what his cognitive functioning will be." It was one breath of declarations that was immediately and forever burned into my soul. Done. I was done. I would never be the same. How could I possibly absorb this? How could I possibly survive this? Why me? Why him? I had taught children with disabilities for years, but Benjamin was going to be more disabled than any child I had ever worked with.

Motherhood had become a fertile ground for sorrow. As a special educator and former professional dancer, I was crushed by the assumed severity of Benjamin's physical and cognitive disabilities. It was as though every fear I had imagined actually came to life. I thought of my students and their

Joanne De Simone is a graduate of Hunter College in New York, with degrees in dance and special education. She has counseled families and taught children with disabilities for the past twenty-one years. She is currently working on a memoir about her experiences as a special educator and as a mother of two children with completely different but equally challenging disabilities and about how her previous career as a dancer supports that journey. She lives in New Jersey with her husband and two sons. She has written for several publications, including the *Washington Post*, the *Huffington Post*, and *Brain, Child Magazine*'s blog. Follow her at https://Special-EducationMom.com.

parents. Until now, I hadn't understood them at all. I wondered if I would ever be able to look at my son without crying. I had failed him. My body had failed him. His future seemed barren, like that of the child I had miscarried before him.

The most difficult lesson for me was learning to focus on the present. I couldn't let my fear of the future interfere with my love for Benjamin. The bond I had with him was strong from birth, and he was an active part of our relationship. Every time I cried, he laughed at me. I could do nothing else but look into his bright, brown eyes and love him even more.

By the time Benjamin was six months old, his daily schedule had been rearranged to include a team of four separate therapists. I was grateful for their presence because I desperately needed to release the idea that I alone had to devise a therapeutic program—I just wanted to be mommy. However, it hurt knowing that my baby needed a team of experts to give him much more than I could ever provide on my own.

Each day was built around accommodating the arrivals of the special educator and occupational, physical, and speech therapists. I was feeling the isolation. The therapies were the number-one priority, and there was no time for the typical activities I thought I'd be engaged in by then. No play dates, baby gym, or music classes. Besides, my version of motherhood was so far from the norm, I wasn't sure how our family would ever fit into the world. Even Benjamin's diagnosis was alienating. Our pediatrician had never heard of lissencephaly.

Frustrated that we couldn't find a lick of information on this rare brain malformation, my husband, John, called a good friend who worked in computers and asked her to look it up. It's strange to think about it now, but it is a fact that when Benjamin was born in 1999, we did not own a computer. Our friend had difficulty finding much information about lissencephaly on the Internet but sent us a printout of a web page that mentioned it. It was from a support group's website. In large artful letters it presented the group's tagline: "Touched Briefly for All Eternity." The connotation was more than a little stunning. Clearly, it wasn't good.

We bought a computer and joined the online support group. The members of the group were my first real lifeline, and I began climbing my way back up to a sanity that had escaped me. The member families completely understood the grief, the loss, the frustration, and the worries about the future. They had more to offer me than anyone else had up to that point. Talking to other parents in similar circumstances was comforting because they just "got it." They had been where I was and had dealt with the same questions. They had some, but not all, of the answers.

I fed off this small yet diverse group of people as if I had been imprisoned and starved. They taught me about the potential physical complications, medications, early intervention, health insurance, therapeutic equipment, and practitioners. I started filing their collective knowledge on every topic for future use. The families were on the front line. Doctors could make recommendations and make decisions based on medical studies, but the support group gave me personal data. I would stay up late cyberchatting with parents about their children. I met several families in person, and on a monthly basis, it seemed, I mourned the death of someone else's child. As with any disorder, the children varied greatly, with a spectrum of abilities. The average life expectancy was two years.

Benjamin's first year of life was compromised by his cerebral palsy and epilepsy, but with medical intervention, he was stable. Although his developmental progress was minimal, it was no longer our top priority. When we blew out the candles on his first birthday cake, we had so much to celebrate. While he was not able to hold up his head, roll over, sit, stand, take one step, or use his hands, he was alive, which was no small feat. If Benjamin was capable of fighting that hard, I had to make sure I was ready to carry him up to the next plateau.

We expanded our team of medical specialists. An orthopedist was monitoring skeletal problems and tight muscle tone. Benjamin was under the care of a gastroenterologist for reflux. A neuro-ophthalmologist tracked him for medication-related vision problems. We had an ongoing follow-up schedule with each provider. We had the strength to manage the juggling act because Benjamin was well. We'd do anything reasonable to help him.

We traveled from New York to Chicago to meet with the most highly regarded specialist in the field of neuronal migration disorders. In his office, we talked about medical management and whether to be aggressive or to just take a care-and-comfort approach. Obviously, those were not decisions we were required to make right at that moment. We would have to wait for Benjamin's medical issues to present themselves, and we would make decisions as needed. John and I realized Benjamin's quality of life was the foremost factor that would determine our course of action.

Before the appointment with the specialist, we had been on an emotional rebound, but seventeen months into the journey, it still hurt to hear the same news over and over again. I didn't like being told that we would be put in a position to make choices that could determine whether Benjamin lived or died. Then I realized we had already begun making those decisions. The seizure medications could kill him, but we were living the disclaimer: the benefits outweighed the risks. I wasn't sure if all the choices would be that obvious. I didn't like that level of responsibility, but it was ours. There was nothing fair about it, but life isn't fair. We learned fast to be grateful for every happy and relatively healthy day Benjamin had. His happiness fueled my strength. Without it, I would be lost and depleted.

While in Chicago, we took a day trip to visit a family from the Internet group who lived in Indiana. Their son, like other children with lissencephaly, had a feeding tube and a tracheostomy. They showed us how they fed him, cleaned all the tubes, and suctioned his trachea. I marveled at their ability to manage it all so routinely. Our doctor had mentioned these types of medical interventions, but discussing them and seeing them in action were two different things. I wasn't prepared to face this extreme.

John and I exchanged glances throughout. We were of one mind thinking about quality-of-life issues, but the definition of "quality" suddenly seemed hazy. I was abandoning the present and speeding ahead to an image of Benjamin without his vibrant personality and laughter. If his health were compromised to the point of needing all this equipment, would our bond deteriorate? Clearly, these parents loved their son. They made difficult medical choices based on their unique understanding of his needs, and they adapted to a role of parenthood consumed with clinical caregiving. Even though it was the right thing for them, I wasn't certain that John and I would make the same decisions. I feared how we would be judged.

As we got ready to return to Chicago that evening, a horrific thunderstorm hit. The house lost power, and we walked out the door as the family's backup generator kicked in. That was a foreign concept for a New York City girl—we truly were in the middle of nowhere. The family encouraged us to stay, but we needed to jolt ourselves back to our present reality. It was dark and the rain was so fierce that we couldn't see two feet in front of us. The only moments of clarity came from the lightning strikes. John drove steadily, never showing trepidation. I was petrified and just wanted the ride to be over. Benjamin was in the back seat, roaring with laughter. Apparently, he loved the sound of the hard rain. I clung to his joy, always a comfort and my guide.

For the remainder of the Chicago trip, we focused on just being a family, which was something that often escaped us at home. There was no therapy schedule. We explored zoos and museums. We took long walks and rode on amusement park rides. It almost felt normal. The winds of Chicago were strong and warm. I was a part of the world again, and I wasn't feeling lonely anymore.

Whatever was to come, our goals were clear. We would be diligent about Benjamin's care. Life span was linked to the level of medical support a child needed. We would continue to seek out the smartest, most compassionate doctors and thoroughly committed therapists to accompany us on this journey. Benjamin would be surrounded by happiness. We would tolerate nothing less from anyone who came into contact with him. John and I were Benjamin's united advocacy team. It was time to go home and get on with life. Benjamin was thriving in his own way. When I opened his door every morning he welcomed me with a smile. Nothing filled me more than the sight of him grinning, his eyes still closed.

He loved the classic children's books *Goodnight Moon, The Runaway Bunny,* and *The Carrot Seed.* We could tell by his laughter and facial expressions that he had playlists of the Beatles and James Taylor memorized. He thoroughly enjoyed watching me dance to his favorite tunes. He loved when John hid behind his high chair and sneaked out to run circles around him. When he listened to our conversations, he always seemed to understand the jokes and laughed at the punch lines.

Benjamin took particular joy in seeing us do any type of manual labor around the house: washing the floors, the dishes, collecting laundry. It was all one hysterical show. I think he was mocking me because when I was pregnant, I often teased that he would one day do those things. He showed me. Looking at him lying on his changing table, I realized that was the way he'd look, ten or maybe twenty years ahead, happy but completely dependent. He was who he was.

I am truly amazed at how clear my insights were back then. Benjamin is fifteen now, and I feel exactly the same way. He doesn't walk, talk, or use his hands. He has endured seven surgeries. Most were orthopedic, but the last was to place a feeding tube. His seizures are present daily. Benjamin is still Benjamin. His smile is wider than ever, and his laughter reminds us to enjoy life's ride. His cognitive abilities will always be unclear, but he has an unmistakable, bright personality. Benjamin has managed to approximate two phrases in his lifetime, "Oh yeah" and "I love you." They define his character perfectly. I couldn't be more proud.

Nowadays, I keep in touch with other families on Facebook. Medical technology has increased the children's life span, and yet I still mourn their passing on a monthly basis. I dread the thought of burying my son. But the idea of John and me preceding him in death fills me with fear. No one can understand, love, and care for Benjamin as well as my husband and I can.

John and I continue to make decisions based on how they will affect Benjamin's quality of life. The choices aren't always obvious. I still do not like that responsibility, but Benjamin has taught me to accept every moment for all its pleasure and all its heartache. I will love him wholly and with brutal honesty until I am no more.

II.4

Conversation with a Mother and Son

An Interview

TRICIA BLACK, MICHAEL BLACK,
AND LEILA MONAGHAN

Background

I (Leila) met Tricia when she took an online disability studies class with me at the University of Maryland, University College, and we have kept in touch ever since through Facebook. Tricia is the mother of two sons. When her older son, Michael, was six months old, he was diagnosed with choroid plexus papilloma (CPP), a rare form of brain tumor made up of benign cysts. Repercussions of Michael's CPP have included numerous medical appointments and hospital visits for a variety of conditions. He has also been a special education student throughout his schooling. When Tricia and I met, Michael was fourteen years old. As he is now over twenty, I asked Tricia and Michael if they wanted to both be involved in a piece for this book. Tricia agreed to interview Michael, and Michael also agreed to interview Tricia. I also asked questions. The interview was done over Facebook messaging, with Tricia relaying her own and Michael's answers. I have edited the exchange for clarity.

The Interview

TRICIA: If you could take away your disability, would you?
MICHAEL: Not really. You just have to accept what you have in life.
TRICIA: Are you happy with life?

MICHAEL: Yes.

TRICIA: What do you not like about having a disability?

MICHAEL: I try to help people, and they push me away because of my differences.

TRICIA: How do you try to help?

MICHAEL: I try to help them out or clean up messes.

TRICIA: Where are the places you feel the most comfortable or most accepted?

MICHAEL: At home, at school, on the train tracks, at Scouts. Oh, and Special Olympics in Maryland. I made a lot of friends there.

TRICIA: What do you think you would like to do in the future?

MICHAEL: Videotape or photograph trains and/or twisters. I would like to make a book with my pictures. I also want to go to school to possibly be a history major. I would like to be a tour guide in a museum teaching about the wars.

TRICIA: How did you feel when you were told by the doctors that you couldn't drive?

MICHAEL: I was really disappointed, but I am okay with it now.

LEILA: What is the most important thing people should know about you, Michael?

MICHAEL: I usually care about people and that I stand up for kids with special needs. And people who have been hit by disasters. Also, I am in the middle—I am normal, but I talk stupid at times.

LEILA: What kind of help do kids with special needs need?

MICHAEL: I know they need help getting around a place (because of being visually impaired or scared), or I help with understanding a lesson.

LEILA: How have you helped when there have been disasters?

MICHAEL: I went to Washington County when a tornado hit. My stepfather and I helped clean up afterwards.

LEILA: What was that like? Were you scared?

MICHAEL: I wasn't scared, but I was very sad. I cried behind the truck. It made me cry because people lost their lives and homes. I was also excited because tornados are very fascinating to me.

TRICIA: Michael has loved tornados since he was nine or ten years old. Michael also assisted an elderly woman when he was touring the Luray Caverns on vacation. She had become overexerted, and he helped her climb the stairs back to the surface. He stayed with her the whole time, consoling her.

LEILA: Michael, what groups are you part of? I saw your Boy Scout troop won a prize.

MICHAEL: I play baseball for the Challengers.

TRICIA: It's a special needs Little League organization.

LEILA: Tricia, can you tell me about organizing the Boy Scout troop and how you got involved with the Challengers?

TRICIA: Organizing the Boy Scout troop was challenging. My husband and I had tried three different troops here in Central Illinois. While they are great troops, Michael just didn't "fit." So we decided to start a troop for those with special needs. The hardest part was finding an organization that would sponsor us. Once the Charleston VFW [Veterans of Foreign Wars] Post 1592 agreed [to sponsor our troop], we just needed to recruit some Scouts. You wouldn't think it would be challenging, but it is. Fortunately, I gained the trust of six wonderful young men with varying levels of needs and their families, and they decided to join Scouts. In the past two years, they have grown immensely and still love Scouts. In March 2016, the troop will gain four Webelos from the Cub Scout pack. I guess we are doing something right.

Challengers was something Michael and I had participated in originally in Maryland up until [Michael was] ten, but when we moved to Central Illinois, there weren't any sports for Michael's age group (age seventeen). So I got this great idea to start my own league. With help from [an] acquaintance, I started planning a softball team through the Mattoon YMCA for Mike. Luckily, someone beat me to it in the next town (which is forty-five minutes away). They joined the Challengers Little League Organization and started the league here. We were excited! Michael did fabulous. He was nicknamed "Babe Ruth" and "Big Mike" 'cause he slams the ball out of the field every time. One time when Michael was up to bat, the athletes' buddies were asked to stand in front of the smaller athletes [to protect them from the ball]. It's fabulous to see Mike's face light up from the joy of hitting the ball and everyone cheering for him. These extracurricular activities that are geared for those with special needs make a *huge* impact on our children's lives.

TRICIA: Michael, what else do you do?

MICHAEL: I also help my mom and dad's friend Todd at the food bank. And I also volunteer at the Douglas-Hart Nature Center.

LEILA: What do you do at the food bank and the nature center?

MICHAEL: At the food bank, I just collect cans and box [them] for those who need food. At Douglas-Hart, I help with the landscaping. This summer I did some mulching and cutting down trees. I got poison ivy twice. I have to be careful of the heat; I am sensitive to it because of my medications.

LEILA: Michael, you should ask your mom some questions.

MICHAEL: Mom, do you like my disabilities?

TRICIA: No, I hate them. They make your life unnecessarily too hard for you.

MICHAEL: How do you live with it?

TRICIA: In all honesty, I can live with it because of how much I love you. A parent should give their unconditional love for their child no matter what.

LEILA: What has been the hardest part of living with disabilities for both of you?

MICHAEL: I could say not having friends (but that answer kinda came from my mom). School was really hard because of being bullied, and learning is difficult for me. Dealing with people's stupidity about disabilities is always a problem.

TRICIA: This is a hard question, for each stage of life has had its own difficulties. Currently, the transition from high school to adulthood is hard. Our compromise was to find a residential group home to allow him to spread his wings. And that plan even seems to be flawed because the group homes are more restrictive than what I allow at home, such as he won't be allowed to go on walks by himself or ride his bike whenever he wants. Growing up, we had a really, really hard time with puberty. Puberty caused a lot of changes, including aggressive behaviors. I had to call child protective services on my own child. That was devastating.

MICHAEL: How are you letting me go out on my own into the community and moving out?

TRICIA: It's really hard because I am afraid you won't come back. I am terrified someone will physically harm you or you might go into a health crisis. I am letting you move out because you are striving to grow. It is my job to give you that freedom to grow, but I fear that someone will break into your home or you won't take care of yourself.

MICHAEL: What are your happiest moments with me?

TRICIA: I have so many happy moments. Usually, my happiest moments are when I see you smiling, and I can tell you are genuinely happy. Most recently, my happiest moment was when you graduated high school! I was told you would never accomplish school. Another moment was when you received your Scout Life Rank.

MICHAEL: What do you think of me when I play baseball?

TRICIA: I think you are adorable! To see you happy makes me happy.

II.5

Taking Disability One Stage at a Time (unless They Attack You All at Once)

CHRISTINA SPENCE

On January 15, 2006, I was in a single-car accident that left me paralyzed from the waist down. My parents were asked if they were familiar with paraplegia, and they prepared to help me deal with a very uncertain future. Over the next few months, I struggled with the loss of my legs and my "normal" status in much the same way that I had struggled with the sudden loss of a family member a few months prior. I was confused, angry, and depressed, and I spent a great deal of time and energy looking back and questioning what had happened and how it could have been prevented. I tried bargaining with God, promising that if everything could just go back to the way it was before, I'd straighten up—that I'd never take anything for granted again. I thought I knew what life with a disability would be like; hadn't I spent my whole life watching how society treated people who were "other" than the status quo, those poor unfortunate souls on wheels and crutches? I had pitied them and had never had the chance or reason to be directly involved with any person with a disability before; the only "knowledge" I had of this life was what society had taught me. I was absolutely terrified.

Christina Spence lives in Maryland with her husband and two daughters and spends her time advocating for disability rights and enjoying the company of her church community.

After being transferred from the acute-care hospital I had been flown to after the accident, my days were filled with learning to live this new life. I had to learn how to do everything in an entirely new way—without my legs. The talented physical-therapy team taught me how to transfer in and out of my chair and how to take care of my muscles to prevent things like atrophy. I was taught how to self-catheterize, and I learned what medications would be essential from then on out. The team was demanding but encouraging, pushing me to challenge myself physically through my recovery, and I started to have some amount of hope that maybe, just maybe, I would be able to push through this life in some of the same ways that I had planned on walking through it before.

But I was still depressed, very angry, and often resentful toward the very therapists who were coaching me. What did they know about it, anyway? Had they ever had to go through any of this? What scared me the most was thinking that something was wrong with me mentally and emotionally as well. I was a strong person. Didn't everyone who visited me keep telling me this? Why was I so angry all of the time? Why were there times when I would fall into tears and not know for sure why? When I spoke of this to my therapists, their only solution was to evaluate the antidepressants I was taking and advise the doctor, and then the doctor would adjust the type or amount of medication and issue it to me promptly. I dutifully took the pills, even knowing in the back of my mind that all they were doing was making me tired, which agitated the negative emotions that were constantly brewing just below the surface. I was never offered a therapist, a psychologist, or a psychiatrist. No one ever attempted to discuss what I was experiencing mentally and emotionally. My entire stay at physical rehab was centered on just that: the physical adjustment to my injury. The psychological adjustments were never even considered.

Over time, with strong family support and a network of a few friends who stuck around despite the bright purple chair I was now confined to, I adjusted. I received spiritual counseling from my pastor. I learned to find humor even in the discouraging moments. While I still had low days when I allowed myself to look back and mourn my losses, and while there were still moments of deep depression, I focused forward. I was put in touch with the Maryland Department of Rehabilitation, which introduced me to the idea of going to college, with the department's assistance. I found others who had gone through similar, acute injuries, and I flirted with the idea of starting a support group. I constantly questioned my thought processes when I became sad or depressed; however, I still felt that this was just a sign of weakness. In my third semester of university, I eagerly signed up for a disability studies course. In the course, I was first introduced to the idea of a stage theory of response to disability, an adaptation of Elisabeth Kübler-Ross's (1969) theory of the stages of grief. I found myself shaking with the realization that I wasn't abnormal, that the emotional journey I had been on since the day of my injury was actually common; this realization brought an instant sense of relief. Almost immediately, I began wondering why I had never been introduced to these stages. It would have saved me countless hours of worry and sleepless nights spent wondering if something was wrong with me, convinced that I wasn't dealing with all of this properly. Instead of medicating me, why hadn't the doctors discussed this with me?

While there have been several different stage theories of response to disability, and no one seems to agree on just one, they are all similar to the stages of grief that lead to acceptance of a loved one's death. In *Disability, Society, and the Individual*, Julie Smart (2001) identifies the different stages typically acknowledged in these theories. Shock is a common first step with an acute, acquired disability; life has changed so abruptly that your mind simply isn't capable of absorbing it all. Smart describes the experience of this stage as being "unable to think or feel" (2001, 242). I remember lying in the hospital, simply nodding at the doctors but not truly hearing anything they were saying to me. I knew that I couldn't feel my legs, and I couldn't talk because of the tracheostomy tube in my throat (until they finally put a speaking tube in, but that was for short periods of time only), but nothing else seemed to be sinking in. As the shock slowly wore off, I was flooded by emotions that were somewhat staved off by the stage of denial that I didn't experience at that time—I felt like I was never really allowed to sink into a denial stage. Instead, I was strongly encouraged by my remarkable support team, both my family and the professional therapists at the hospital, to accept my new reality.

Denial is also referred to as "defensive retreat" by Smart. She explains, "Denial can take three basic forms: (1) denial of the presence of the disability, (2) denial of the implications of the disability, or (3) denial of the permanence of the disability" (2001, 242). Denial of the full implications of an injury and the subsequent acquired disability is common, not only for the patient but for family members as well. Believing that the disability will not truly be permanent, or that there is some miracle solution for it, can actually be beneficial in that it "can prevent what is called 'emotional flooding' and allows the individual to gradually assimilate both the permanence and the full implications of the disability" (Smart 2001, 242). My mother told me a story about a nurse in the trauma ward at the inpatient hospital where I was initially treated. Apparently I would repeatedly bang on my legs and then make a "why" motion with my hands. While I have no memory of the first few weeks in the hospital, my mother believes that this was an effort to learn why I couldn't feel my legs. At one point, a nurse told me that I should just accept it and stop having such a tantrum, that of course I couldn't feel my legs and I would never feel them again because of the spinal-cord injury.

While my mother made certain that this nurse was never again allowed in my room, she has told me that I quit asking why in any capacity from that day forward; I seemed to regress to a state of shock for a few days, and then the tears and anger began.

As Smart explains, the "depression or mourning" stage begins when a person looks forward and "struggles with questions of an uncertain future and an uncertain identity" (2001, 243). I was faced with being a single mom, at the relatively young age of twenty-four, without the use of my legs. I was absolutely terrified and, in a way, felt that I had lost part of myself, that someone had indeed died. I had been socialized with certain beliefs of people with disabilities, and none of them were encouraging to me. While I was raised in an upper-middle-class, educated white family and was taught not to hold prejudices, I was certainly not used to belonging to a minority group. I was no longer "normal," and I longed for the girl I thought I used to be, not capable of realizing that I was still that person, regardless of whether I was walking or pushing. The depression was overwhelming, and I rapidly pushed everyone around me away and allowed myself to sink into it.

Almost simultaneously, I fell into the stage of personal questioning and anger: "Why did God allow this to happen to me?" (Smart 2001, 244). Again, as a single mom of two, and, at twenty-four, in what I considered the beginning of life, I couldn't believe that any fair God would allow this to happen. A nun who made rounds at the hospital attempted to visit and pray with me many times, and this stoked the flames of my anger at God. The only person I was angrier at by now was myself; how on earth could I have allowed myself to take the chances that had led to this? I was fresh out of a divorce, deeply unhappy, and self-medicating. I got into a car with someone who was as intoxicated as I was, and I have lived with the consequences ever since. I could, and did, spend entire days mentally abusing myself. I alternated between crying from the depression and begging God to please fix all of it somehow. I continued to go through these stages until, with the help of my family, I began to accept what had happened. They struggled to show me that life would go on, perhaps different than I had ever expected it to be but fulfilling all the same. Therapists showed me how to handle everyday situations from a seated standpoint, and I learned how to manage my body in new ways. I had two wonderful children watching expectantly, which helped me reach a certain level of "integration and growth" (Smart 2001, 245). This level has also been called "transcendence" by Carolyn Vash and Nancy Crewe (2004, 154) and is reached when an individual has accepted the changes caused by her or his disabilities.

This last stage occurs, according to Smart, when a person "(1) understands and accepts the reality and implications of the disability, (2) establishes new values and goals that do not conflict with the disability, and (3) explores and utilizes his or her strengths and abilities" (2001, 245). I came to terms with the changes that my body—and, in turn, my entire life and future—had been through, and I adapted. I committed myself to researching all the available assistive technology and changing my plans for the future accordingly. Since my accident, I have met a wonderful man whom I married in October 2010, and we are now living as a family with my daughters in my new accessible home. Being disabled has also opened up a wide range of friendships and career possibilities. When I was nondisabled, I would have ignored many of the close friends I have now, the brilliant, accepting, encouraging people who buoy me up in so many ways. Thinking about my future, I see so many different fields in which I can help others, sharing what I have learned with people in situations similar to my own. The whole experience of being disabled has opened my mind in ways I could never have anticipated.

While there are certainly advantages to understanding stage theory, and I believe wholeheartedly that every therapist should be educated about the general themes behind these theories, it is also important to understand that coming to terms with an acquired disability is not a sequential experience. Most people with disabilities such as spinal-cord injuries will find themselves cycling through these stages as they continue through life and are challenged further because of their disability. I still fight these waves of emotions on a regular basis as I try to navigate the world. For example, I find myself angry at medical professionals who willfully disregard my knowledge and experience with my own condition. And in the rural area where I live, even simple tasks can become complicated. I may have accepted my disability and my limitations, but I still have periods of depression and anger and—every year around the anniversary of my accident—personal questioning. As my children get older and there are many things I cannot do with them (rollerblading in the park, ice skating, climbing on the monkey bars, and rolling snowmen in the yard), I experience periods of mourning, wishing for the full use of my legs.

I do believe that my initial recovery may have been impeded because my emotional and mental well-being were not addressed as thoroughly or directly as my physical recovery. My physical needs were well taken care of, but if my therapists had talked to me about what I was experiencing and explained the normalcy of the stages, I believe that my process of recovery would have been much smoother. It is essential for everyone, especially the medical workers who help guide us through our recovery, to understand the impact of emotional well-being on physical states. Simply taking a pill can't help us through the stages that many people with acquired, acute disabilities face. It is only when I took a disability studies course that I realized how normal my reactions to my new circumstances were.

REFERENCES

Kübler-Ross, E. 1969. *On Death and Dying.* New York: Macmillan.
Smart, J. 2001. *Disability, Society, and the Individual.* Austin, TX: Pro-Ed.
Vash, C. L., and N. M. Crewe. 2004. *Psychology of Disability.* 2nd ed. New York: Springer.

II.6

My Brother's Traumatic Brain Injury and Its Effect on Me

M y brother Richard Kidd experienced a traumatic brain injury (TBI) on December 31, 1987. At the time of his accident, I was nondis-abled. However, since surviving my own TBI in a car accident on May 17, 2005, Richard's significance in my life has led to an evolution of my beliefs about persons with disabilities (PWDs).[1]

My embrace of Richard's life is not an intellectual exercise but, rather, a profound need to identify with and accept Richard and then to attempt to resolve the disregard and neglect exhibited by others toward him. Richard is the touchstone of my new identity as a disabled person. This new identity has altered my view, from regarding PWDs as sources of abject pity to valuing the lessons we teach about the quality of humanity and validating our roles as vital members of the community. But if it were not for my own experiences of living with TBI, it is unlikely that I would have altered my view

---

Douglas Kidd, since his accident, has achieved a bachelor's degree in history and a master's degree in liberal studies with a concentration in disability studies. Currently, he is a qualified health home specialist for Harbor and the founder and owner of Undistracted Driving Advocacy, LLC. He leads the Greater Toledo Brain Injury Support Group, and he is a member of the Toledo/Lucas County Commission on Disabilities and a member of the board of trustees of the Ability Center of Greater Toledo. In addition to being a published poet, he has published in the Johns Hopkins University journal *Narrative Inquiry in Bioethics* and the *Review of Disability Studies*.

of disabled people. Christmas Day, 1987, was the last time I would see the old Richard before a car accident changed our lives forever. As the family member of a TBI survivor, I lost the Richard I knew on December 31, 1987. Our mother, Mary, called to inform my twin brother, David, and me that earlier that evening, Richard had been hit by a car.

Richard had multiple fractures to both legs and a severe head injury. The accident occurred when Richard attempted to cross a street as a pedestrian in Indianapolis, Indiana, and a car with the headlights off collided with him. After that, the driver ran Richard over and then fled the scene. We know this because a friend of Richard's had just stepped out of the street and witnessed the horrendous accident. We learned that the car smashed Richard's legs, and the force of the collision caused a closed head injury. What are endlessly agonizing for me are the images of my brother during those horrifying few seconds. Also agonizing are the endless "what if" questions that come unbidden as I replay the imagined events of the accident in my mind: What if the driver had had the car lights turned on? Surely, he or she would have seen Richard and would have stopped the car in time to avoid the accident. What if Richard had looked to his right just before impact? Richard might have reflexively stopped in his tracks and proceeded no farther. What if Richard had been mere seconds earlier or later? Surely the accident never would have occurred. We learned that Richard lagged seconds behind the friend who had just stepped out of the street when the car barreled into Richard. We were informed that when the front of the car struck Richard, he was thrown many feet before he came to a stop in the road.

Upon our arrival at Wishard Memorial Hospital in Indianapolis, Indiana, on January 1, 1988, our first consultation with a doctor left us hopeful. She relayed that Richard was still alive. The doctor informed us that Richard had multiple compound fractures to both legs and a closed head injury. The doctor told us that a standard medical procedure of the time, although it seems almost like a procedure belonging to a medieval torture chamber, was to drill small holes into Richard's skull. The doctor explained that this procedure was necessary to lessen the damage caused by the intracranial pressure that developed as Richard's brain absorbed forces of the collision. Additionally, we were told that the procedure was performed to lessen the effect of the brain swelling that had already occurred and would occur in the hours to come. (When I had my accident in 2005, doctors did not drill holes into my skull—perhaps because of changes in the management of this type of injury.) Richard's doctor informed us that major complications of brain injury occur as brain tissues swell and tear on bony structures in the skull. Richard also faced additional complications because his heart had stopped beating, and he had ceased to breathe for an unknown period of time following the accident. Doctors told us that when respiration ceases, secondary brain damage occurs.

As doctors worked to stabilize Richard's injuries in the intensive care unit (ICU), periodically a doctor would come to the waiting room to update family members on his condition. During one such visit roughly two days after the accident, a doctor informed us that, given the severity and number of brain hemorrhages Richard had experienced, and the multiple compound fractures to his legs, Richard faced a long and uncertain recovery. She said that Richard's survival in that moment was far from certain, but extraordinary medical efforts could be made to save his life. The doctor then asked our family if we wished doctors to make extraordinary efforts to preserve Richard's life. This is by far the most difficult question I have ever been asked. As we attempted to process the situation, the look of concern on the doctor's face indicated to me that Richard would be severely impaired for the rest of his life. I interpreted the doctor's nonverbal signals to mean that, in her opinion, it would be better to let Richard die than to force him to live a life with profound physical and cognitive impairments.

Perhaps I am wrong by suggesting that the doctor intimated this, but I cannot escape the feeling that she thought it would be better for Richard if he were to die. What I gathered from the doctor's nonverbal communication in the ICU waiting room speaks to many people's view of the subjective quality of life of disabled people. Given my family's complete lack of knowledge about a possible life as a disabled person with profound impairments, the doctor's seeming assumption that we would share the idea that Richard's survival might not be worthwhile seemed to me to be impossibly unfair. We felt that if Richard had survived the accident, he deserved every life-saving technique available, and we emphatically requested extraordinary efforts to save Richard's life.

This period was the first time in my life when I felt estranged from nearly everyone I encountered, except Richard and some members of my family. I remember friends and acquaintances discussing the problems in their lives at that time, issues that by comparison seemed petty and trivial. The first six weeks of 1988 passed in a blur. It was a routine of Monday through Friday at work in Toledo, Ohio, and then weekend trips to Indianapolis to visit Richard. Concern over Richard's survival seemed to dominate every waking moment. My anxiety over Richard was reduced during mid-February of 1988, when he returned to Toledo. Richard came back to Toledo as soon as doctors felt he could safely meet the demands of traveling the nearly five hours from Indianapolis by ambulance. As I recall, I was a nervous wreck that day while Richard was transported from Indianapolis. I kept having a recurring feeling that the trip would prove too much for Richard. However, this irrational fear proved untrue; Richard was well secured and protected by ambulance personnel for the trip to Toledo Hospital.

Eventually, he was moved to a well-known coma management program at a hospital in Green Springs, Ohio. It was in Green Springs, after approximately nine or ten months, that Richard surfaced. One of the first indications we had that Richard was no longer in a coma came the first time our mother heard Richard speak. For many months, Richard's roommate at the hospital had engaged in a characteristic trait that many with brain injury exhibit—perseveration—which manifested in his continually calling out, "Help!" I am sure this repetition and stimulation helped Richard greatly to resurface. One day, as our mother waited with Richard in a hallway of the hospital, she heard him call for help in a faint voice. "Help" became the first word Richard spoke in nearly a year.

My mother asked him, "Is that you in there, Richard?"

After a long delay, Richard answered in a voice as soft as a whisper, "Yes."

My heart leapt with this news. For me, this was an absolute high point of the year. Over the course of the next few months, Richard regained an awareness of the world. Richard's steady improvement was underscored one day when he responded to a question I asked him. I was beyond excited that my brother was on his way back to a life!

On March 7, 1989, nine days shy of his twenty-seventh birthday, Richard was transferred into the rehabilitation unit (Keller 2011). It was there, over the course of the next few months, where therapists greatly assisted Richard by teaching him how to hold a spoon, gather food from a plate, move the spoon to his mouth, and then swallow the food. Therapists worked with Richard so he was soon able to hold and then take a drink from a cup or glass. Given where Richard had been only months before, these were major victories for him. Because of this progress, I distinctly remember saying to my mom that I could see a time in the future when Richard would completely recover his life. I even said that Richard would one day find another person and then fall in love. However, sadly, this hope would later prove false, as Richard's capacity to interact with others does not support his ability to develop an intimate relationship.

We were informed by a social worker at the hospital that the State of Ohio would provide Richard with funding to pay for physical, occupational, and speech therapies, so that he might regain as many abilities as he could, but only for a limited time. State-sponsored rehabilitation ended as Richard plateaued when therapists attempted to teach him the skill of using a motorized wheelchair. Richard failed to learn how to use the chair because he did not possess enough awareness of the world. I have witnessed others manipulating wheeled devices with parts of their face and body, but this requires an individual's will to initiate the action, and Richard does not possess this ability. Because of a lack of private insurance and because our family did not possess the resources to pay for ongoing rehabilitation, sadly, real efforts to rehabilitate Richard ended.

We have learned that when there is no money from the family or state to pay for rehabilitation, nursing homes do not attempt to restore residents to an independent-living lifestyle. It is less expensive for staff to simply spoon-feed a resident than to take the time to supervise the development of an individual's abilities for self-care. In my opinion, the dependence nursing homes foster in their residents only ensures the need of their future services. On April 7, 1989, Richard entered into custodial care at the first of the nursing homes he has lived in for more than twenty years. Richard's first nursing home was located in Fremont, Ohio (Keller 2011). Sadly, as rehabilitation efforts for Richard ended, so did my involvement in his life.

One of the toughest adjustments I have been forced to make in life is accepting the new Richard that emerged following his accident. The drastic changes brought on by his altered life were too many and too much for me to bear. Only two years before his arrival in Fremont, Richard was a vibrant young person, full of potential. I had reconnected with Richard after he spent four years driving a tank in the United States Army, from 1982 to 1986. The sibling rivalry issues we had when we were younger had largely been resolved. We were both in our twenties, kept in regular touch, and looked forward to seeing one another when we could. Richard was one of my best friends, and I still miss him. It was extremely difficult for me to accept the loss of the brother I once knew, so I removed myself from his life. There were times I went six to eight months without seeing him. My withdrawal from Richard went on for nearly two decades. The more Richard needed me, the further I removed myself from his life. This is a hard realization to reconcile about myself, but it seems that as hope for Richard resuming a "normal" life ended, so did my involvement in his affairs. Despondently, I referred to Richard as a door to pain that I did not wish to enter. During this time, I could not get past the extent of Richard's impairments. To be honest, while I did not realize this at the time, I considered Richard to be completely "other," and thus I avoided him. This distance from Richard did not fully end until I gained an appreciation for how life is for some TBI survivors, when I became one myself.

Just like Richard, I became injured—emotionally injured—when his accident occurred on December 31, 1987. Then, in May 2005, I, too, experienced a TBI, which was the start of feeling closer to my brother. Although my accident was somewhat different from Richard's, involving an SUV hitting the midsection of my car at approximately fifty miles per hour in an intersection, my life after a brain injury has given me insight into his life. I was in a coma for nearly a month, and once I had recovered from a deadly bacterial infection with methicillin-resistant *Staphylococcus aureus* and my injuries began to stabilize, my survival looked increasingly more certain. Evidently, the most essential aspects of me emerged through the trauma. My wife, Nora, recalls that as doctors attempted to characterize the many variables influencing my survival, they would say that if I came through a particular episode, I would face another hurdle. While my chances of survival increased greatly during the second month after my accident, my social (re)integration was far from certain. Because of the severity of my TBI, amnesia dominated my experience during the second month. I do not recall this time, although I have been informed that I spent many hours sleeping—a sharp contrast to a short time later when I became extremely agitated, at one point pulling the tracheostomy tube from my throat. Later, I experienced delusions, and then—it is strange to write this—it seems that I fully emerged one day in mid-July 2005. Nora had given me a journal in which to record my thoughts and feelings. It seems to me now as if all of a sudden I was aware that I was in a hospital bed and I was back, and I had to begin the process of reacquiring information in a simple way, similar to how many children gain knowledge of the world.

It is impossible for me not to recognize the amount of emotion I have invested in Richard. Perhaps logic fails, but I feel extremely close to Richard. Since my own brain injury, I fully acknowledge the harm caused by a hit-and-run driver nearly twenty-five years ago, and, at the same time, I no longer see Richard as "the other." It is not an intellectual process of identification that I have with him but rather a visceral and emotional connection. Richard is the touchstone of my new identity as a TBI survivor, and his life anchors mine. I resonate with him because our experience diminishes our capacity to cope with social expectations and meet some of life's demands. I resolve and renew my emotional connection and commitment to him.

While physical recovery is largely complete, my cognitive and emotional growth and (re)adjustment continue to the present day. As it is the lens through which I perceive and seek to (re)engage the world, I fully embrace a disabled identity. Being disabled is a source of strength that has enhanced the expression of my humanity. On June 12, 2014, I was able to express this in a paper I presented at the Society for Disability Studies conference. The title of the paper is "Surviving Traumatic Brain Injury: Exploring the Lives of Two Brothers," and in it I explore the evolution of my relationship with Richard and my understanding of disability. On May 18, 2015, I presented a paper titled "Disability Studies' Influence on a Profoundly Altered Identity" at the Pacific Rim International Conference on Disability and Diversity. The paper explores how pursuit of a graduate degree in disability studies became pivotal as I assumed a disabled identity.

NOTE

1. On May 17, 2005, I failed to yield at an intersection, and an SUV smashed into my car. My major injuries included multiple hip fractures, a crush injury with compartment syndrome to the lower right leg, multiple internal injuries, and severe brain hemorrhage. In addition, I experienced two cardiac arrests. I spent nearly thirty days in a coma and had amnesia for forty-five days. Fifty days of physical, occupational, and speech therapies marked the beginning of recovery.

REFERENCE

Keller, D. 2011. *Options for Tomorrow: Richard Kidd*. Toledo, OH: University of Toledo.

PART III

DISABILITY AND COMMUNICATION

THIS PART BRINGS TOGETHER narratives focused on the complexities of communicating about the **bodymind** experience of disability, with chapters focused specifically on communication marked as "disordered." From differing starting points, all of the narratives explore the ways typical social expectations of communication often impede mutual understanding. Contributors discuss provocative social tensions around disability and communication, including pressures of **normative speech**, repetitive conversations extracted from and expected of disabled people, and the complexities of disability disclosure. Contributors also challenge prescriptive expectations within disability politics itself, asking, for example, if some conversations—especially those around cure—are curtailed or forbidden within activist communities. Ultimately, this section aims to connect these multiple layers of communication.

Joshua St. Pierre, in Chapter III.1, shares his experience with stuttering and addresses the intense social pressure for normative speech: speech that is seen as clear, fluent, or appropriate. St. Pierre's narrative provides poignant descriptions of other people's expectations and their reactions to his stutter—usually manifested by rejection and impatience. Challenging this social pressure, he situates the problem as a relational one, inviting readers to take part in relocating the performative demands in such encounters.

While stuttering is a communication-related disability, hidden disabilities also compound the complexity of communicating one's access needs and experience. Catherine Graves, in Chapter III.2, explores the nature of the **nonapparent disabilities** she has, the ongoing pain and other effects of fibromyalgia and rheumatoid arthritis. To her frustration, nondisabled people can be unwilling to accommodate her disability because she appears able-bodied—her pain, fatigue, and feeling of sickness are not readily apparent. Graves ponders what it would be like if she could communicate her disability with visual cues to make her pain more recognizable.

Deafness is another nonapparent disability that directly impacts communication. Centuries of hearing communities and professional institutions have viewed deafness within a **medical model**, seeing it as something to be remedied with oral education practices in which children have been forced to speak and lip-read, or to use hearing aids or cochlear implants (Monaghan, Schmaling, Nakamura, and Turner 2003). In the past and today, however, many Deaf people have viewed, or do view, deafness through a **cultural model**, seeing themselves as having "their own language, values, rules for behaviors, and traditions" (Padden and Humphries 1990, 4). Sign languages like American Sign Language (ASL) both make deafness visible and serve as the binding force for long-standing Deaf communities. One value often held within Deaf communities is in fact a dismissal of the label "disabled" to describe deafness. Instead, many prefer a **minority model**, identifying deafness and the use of sign languages as a trait of a linguistic or ethnic group.

Blake Culley grew up deaf in a family without any connection to Deaf culture or ASL. In Chapter III.3, she describes the distinct pain of what Rosemarie Garland-Thomson (2011) calls **misfitting**, first in her hearing family and among hearing peers and then as a deaf person neither fully fluent in ASL nor accepted in Deaf culture. For Culley, communication is fraught with misunderstanding and isolation, but ultimately the Deaf community provided a long-awaited home. By contrast, for Tasha Chemel, joining the blind community has been more complicated. She appreciates the political history of blind and disability activism that has paved the way for her as a young blind woman, but she also wonders if there is room in disability studies to talk about *wanting* sight. Her narrative in Chapter III.4 resists constructing her desire for a cure as simply ableist and asks instead where this desire might cohere within a politics of disability.

Leigh A. Neithardt, in Chapter III.5, and Leslie Johnson Elliott, in Chapter III.6, expand on themes of nonapparent disability and **social misrecognition**, in which people with disabilities are treated with suspicion or excessive, misplaced concern. Neithardt, born with cerebral palsy, beautifully captures her frustration with tiresome inquiries from strangers. The invasive question "What's wrong?" forces her to engage in unwelcome conversations. At the same time, she does not want to cut off communication completely. Reflecting on such encounters, she invites and imagines a different kind of engagement and curiosity on the part of concerned acquaintances—one involving active listening and taking responsibility for false assumptions. The awkward conversations Neithardt describes are part of what Jackie Leach Scully calls the **hidden labor** of disability, or the energy expended by disabled people "to manage or manipulate the presentation of their impairment to others, and their own and others' emotional responses, in order to achieve their goals" (2010, 25). Such unrecognized labor of explaining one's disability is an enduring concern in disability studies. Elliott, for example, describes the labor involved in her struggle to communicate effectively the material effects of hidden disabilities, in her case lifelong migraines and depression. She points out that while these conditions affect her life, the more acute suffering results when others, including family, friends, teachers, and medical professionals, fail to understand—or worse, refute the reality of—her experience.

Overall, these chapters provide insights into the profound **gaps in communication** that reinforce ableism, demand extra social labor from disabled people, or pressure people into **silence**. These narratives demonstrate how normative perspectives held by many people and institutions often require people with disabilities to do a great deal of work in order to communicate their needs and desires, let alone for their perspectives to be understood and made welcome.

Reference the boldface terms as themes for discussion, and consider the following questions as you read the chapters in Part III:

1. How do normative social expectations of communication often impede mutual understanding? What crucial insights do people with speech and hearing differences have to offer about clear communication?

2. Are some conversations curtailed or forbidden within disability studies? Where might individual desires for cure be situated within the broader politics of disability justice?

3. Several authors discuss the social pressures and labor involved with addressing disability-related questions from (sometimes well-intentioned) acquaintances and strangers. How do these issues affect disabled people? What ideas can you pull from these narratives for different, more productive types of conversations? What kind of work could nondisabled people do in order to share in this labor?

Suggestions for Related Readings

- As he comes to understand the sociopolitical dimensions of disability, Joshua St. Pierre (Chapter III.1) begins to see communication not as his failure but as a shared responsibility. How does this insight apply to other narratives in the collection—and to thinking about access more broadly? St. Pierre also describes an empowered disability identity, which can be put into conversation with many other chapters, such as those by Allegra Heath-Stout (V.1), Adam P. Newman (VI.4), and Rebekah Moras (VI.5).
- Pair Blake Culley's chapter (III.3) with Denton Mallas's chapter (V.6) to discuss deafness, Deaf culture, and their relationship with and difference from disability.
- Compare Tasha Chemel's desire for sight, described in Chapter III.4, with Caitlin Hernandez's struggle with blindness and vulnerability, discussed in Chapter IV.2. Emily K. Michael, in Chapter IV.3, also discusses her vision impairment and markers of blindness. How do these three very different perspectives complicate and enrich your thinking about blindness, sight, and the social dimensions of vision and visibility?
- Catherine Graves (Chapter III.2), Leigh A. Neithardt (Chapter III.5), and Leslie Johnson Elliott (Chapter III.6) all discuss themes of recognition and misrecognition of disability. Connect these chapters with those of Emily K. Michael (IV.3) and Garrett R. Cruzan (IV.4) to discuss the differences and similarities between (hyper)apparent, variably apparent, and nonapparent disabilities. Other narratives focusing on these issues include the chapters by Shayda Kafai (I.2), Elizabeth Allyn Campbell (II.2), Allegra Heath-Stout (V.1), Nancy La Monica (V.2), and Suzanne Walker (V.5).

REFERENCES

Garland-Thomson, R. 2011. "Misfits: A Feminist Materialist Disability Concept." *Hypatia* 26 (3): 591–609.
Monaghan, L., C. Schmaling, K. Nakamura, and G. H. Turner. 2003. *Many Ways to Be Deaf.* Washington, DC: Gallaudet University Press.
Padden, C., and T. Humphries. 1990. *Deaf in America: Voices from a Culture.* Cambridge, MA: Harvard University Press.
Scully, J. L. 2010. "Hidden Labor: Disabled/Nondisabled Encounters, Agency, and Autonomy." *International Journal of Feminist Approaches to Bioethics* 3 (2): 25–42.

III.1

Voicing Disability with Disabled Voices

Reimagining a Stuttered Identity

JOSHUA ST. PIERRE

I can't remember life before my stutter, but I am told that the stutter began
when I was four years old and my family moved to an unfamiliar town.
Stuttering is experienced differently by different people, but for me it
involves regularly having a word stuck in my mouth, a silent "block," which
I attempt to overpower by facial tics, by going back a few words to get a
running start, or by forcing my way through with gusto. Other times I repeat
the first syllables of words, especially those starting with *l* or *s* sounds, until
I'm able to push through and complete the phrase. When I do get on a roll, I
will often keep on going until I am out of breath, as stopping could result in
another block. Like many who stutter, I have trained myself to avoid trouble-
some words and will often change my phrasing on the fly if I sense I am
about to become stuck. For me, stuttering is manageable but always obvious
to those who hear me.

Joshua St. Pierre is a Ph.D. student in philosophy at the University of Alberta. His
current research examines the relations between speech, embodiment, and disability,
looking specifically at the generative breakdown of speech as a performance of rational human and posthuman identity within political economies. He has published on
speech disabilities in the journals *Hypatia* and *Communication Theory* and in the book
Literature, Speech Disorders, and Disability: Talking Normal. He is a cofounder of the
Did I Stutter Project.

Growing up with a stutter in a world that expects a certain pace and efficiency in oral communication presented many challenges. Like many who stutter, I routinely pretended not to know the answer when called on in class and avoided speaking up as much as possible. School presentations were dreaded and cumbersome. In one classroom, my five minutes expired only halfway through the three pages I was required to read, and the teacher asked me to sit down. Most of the time, even though my pace of communication was accommodated for, I was painfully aware by the end of a labored presentation that some of my peers had been caught up in willing me to just get through it, instead of actually hearing much of what I had to say.

Combined with the pressures faced by every adolescent—to fit in, talk to crushes, and try to establish a personal identity—life was often difficult. I was ashamed not only of how I spoke but also of myself. Since I had been continuously taught that my stuttering was a problem and since speech plays such a primary role in the presentation of one's self, I could not escape understanding myself *through* my stutter. I became convinced that everything I did was interpreted by those around me as either because of or in spite of my stutter. I was left sealed within and reduced to my body.

Even though I had an active social life and had developed good friendships, the feeling of succeeding despite my stutter persisted, as my stutter would often protrude to cause hassle and embarrassment. I remember one conversation when, while forcefully trying to push out a word, I inadvertently spat in a friend's face. I distinctly recall his look of horror and revulsion before he quickly regained composure. The ensuing social niceties could not cover the deep shame I felt at being unable to control my body. So many social interactions rely on a certain timing and control: jumping into the conversation before the topic moves on, finishing the punch line of a joke before everyone figures out what's coming, relaying a string of numbers on the phone without confusingly repeating any, ordering at a drive-through as the queue grows longer, introducing friends whose handshake has passed the allotted time. Daily life could become stressful at any point.

Yet perhaps the most challenging aspect of having a stutter is not the mundane, present-day difficulties but the terrifying prospect of the future. I can vividly remember worrying whether I could get married or garner the respect of my children. As I realized I had interests and skills in academia, my fear of the future took on a more concrete form: Would someone hire me if I could not present or teach in the normal manner? Could I provide for a family? Should I choose a career in the trades instead, even though that is decidedly not where my talents lie? When I decided to apply to a master's degree program in philosophy, I felt like it was the riskiest decision of my life.

It was during this graduate program that I encountered disability studies. Prompted by both my experience of stuttering and an introduction to disability studies in a feminist philosophy course, I undertook a project—from which many of these present reflections are derived—of interpreting stuttering through disability studies (see St. Pierre 2012). Studying disability theory was revolutionary for me, as it helped me understand that disability as an individual, biological "malfunction"—the medical model—is only one reading of disability, and a poor one at that. Two of the influential books I read during this time were *Enforcing Normalcy* by Lennard Davis (1995) and *Disability, Self, and Society* by Tanya Titchkosky (2003). Rather than understanding disability as a problem to be overcome, these theorists conceptualize disability as a lens that makes the ableism of our world apparent. As Titchkosky notes, "Disability provides the occasion for us to understand the hegemonic character of ordinary life, and to disrupt and question the taken-for-granted expectation that ordinary life is merely an ordinary matter" (2003, 23). Our commonsense understanding of disability is not objectively given, as the medical model would have us believe, but has a specific and contingent history. I began to ask myself how many of the personal and social "problems" my stuttering caused me were actually due to ineffectual communication, how many were due to my fear of inconveniencing those around me, and how many were simply a result of not wanting to be different from what our culture had deemed normal.

In the midst of all of this reading, I was chatting with a coworker at a summer job who recurrently asked me to repeat myself. I would laboriously finish a sentence, only for him to say, "Huh?" in a distracted voice and expect me to begin again. It suddenly occurred to me that I was going to all this effort to speak as clearly as I could, and he was putting no effort into trying to hear what I was saying. Communication, I realized, is not a one-person task but relies on both speakers and hearers. The problem of stuttering as a breakdown of communication, therefore, cannot solely be conceived as *my* problem as the disabled speaker. Rather, I realized that the breakdown must occur *between* the speaker and the hearer, insofar as the hearer, in this case my coworker, does not always hear or make the effort to hear.

This attention to the dialogical nature of my stutter announced a shift in how I would understand my disability and the others' responses to it. I realized that stuttering and the shame it caused me could not properly be explained by the mere physical difficulty of vocalizing certain words; our culture's approach to stuttering is primarily a discrimination against certain ways of communicating and using one's body. Stuttering is a problem because our culture places so much value on efficiency and self-mastery. I speak horribly inefficiently and involuntarily stick my tongue out of my mouth and grimace in an attempt to get words out. These things mark my speech as abnormal, undesirable, and aesthetically displeasing in our culture, and so it becomes awkward for me to speak and for others to listen.

Realizing that my manner of communicating is interpreted as abnormal and as a disability by others because it conflicts with a particular set of values and social structures, I came to the understanding that stuttering is not primarily about my body being "wrong"; rather, it is a form of ableist discrimination. In much the same way that a girl who doesn't like her shape or features might be encouraged to accept her body and resist the unfair standard of beauty our culture presents in magazines, I saw that it might be possible to accept my speech by recognizing that it was these larger cultural expectations that marked me as abnormal and wrong. This realization allowed me to reinterpret much of my previous experience, as well as my current identity, relationships, and goals.

As I developed this research, I distinctly remember seeing the world differently. Rather than being ashamed when people shifted uncomfortably and their attention trailed away as I stuttered, I became frustrated with their expectations. For not only were such people hearing poorly, they were completely unaware that they had any role in the communicative process. Far more than my halted words or "distracting" facial tics, the *problem* was that our society does not teach us to listen generously and be attentive to abnormal voices, paces, and bodies. Having been to speech therapy for much of my life and hearing day after day that if I wanted to be taken seriously, I needed to learn to speak "properly," it was immensely empowering to realize that this burden was, in fact, asking me to live up to oppressive expectations of communication.

This reconceptualization of disability has given me immense confidence in doing things that I used to fear greatly. I no longer take a deep, stressed breath before picking up the phone or hope to avoid meeting new people, and I no longer feel the massive pressure to "fix" my speech before pursuing a career I will enjoy. It is immensely relieving to be freed from the pervasive cultural narrative that stutterers can "fix" themselves with enough determination. Conceptualizing disability as discrimination against "abnormal" bodies means that those who are disabled come up against challenges that cannot be overcome by sheer determination, since we are up against immense cultural discrimination. Nevertheless, in the face of structures of oppression, it has been immensely helpful to find a new framework from which I can understand myself and resist normalization.

It is here that engaging in disability studies has perhaps most affected my personal identity. As I mentioned above, up until recently, I have felt defined by my stutter in a very real way, and, subsequently, I have been marked by shame and self-hatred. In an interesting twist, I still define myself through my disability in a primary way. But now, rather than being shameful, the fact that I stutter is (slowly) becoming a source of pride, because stuttering invites me to continually resist the communicative expectations that are supposed to make me feel ashamed. A world that normalizes bodies and discriminates against those who do not fit is not the world I want.

My wife asked me during this learning process if I would keep my stutter if someone magically gave me the choice of having it "cured." Up until recently, this had always been a nonquestion. For most of my life, I have daily wished to no longer stutter and thus to be like everyone else. However, this time my answer was different. My voice sounds the same now as it always has. The difference is I am no longer ashamed of it. People speak in many different ways, and we all have a right to be heard. For me, disability theory is not abstract; it has had a profound influence on how I conceive of myself and the world I live in.

My discussion here has centered on the physical voice, but it is significant that in the cultural imagination, "having a voice" also denotes the possession of agency. While my voice (in both senses) is disabled, people with communicative disabilities are certainly not the only disabled voices that must work hard to claim agency—the right to be heard without being treated as shameful and deficient. Thus, the process of claiming space for the particular way I communicate has also been an act of making room for others and demanding that differences aren't grounds for exclusion. I have learned that perhaps the appreciation of differences requires ears to hear those who have been speaking all along.

REFERENCES

Davis, L. D. 1995. *Enforcing Normalcy.* New York: Verso.
St. Pierre, J. 2012. "The Construction of the Disabled Speaker: Locating Stuttering in Disability Studies." *Canadian Journal of Disability Studies* 1 (3): 1–21.
Titchkosky, T. 2003. *Disability, Self and Society.* Toronto: University of Toronto Press.

III.2

Fibromyalgia Syndrome

CATHERINE GRAVES

My name is Catherine Graves. I am a thirty-four-year-old working professional, college student, daughter, and friend. My thirties have been tumultuous. I started a new job, filed for bankruptcy, separated from and divorced my spouse, moved back into my parents' home, and then moved into my first apartment. And though you would not know it by looking at me, I have three invisible disabilities that affect my daily life: fibromyalgia syndrome, anxiety-depressive disorder, and rheumatoid arthritis (RA). All three conditions affect my daily functioning, but here I focus on the fibromyalgia. Fibromyalgia syndrome (FMS) is

> a chronic health problem that causes pain all over the body and other symptoms. Other symptoms of fibromyalgia that patients most

Catherine Graves is a native Marylander living with chronic invisible disabilities. She has over fifteen years of experience working in the disability community as a residential rehabilitation counselor and house manager and as an information and media specialist for a federally funded library and information center on disability and rehabilitation. Graves received her bachelor's degree in social science from the University of Maryland University College (UMUC) in 2010 and obtained her information and referral certification from the Alliance on Information and Referral Systems (AIRS) in 2015. She is also a member of Maryland Theta, the UMUC chapter of Pi Gamma Mu, the International Honor Society for the Social Sciences. She currently resides in the Baltimore area with her beloved cats.

often have are tenderness to touch or pressure affecting muscles and sometimes joints or even the skin, severe fatigue, sleep problems (waking up unrefreshed), [and] problems with memory or thinking clearly. Some patients also may have depression or anxiety, migraine or tension headaches, digestive problems . . . , irritable or overactive bladder, pelvic pain, [and] temporomandibular joint disorder. (Crofford 2015)

It is unclear what causes FMS. It is speculated that major physical or emotional trauma and genetics play a role. Fibromyalgia syndrome is more prevalent in women and in those who already have a rheumatic condition such as RA (Crofford 2015; for more information on RA, see Ruderman and Tambar 2013). I certainly experienced stressful, life-changing events, and I was in a major car accident in October 2001. All these factors, or perhaps none of them, may have contributed my development of FMS.

My journey toward a medical diagnosis began in the late summer of 2007. When I began a part-time job as a bookseller, I began experiencing noticeable chronic pain and fatigue. I figured that my body was rebelling against the physical demands of a retail job. I began to notice that the pain seemed to worsen the more physical activity I demanded of my body. I had heard of FMS through my work with persons with disabilities and acquaintances who had the condition. One evening, while shelving books at work, I picked up a copy of *Fibromyalgia for Dummies* (Staud and Adamec 2007). As I read through the laundry list of symptoms, I realized that they all sounded hauntingly familiar. The next day I researched FMS online and came across the "Chronic Fatigue Syndrome/Fibromyalgia Symptom Checklist" (Berne 2014). I was disheartened as I went through the various categories and checked off almost all the symptoms.

I decided that it was time to speak with my primary care physician and insist on a referral to a rheumatologist specializing in FMS. Previous attempts to discuss my chronic fatigue and other symptoms with my primary care physician and other specialists were often met with skepticism. Because I had a documented anxiety and depressive disorder, doctors associated my FMS symptoms with those disorders. I had to prove that I was mentally stable before I was taken seriously. By late 2007, I was finally evaluated by a rheumatologist. Since there are no definitive medical tests for FMS, specialists rely on type and duration of symptoms and an examination of eighteen characteristic tender points. In order to be diagnosed with FMS, an individual must have pain in eleven of the eighteen tender points. Based on my symptoms and the results of the examination, the rheumatologist diagnosed me with FMS.

I experience chronic fatigue, aches, and pain *every* day. In hindsight, I realize that I probably have had FMS for a long time. For example, I would feel severe physical exhaustion and pain after spending the day at the Maryland Renaissance Festival or any other energetic activity. The best way to describe the experience of FMS to one unfamiliar with the condition is to equate the pain and fatigue to the worst case of the flu you have ever had—except this bout never ends.

A few months after I received my FMS diagnosis, I applied for an ADA-accessible parking permit. Those with FMS refer to their bad pain and symptom days as "flares." I decided that, while I have more good days than bad, having the ability to park closer to my destination when I am experiencing a flare would be ideal. I used to be one of those people who would look at seemingly able-bodied people parking in accessible parking spaces and assume that they must be fine. But now that I'm the one being judged by others, I have a whole new perspective on the stigmatization that individuals with invisible disabilities experience. I look younger than my thirty-four years, so I know that people must be thinking, "What could possibly be wrong with her? She looks so good." Little do most people know that I feel a hundred years old, and everything I do some days can be a major effort.

As a woman living on my own and on a single income, finances were limited. In an effort to save money, I began to take the Maryland Area Regional Commuter (MARC) train to work. In the mornings, it is easy to find a seat because my stop is early in the route, but during the evening rush hour, it is impossible to find an available seat. Standing for long periods of time is extremely painful and difficult. Since I know I don't appear disabled to most people, I felt uncomfortable asking for accommodations on the MARC train. I researched the disability services available and discovered that, if I obtained a disability ID card from the Maryland Transit Administration (MTA), I could receive a discount on my fare, and the MTA and MARC staff could request a seat on my behalf. I hadn't had the opportunity to go to the only office in Baltimore to get my ID card, but I was assured that as long as I showed the disability certification card that was issued to me by the motor vehicle administration along with my disability placard, I would have access to a seat.

One evening, I attempted to board the train and asked the MARC conductor to assist me in locating a seat. He ignored my request despite my visible discomfort and the use of a cane. I stood in the entryway between the train cars while he reviewed my documentation and then lectured me on the proper documentation I lacked. At this point, the pain and frustration upset me so greatly that I exclaimed, "Can I get some assistance now in getting a seat?" Many of the riders witnessed this exchange, and several people offered their seats to me. By then, I was in a lot of pain, which the stress, humiliation, and anger only exacerbated. I took to carrying a fold-up cane when riding the train after this incident so people might recognize me as disabled.

Otherwise, I just looked like a young, perfectly healthy adult. I researched the contact for ADA complaints for the MARC train system and filed a complaint. However, this person was never removed from his position, and I had to deal with him daily. I learned who the nice conductors were. Having my disability ID card and my cane made seeking accommodations easier but no less embarrassing or stigmatizing.

Before my diagnoses, I was already familiar with people with disabilities and disability issues. I have almost ten years of disability-related work experience, including working for the National Rehabilitation Information Center as an information specialist. While I had been dealing with the symptoms of my conditions for some time, having a medical diagnosis was the first step toward perceiving my disabled identity.

At first, it was very difficult to perceive myself as a person with a disability. I felt like I was deceiving everyone, because I appear to be young and healthy. Most of my friends had not heard of FMS, and some shared the common misconception that individuals with FMS are just lazy or need to get into better physical shape. My family was fairly understanding and accepting. My best friend still does not perceive me as an individual with a disability, because to him, I appear to be highly functional. He perceives me as being just me—medical conditions and all—and doesn't perceive me as "handicapped." The depression I felt was due not to my disability status but to the reality of living with chronic fatigue, pain, and the other symptoms of my conditions. Even now, months and years later, I find that my perception of being a person with a disability varies depending on how I feel on any given day.

It is extremely disheartening to know that you will almost always be in pain and tired. We have all had the headache that won't quit, and just a few hours of pain can make us tired, frustrated, and agitated. I mourned for the loss of my dexterity and my ability to be carefree and socially and physically active. I questioned whether my conditions, especially my FMS, were some kind of retribution from the cosmos or bad karma. I found myself retreating from social interaction and becoming more mindful of every activity. With FMS, I definitely have to listen to my body. I integrated a mindfulness approach into my life, in which I am aware of my body and what it is telling me. If I have a particularly rough day with pain and fatigue, going grocery shopping and then going home to make a four-course dinner might not be the best idea. Instead, since I know my physical and mental limits have been reached, it might be a good night to get take-out on the way home. I also learned to be okay with not accepting invitations or participating in various activities that I knew would result in a flare. I know that I have to plan for events and outings that require me to be standing or walking around for a good bit of the day (for example, the Maryland Renaissance Festival). By being mindful and aware of how my body handles socialization, I may want to consider not doing more than one activity in a weekend, or else I will be useless when the workweek comes around.

Since I am a divorced, single woman, I have to consider whether to reveal my invisible disabilities to potential dating partners. I do not make an effort to hide my conditions. I mention that I'm on medications, and I will readily use my disability placard when out and about. If someone asks me about my medication or placard, I will explain that I have FMS and RA and what those conditions are. While I'm not uncomfortable disclosing my disability status, disclosing and discussing my conditions does makes me anxious that I will be stigmatized. I do worry that my conditions will make it difficult, if not impossible, for me to find and maintain a long-term relationship. I believe that I had both FMS and RA while married and that the physical strain of these conditions on my body contributed to some of the problems in the marriage. FMS and RA can be extremely emotionally and physically draining on an individual and his or her significant other. Individuals with FMS and RA require partners who are willing to educate themselves about how these conditions affect their loved ones and to be understanding and patient. I often joke that I have a better idea of what I don't want in a relationship than of what I do want. I know that honesty, empathy, and understanding rank right up there as qualities I would like to find in a special someone. Ironically, my ex-husband has moved on to be in a relationship with an individual who has FMS.

Living with the symptoms of these disabilities is challenging. Because my pain and fatigue are invisible, people usually assume I am fine. The natural tendency is to associate disability with physical appearance. If you don't look sick, you must not be sick. I often wish I changed colors to reflect my pain and fatigue levels, so I could say, "See, I told you I don't feel well." FMS and RA are not immune to common misconception. The stigmatization that people with invisible disabilities experience is that we are not taken seriously by the medical community or by society (Parker-Pope 2010). We have to fight twice as hard to prove that we qualify for Supplemental Security Income (SSI) or Social Security Disability Insurance (SSDI). We are told that our pain, fatigue, and other symptoms are all in our head. Our requests for accommodations in the workplace or academic environment are less likely to be taken seriously. Family members, loved ones, and friends—whom one would expect to be understanding, accepting, and supportive—are often the worst perpetuators of ignorance, intolerance, and stigma.

Education and community are extremely important for all individuals with disabilities but especially for those with invisible disabilities. The Internet has become a valuable resource for information on all conditions and diseases associated with disability. Disability-related organizations help reduce misconceptions and reduce the stigma associated with particular disabilities. Online chat groups and websites allow individuals with disabilities to connect with each other and find empathy and support that they may not receive elsewhere. This camaraderie is especially important for individuals with invisible disabilities. There is an old saying: "Don't judge a book by its cover." While the saying may be a cliché, invisible disability provides an example of how individuals' appearance, their cover, does indeed not tell the whole story.

REFERENCES

Berne, K. 2014. "Chronic Fatigue Syndrome/Fibromyalgia Symptom Checklist." Available at http://www.anapsid.org/cnd/diagnosis/berne.html.

Crofford, L. J. 2015. "Fibromyalgia." Available at http://www.rheumatology.org/I-Am-A/Patient-Caregiver/Diseases-Conditions/Fibromyalgia.

Parker-Pope, T. 2010. "The Voices of Fibromyalgia." *New York Times*, March 3. Available at http://well.blogs.nytimes.com/2010/03/03/the-voices-of-fibromyalgia.

Ruderman, E., and S. Tambar. 2013. "Rheumatoid Arthritis." Available at http://www.rheumatology.org/practice/clinical/patients/diseases_and_conditions/ra.asp.

Staud, R., and C. Adamec. 2007. *Fibromyalgia for Dummies.* 2nd ed. Hoboken, NJ: Wiley.

III.3

ASL in a Hearing World

BLAKE CULLEY

"Please do not sign—I rather hear you voice!" screamed a five-year-old, deaf,[1] blond-haired, blue-eyed kindergartener named Brittnie Culley.[2] Yes, I yelled at my speech therapist to make her speak rather than use sign language. I thought using sign language labeled me as "special." My parents don't know sign language, my siblings don't know sign language, and the rest of my family members don't know sign language. I definitely did not want to know sign language, either, because outside my elementary school, no one else knew sign language. English was my first language, and I intended to keep it that way.

I had learned to view sign language as a negative practice, in that it formed my social identity as deviant from everyone else. I hated eyes on me whenever I used sign language. I worked to speak really well and wanted to make sure my speech was up to par with that of hearing people. I stepped

Blake Culley was born and raised in Ventura County, California. She is the only Deaf member on both sides of her family and spent her childhood learning to accommodate within a world she found undesigned for her. Until her junior year of high school, she attended public schools with small deaf programs. She became mesmerized by the Deaf World when she attended an all-Deaf school competition at age fifteen. She then transferred to the "Deaf School World," and the rest is history. Now in graduate school at Gallaudet University, she is majoring in school psychology with a subspecialty in deaf and hard of hearing children. She hopes to help deaf children in mainstream schools find their identities as deaf persons.

out of my boundary as a deaf person to accommodate hearing people by communicating in the way that is most convenient for them—speaking and relying on my hearing aid. (Hearing people are those whom deaf people refer to as hearing-able people). Being deaf was not really the issue; the issue was using sign language and the way that it marked me visually as different. My aunt always told me as I was growing up, "You know, you are very special; you can't hear and you can speak." She was right; none of the deaf people I knew could speak as well as I could. At first, I did feel special. But later on, I felt really "special" and judged negatively, as kids who have "special needs" often are.

Erving Goffman wrote, "Society establishes the means of categorizing persons and the complement of attributes felt to be ordinary and natural for members of each of these categories" (1963, 2). Generally, deaf people cannot speak. People need to hear to be able to speak easily. Many societies have viewed deaf people as subhuman because they could not speak and communicated through sign language. When William Stokoe, considered the father of the linguistics of American Sign Language (ASL), identified ASL as a true language, Deaf people redefined themselves as a linguistic minority. However, stigma around deafness remains. I tried to suppress the stigma of being deaf from my hearing classmates because I wanted to be "ordinary and natural" like everyone else. Hearing people have looked down on deaf people and considered us "deaf and dumb" because we cannot speak. I went to the audiologist countless times to receive new hearing aids and ear molds, and I had to make sure that my hearing aid could be amplified enough so I could hear. Instead of my mother researching Deaf culture and making sure I had the best education in a communication-accessible classroom, she viewed my deafness from a medical perspective, something to be fixed with technology.

I was placed on a bus every morning to ride to a school thirty minutes away because it was the only school that had a program for deaf students. I envied those who lived close to their school and were able to walk there. In preschool, I was in a classroom for the deaf, although I do not remember this. In kindergarten, this kind of classroom was not challenging enough for me. I do remember clearly when I went into the first grade with an interpreter by my side, and all the students in the classroom could not take their eyes off me. I couldn't stand the thought that I was coming off as the deaf girl who used sign language and did not belong in the classroom. I tried to be as normal as everyone else in the classroom, and hence I wanted my speech therapist to use her voice. I loved going to speech-therapy classes, because I knew that the teachers were going to help me speak clearly and interact better with my classmates. I tried to give my classmates the impression that I was not like the other deaf students, those who were behind in their education.

I made a special effort to participate in the games of my hearing class-mates during recess.

"Red Rover, Red Rover, please bring Brittnie right over!"

Even when trying and trying to pay close attention to my playmates, I could almost never catch my name. All the playmates would stare at me to let me know that they were calling my name. By the time I ran over, they had the time to clench onto each other so tightly that I couldn't break the chain. (The concept of the game is to form two long chains by clenching arms together, and when one side is ready, everyone huddles and decides on a name. After the line is formed again, they chant and call the person over.) After continually not being able to break the chain, or not even being called anymore, I was humiliated, and the game stopped being fun. I thought it was normal for classmates to treat me the way they treated the other deaf students. It was clearly a game for kids who could hear their names being called, which was something I couldn't do.

At the same time, whenever I hung out with the deaf students, I couldn't understand them because they signed. I had lousy signing skills. I just sat in the sandbox by myself, minding my own business. My rejection of signing was motivated by my desire to fit in with the "hearing" culture. I had to act just like a hearing student, so I could blend with everyone else in the classroom. During school hours, I had speech therapy sessions every day for one hour. One of the biggest struggles I had in the classroom was being able to understand the other students without relying on the interpreter. I was always two or three seconds behind; I would laugh at something that had happened earlier because the interpreter often had to relay to me what had happened before I understood.

In my sophomore year in high school, I took a geometry class. I still had the mind-set of not relying on interpreters and relying on my hearing instead. Also, it did not help that my interpreter was not competent in sign language. For me, geometry doesn't require intensive explanation. I could just read the chapter and understand the formulas right away; hence, it was easy to work on my geometry homework in class and get ahead while I could. However, my geometry teacher was very particular with me. He always made sure that I was paying attention to my interpreter. He was always checking up on me, which I felt was a little excessive. He did not treat the rest of my classmates the same way. One day, I had my head down and was working on my geometry problems. Of the rest of the class, some students had their heads up, facing the whiteboard, but others had their heads down reading their books, doodling, or looking at their cell phones.

My teacher came up to my desk, kneeled down, and slammed his hand on my desk, causing me to jump in my seat. I looked up with my heart racing, and he clearly said, "I need you to watch your interpreter while I am teaching. It is rude not to." He got up and proceeded to teach. I looked around and all eyes were on me. My interpreter just sat there, shrugged and gave me a look like she was disappointed in me. I felt mortified.

The same classroom woes carried on into my home. I was often assigned housecleaning chores, and my parents checked on me to make sure I had finished my homework and that I was finding something to keep me busy. During dinnertime, everyone in the family had to eat together. Based on my understanding, there was no talking allowed during meal times, but, ironically, it was okay for my parents, brother, and sister to converse. I was better off being left alone than understanding only 20 percent of the conversation, anyway. I was better off not having to hear the words, "I'll tell you later" and "Oh, never mind; it's not that important." Those words made me feel not important at all, just because I couldn't understand what people had said. Bonding with my family felt nearly impossible.

As much as I hated going to the audiologist, it was one of the only times I could bond with my mother. My mother took me to the audiologist at least four times a year to be tested to ensure that my hearing did not worsen over time and that I could still hear almost like a hearing person. I felt like a little laboratory rat because I had to test hearing aid after hearing aid. My deafness was constantly viewed from a medical perspective. My parents were not exposed to the idea of using sign language; nor were they made aware of how my social skills, intelligence, and personality could have flourished if my family and I had been able to have access to clear communication. Audiologists, my parents, my speech therapists, and my teachers focused on making sure I was able to hear as well as possible. My hearing aids and I were inseparable.

From the time I was very young, the first thing I did when I woke up was put on my hearing aids. They became a huge part of my life. I knew that I must wear them at all times. I was never once given the option to either wear my hearing aids or not. As a child, I always thought they were required because I had to fit in with the hearing world and with my hearing family. I accepted that "requirement" because I thought it was the right thing to do. My mother always made sure I had on my hearing aids. I became very upset if my hearing aids were lost or damaged, and I remember that when they broke a couple of times, I had never felt so alone. My brother and sister never bothered to talk to me because they knew I couldn't hear and understand. I had incompetent lip-reading skills because I had relied on my hearing aids to understand. Now that I have the choice to either leave my hearing aids on my nightstand or put them on, I still have the need to put them on. Wearing them has become a part of me, just like putting on my glasses.

When I was growing up, my signing skills were incompetent, but my speech was nearly impeccable, and I thought I was better than all the deaf students because I hung out with my hearing classmates. For high school, I finally went to a school that was nearby. My high school had a bigger deaf program, and I met more deaf students. I made my first friend; her name was Julia, and she was deaf just like me. She was smart and funny, and I was finally able to chat with a deaf person who had the same intellectual curiosity as I did. She told me that her parents, along with her sister, aunts, uncles, and cousins, were deaf. I was in awe because I never knew that even existed. A deaf family? Complete communication using ASL? What?

I was invited over to her house on a weekend, and I was culturally shocked by the environment: the family had flashing lights for their doorbell, a TTY device, and closed captioning on *all* televisions, and all of the members in the family were Deaf and using American Sign Language. At first, Julia was very nice to me because she knew that I was not exposed to deaf families and that I did not use ASL as my primary language. This moment was a huge turning point in my life because it ignited a drastic perceptual change toward my Deaf identity. I finally figured out what was missing from my life—the ability to get around without relying on my unreliable hearing.

It wasn't easy, though, to find my place in this new world. I think I am a funny girl, but none of my Deaf schoolmates thought I was funny, because I couldn't tell jokes properly. Whenever I told a joke, my friend Julia would look away and not even acknowledge me. I didn't understand why she and my other Deaf peers would do that. Finally, I was fed up and asked why they thought I wasn't amusing. They told me it was because my signing skills really sucked, and they were fed up with me having to ask them to repeat parts of conversations whenever I didn't catch what they were trying to say.

I was hurt, of course, because growing up, I thought sign language was not important and that being able to speak was better than not being able to speak. This was the point where I finally recognized myself as a Deaf person, and realized I needed to analyze my reasons for not wanting to learn sign language. I could not be accepted in both worlds—the hearing world and the Deaf world. I was stuck in between because I was not accepted in the hearing world and I struggled to keep my membership in the Deaf world.

My sophomore year in high school, I found out that there was a school for the Deaf. My parents immediately said no when I told them about it. The school was nearly three hours away from my home, and I would have to live in the dorms. My parents couldn't fathom the thought of letting me go and seeing me only on the weekends. After months and months of trying to convince my parents to let me go there by purposely letting my grades slip and blaming the lousy interpreters, my parents decided to let me transfer there.

The first day of school, I was bombarded with the speed of everyone's hands. I was awestruck by the beauty of ASL and how everyone communicated with each other in ASL: the teachers, students in the classroom, the classroom aide, and even the principal. I learned to improve my ASL skills and to really embrace my true inner language.

I have come to understand the core concepts of being Deaf. Living with the stigma and the medical model of deafness and being acculturated into the hearing world have given me a good understanding of how my Deaf identity has been shaped over the years. Before meeting Julia and attending the school for the Deaf, I never knew there was a cultural model within the Deaf community or that my parents and audiologist viewed my deafness through the medical model. They truly wanted me to become as hearing as possible; in the process, they neglected the fact that I needed to embrace ASL and learn Deaf culture values to flourish into my true identity. I had wanted to minimize the stigma of being deaf as much as I could in mainstream classrooms. I sought recognition as an ordinary and natural member in the hearing world. I wanted to demonstrate that I was just as smart as everyone else in the classroom, instead of being perceived as "deaf and dumb" or not an equal. When my identity as a Deaf person started to develop, I created boundaries to the hearing world and the Deaf world. I realized that I needed to learn how to keep my membership in the Deaf world, and that is when I was motivated to improve my ASL and seize my deafness as my Deaf identity. Being Deaf is not a disability. We are a linguistic minority that I am proud to be a member of, regardless of any struggles I have been through or may face in the future.

NOTES

1. There is a distinction within Deaf studies between being audiologically deaf and culturally Deaf.

2. Blake Cullie now identifies as transgender and has formally changed her name from Brittnie to Blake. "She" and "her" are still Blake's preferred pronouns.

REFERENCE

Goffman, E. 1963. *Stigma: Notes on the Management of Spoiled Identity.* New York: Simon and Schuster.

III.4

Bumping into Things while Treading Carefully

On Narrative, Blindness, and Longing for Light

The glare of light skating across the water.
The most strident reflection
I have ever seen.
Is that horizon?

Blue is cold.
My skin told me so.
Is that horizon?
Notes falling into scale.
Fingers edging a water glass . . .
Are they horizon?
. . .
The horizon doesn't know or care.
She just wants me to wash and plait her hair,
imperfectly,
with my wounded hands.

      —TASHA CHEMEL, "Attending Horizon"

Tasha Chemel is a poet, potter, and teacher. She recently received a master of arts in education from Harvard University. Currently, she is working on a project that could help people with retinal diseases experience some aspects of sight, if they so choose.

Acknowledgments: This chapter would not have been possible without everyone who has supported me on this mixed-up journey. Thanks go to Brian Mooney, Tom Howe, and the Putney School. Thanks also go to my family and friends for their laughter, understanding, and love. Finally, thanks go to Carolyn Tyjewski, who taught me to hold on to my humility, to be aware of how my own sensitivities can cloud my arguments, and to consider carefully the consequences of my words. Some sections of this chapter are taken from two of my essays, "In Search of the Ordinary" and "An Inconvenience for Whom?" These can be found at http://www.blindnessandarts.com/documents.html.

In summer 2011, I attended a weeklong poetry workshop in Vermont. At the end of the session, I submitted a collection of poems titled *Longing for Light* to a prominent literary magazine. My cover letter began, "My name is Tasha Chemel. I am twenty-six years old, I have been totally blind since birth, and I really, really want to see." When I wrote these words, a thrill buzzed through my body. I felt rebellious, as if I were a teenager taking her first unsanctioned nighttime drive, with the windows down and the music loud. I was also filled with a warm sense of gratitude for the encouragement and support of my teachers and classmates. My poetry stood on its own two feet. For once, no one told me not to allow myself to be victimized by blindness or to "shift my focus" and "put a different spin on things." No one compared my desire to see with their own desire to be rich, as my mother had done recently. Rarely do I feel so understood, so loved for who I am— longing for light and all.

The eye condition responsible for my blindness is called Leber's congenital amaurosis (LCA), which is an inherited retinal degenerative disease. I have very limited light perception, but my vision fluctuates somewhat. On infrequent occasions, I can see some shadows, colors, contrast, and reflection. Even with my extremely limited sight, I am always amazed by how many visual concepts intuitively make sense to me. I know, for example, that white can look slippery, and that burnt orange can be described as sun embers. Having this visual awareness isn't easy, though. It's like walking around with a splinter in your left hand, painful and almost impossible to ignore. It's as if I'm a character in a fantasy novel who is stuck between two worlds, neither of which quite feels like home.

I have wanted to see ever since I was very young. Fortunately, my desire for sight is not completely unrealistic. My family and I have always kept abreast of the latest developments in stem-cell treatments and gene therapy. A clinical trial for my LCA gene mutation is slated to begin in one to two years, though I might not be eligible for the trial because of the severity of the damage to my retinas.

For the sighted, my proclamation that I would like to see might not appear to be very earth-shattering. After all, we live in a world wholly obsessed with the visual, and most people cannot imagine what life would be like without their sight. However, I have found that some people are disconcerted by my loss. They ask, "How can you miss something that you've never had?" My splinter metaphor doesn't quite make sense to them. Others say that I am inspirational and that I am better off without sight in the first place.

For me, the most perplexing reaction to my attitude toward blindness comes from the blind community itself. When I tell other people who have been blind since birth that I have always wanted to see, many of them say that they treat blindness as a fixed part of their identity, like hair color or being male or female, and that they can't even conceive of having sight. Some blind people to whom I have spoken do want sight, but mainly for practical reasons, such as gaining the ability to drive.

Recently, one blind person told me that she believed I was "trained" and "socialized" to want sight, because wanting sight is what society expects of me. Similarly, some blind people say that my philosophy of blindness is offensive because it is supportive of a medical model in which disability is seen as an individual affliction or tragedy. In general, proponents of the disability rights movement favor the social model of disability, which states that people are disabled by the barriers society puts in their way, not by their physical impairments (Oliver 1996). Given this perspective, it makes sense that blind people who favor this model might choose to look upon my grief for my sight as destructive because it sends the message that blindness is a tragedy and that blind people are pitiable victims. I have been told frequently that if I became more independent and developed stronger blindness skills, my sense of loss would disappear, and I would be able to construct a pride-based blind identity. To some extent, I have constructed a pride-based identity as a disabled writer and activist, but such an identity does not mitigate the acuteness of my dysphoria—my desire to see. The social model only partially accounts for my lived experience. I have no desire to judge others, however, so I fully support disabled people who embrace this model.

Though the social model is not overtly prescriptive, any theory is prone to misinterpretation and misapplication. When I speak to blind people who belong to one of the major blindness advocacy organizations, I often feel judged for being too whimsical, for being a victim, for not being independent, skilled, or accomplished enough. My friend Caitlin and I have even coined the term "blind police" to refer to people who seem to hold these views. Somehow, moral judgments have become tangled up in disability politics, and the social model has played an unintended role. Bill Hughes (1999), Eli Claire (2015), and other disability studies scholars critique the social model because it tends to minimize the significance of impairment or the embodied nature of disability. Embodied accounts focus on how disability affects how we relate to our own bodies, both positively and negatively, and how others relate to us. They often do not shy away from topics such as pain, vulnerability, and dependence. In contrast, the social model makes the assumption that all people with disabilities aspire to independence and self-sufficiency. By overlooking the embodied nature of impairment, and by marginalizing those who wish to seek a cure for their disability, "dogmatic renditions" of the social model are inadvertently silencing individual voices within the disability community (B. Hughes, personal communication, March 27, 2010). I have not met many other blind people who share my desire for sight, and I worry that the absence of an alternative to the social and medical model sends a message to blind people that it is not safe to talk about their desire for sight. If they do, they risk censure from the blind community.

When other blind people say that I am in danger of letting myself be victimized by blindness, I usually tell them that I believe that for all of us, blind and sighted, longing for what we do not have is just part of being human. I also tell them that my father died of cancer when I was sixteen years old, and I have found a way to honor my grief and his legacy while still living a full life. For me, as complicated and messy as it often is, my relationship with blindness is much the same.

In my personal and academic life, I search for ways to experience and express this messiness. I would like to join the group of disability scholars who are creating alternatives to the social model (e.g., Lang 2007; Swain and French 2000). I want to approach the world through stories, through a celebration of the cacophony of individual variation. I am currently a third-year doctoral student in marriage and family therapy at Antioch University New England. In my clinical and academic work, I am influenced by postmodern approaches to therapy, such as collaborative language systems and narrative therapy. In my doctoral research, I plan to develop a narrative framework of disability. I will use the postmodern concept of deconstruction to reveal and challenge unspoken, taken-for-granted assumptions about blindness. Michael White, one of the creators of narrative therapy, refers to these assumptions as dominant discourses (White 2007). Examples of dominant discourses of blindness include the idea that viewing blindness as a loss is destructive, that blind people must be either victims or heroes, and that independence should be a first priority for all blind people. A narrative approach to disability honors the uniqueness of each person's story of disability and recognizes that the telling of these stories is shaped by personal, familial, cultural, and political forces. I have decided that sharing some pieces of my own story is an initial step toward the development of a narrative perspective. It is also my intention to engage others by stimulating dialogue and curiosity around these issues. The four personal narratives I have selected involve my relationship with my mother and her work as a visual artist, my experiences as a child and teenager at school and in a summer rehabilitation program, my mother's approach to parenting me, and speculation about the future.

The Language of Snakes

My mother is an artist. Two summers ago, she became intrigued with a snake that had made a home for itself in our front yard. Usually, she is not particularly fond of what she calls "creepy crawly things," so I couldn't have been more surprised when Dudley—she named him for the street on which we lived—became a permanent fixture in her summer routine. Early each morning, she would wait for him to make an appearance so she could collect the skin he molted and trace its spirals with her acrylic paints. These sketches were the precursors to her most recent paintings, which resemble blocks of text one could find in a book. When I ask her to describe her work, her descriptions of these paintings are as fragmentary and fleeting as the paintings themselves. She has told me that none of the letters recognizably belong to the English alphabet or that of any other language, and I can imagine that her desire was to give a new freshness to the act of reading and to express her ambivalence toward writing.

My mother becomes easily impatient with words and stories, with the stale minutiae of details, and her life and her art are a reflection of this impatience. At our Rosh Hashanah dinners, for example, there are no apples and honey. Instead, there are apple wontons with caramel sauce and homemade apple ice cream. Her paintings are not about the comforting familiarity of words but about the primeval journey we took as a species before there were words. The alphabets are composed of variations of the mandala, the spiral, the cross—all of which are universal symbols that can trace their origins to the Jungian concept of the collective unconscious, the stored knowledge of our species that dates to prehistory.

In contrast, I am an artist-writer who is trying to unlock concepts like perspective and shading and depth. There are times when the lock doesn't seem quite so intimidating, and I believe that my mother has the key to that door. We collaborated on some paintings together one year, and now that my vision has improved a fraction, I'm eager to try it again. But some invisible force always seems to distract us.

"I was riding in Dan's car yesterday, and I saw bits and pieces of the houses on Dolores Street through the window," I tell her. "The hill was so steep, I thought the car was going to fall off."

"Wow," she says. "That's wonderful. You experienced that visual fear." But then she ends the conversation before I can tell her anything else. The phone is ringing, or the asparagus is starting to burn. The key crumbles in my hand, a relic from an alien dimension that shouldn't exist, and I realize, again, that no one else's words will ever be enough for me.

Victim or Hero?

I am eleven years old, and I have forgotten the way to my science classroom. All the narrow hallways feel the same, and my cane provides little information about my precise location in the maze. For a time, I wander aimlessly, my efforts at reorientation becoming less systematic by the minute. Just when I feel that I am about to break down completely, my aide comes up from behind me. "Do you know what you did?" she asks, her reproach and disappointment evident. Unbeknownst to me, she has been watching my struggles all along.

The summer I was fifteen, my parents sent me to Youth in Transition, a summer rehabilitation program at the Carroll Center for the Blind. I had difficulty making friends among the students, many of whom did not understand why the program's one-size-fits-all philosophy made me feel so uncomfortable. The one other like-minded student was expelled soon after classes began. With a few notable exceptions, the teachers brushed off my attempts to form closer relationships with them because, they said, "You need to improve your social skills through interacting with your peers." The classes were intended to teach us "activities of daily living," like orientation and mobility, basic cooking, and personal hygiene, but most of the lessons seemed irrelevant to me. I had no interest in learning to make Hamburger Helper, and I was disgusted by the prospect of cutting ham, because, at that time, I was a practicing Jew. Even more problematic was that the staff rarely acknowledged the feelings of vulnerability that learning such intimate tasks sometimes evokes. I often found myself resenting the fact that while my best friend from high school enjoyed the dubious pleasure of supervising rambunctious day campers, I was struggling to assemble a tuna sandwich. Like all learners, I am most motivated to acquire new skills when I have an intrinsic desire to apply them to my daily life. Teenagers are very present-focused, so even though I was told repeatedly that I'd use these skills in college, that time felt so far into the future that it held little meaning for me. The program would have been more helpful if the staff had been more attentive to who I was as an adolescent learner. For example, instead of telling me not to wear high heels because they were impractical, my teachers could have helped me learn to walk in them safely and gracefully. When the end-of-summer evaluations came in the mail, I discovered, to my dismay, that I had earned only 80 percent for "use of a napkin" and 70 percent for "attitude" and "hand strength." For someone who has considered herself to be a perfectionist and an overachiever, and who has always been proud of these attributes, those low scores were a bitter and demeaning pill to swallow.

In a college creative writing class, I was suddenly compelled to tell this story and others like it. My intention was not to garner people's pity for the poor little blind girl but rather to earn their curiosity, validation, and understanding. In a thinly veiled attempt at fiction, I described a typical school day in painstaking detail: what it was like to go to great lengths to print out my homework on the school's one accessible computer, only to find that the ink had run out and I would be penalized for lateness. I was saddened by my professor's response. He told me that although he liked the concreteness of my writing, "victim stories [were] more interesting when they [were] complicated" and that he felt that I had "written about an unmitigated, probably unrealistic, oppression." In his final comments, he praised me for "never asking for anything special" and wrote that it seemed odd to him that "only in stories" was I a victim. "If you're also a person who sees herself as a victim," he wrote, "you hide it well."

I felt chastened by those words, and I began to question the content and relevance of the stories I felt I needed to write. Was I exaggerating? Had I really been the victim of "unmitigated oppression," or was this just my distorted perception? And even if my perception was correct, were these stories even worth telling?

To Cane or Not to Cane

On our way back from the Massachusetts Eye and Ear Infirmary last spring, my mother and I had a horrible fight. I'd just found out that the doctors there couldn't perform a test I'd been anticipating for over a year, a test that might tell me whether I'm eligible for a gene-therapy trial. My mother was angry with me because I'd talked to her ex-boyfriend, Julian, about her inability to support me when I become this emotional, when I insist upon entering a crisis state instead of being philosophical. Gene therapy is still years in the future, after all.

"You just lump me in with all the other people who don't get you and your blindness," she said. I told her that she was mistaken, but I protested too much. A resin of truth coated her words. She has told me many times that the first parenting book she read after I was born said that a lack of independence, rather than blindness, is the true disability. When I was growing up, she was always telling me how important it was for me to use my cane correctly, to get oriented to my surroundings to keep myself organized, and to learn to cook and fold laundry. "Be systematic," she'd always say. When she tried to teach me blindness skills, usually with little success, I found myself wondering what the blind police had done with my disorganized, spontaneous, decidedly nonsystematic mother.

"I just wanted to make sure that you would be all right when you moved out on your own," she told me later.

According to narrative therapy, the parenting book my mother read supported a dominant discourse of independence (White 2007). In the blindness community, the assumption that independence should be the top priority for all blind children often goes unquestioned because we have been explicitly and implicitly told that to question it is forbidden.

It took twenty years before my mother began to partially join me in my questioning and contestation of this discourse. I spent most of that time feeling invalidated and inadequate because I was never quite independent enough. Sometimes, I still feel that way. The stubbed toe I received last week, when I blithely chose not to use my cane, because I had mistakenly assumed that my mother would alert me that there was a crack in the sidewalk, is a tangible reminder that all is not well. "Use your cane. It's not my job," she had said. I am curious what it would be like if I had grown up in a world where my mother and I could have been messy, disorganized, interdependent artists together and she would not have felt so pressured to mold me into her very opposite.

Where Do We Go from Here?

Though my intent is to contribute to the growing literature critiquing the social model of disability, my own experience has taught me that blaming or judging others who hold different views is not the answer. I have deep compassion for my mother, who is doing the best she can to make her work accessible to me, and who latched on to a discourse that was empowering to her in a difficult time. What would have happened if she had not read those words about lack of independence and had gone in the opposite direction, never allowing me to do anything for myself?

Julian and I are having dinner at a Thai restaurant. I am telling him things I shouldn't, about the way my mother has overinvolved me in the drama of their relationship. "You complain about it, but you don't tell her to stop," he says. "It's just like all the boxes and other crap she leaves in the garage. You just trip over them constantly, and you never tell her to move them." Julian is right. I don't tell her because I know that she will always have the upper hand in these kinds of arguments. If I appear to be in denial about my own blindness, if I treat it with my trademark humor and irreverent casualness, what right do I have to criticize her for following my lead? I am complicit in her denial. I'm an adult now. I can be responsible. I can put my foot down and insist that everything needs to be in the same place, that she absolutely must not leave suitcases in the middle of the hall for me to trip on, that she shouldn't leave wineglasses in the middle of the counter for me to break.

But I only halfheartedly say these things. I'm too busy falling in love with my own reflection: my mother's daughter, the epitome of the free spirit, the woman who is too artistic for paratransit, with its rigid schedules and smelly vans, who agrees that the ugly contrast of braille labels against the purity of our cabinets outweighs all the helpfulness that such labels would provide. To blame my mother for the origin of these attitudes would be inaccurate and unfair, but at the same time, I don't see them as wholly my own. Instead, I think in circles. I see my views on blindness as stemming from our unique cultural and family context. The unrelenting materialism of South African Jewish values clashes horribly with the pragmatism of blindness culture. Of course I am confused.

My confusion has compelled me to be interested in family stories, in how realities duel and interact. If a therapist who was indoctrinated with the professional discourses about blindness were to meet with our family, she probably would either blame me for being a bad blind person or blame my mother for being a bad mother of a blind child, for not being Super Blind Mom and placing braille labels on every single surface, regardless of the ugliness. My dream would be for a therapist to be curious about each of our realities, so that blame could no longer thrive. Instead of chastising me for refusing to accept blindness, a therapist working from a narrative perspective might instead ask about the intentions, hopes, and other qualities that allowed me to continue to refuse to welcome blindness into my life, despite the insistence from others that I must do so. She might also work jointly with my mother and me to see if my desire to emulate her as a visual artist could become a source of joy for both of us, rather than simply an unwanted tension in our relationship.

I know that the path I have chosen will not be an easy one. Both blind and sighted people, including my own mother, might not like all the things that I have to say. But I have experienced firsthand the positive effects of adopting a narrative approach to disability, and it is my most fervent wish to make those effects available to others. These effects include curiosity, empathy, and compassion, directed toward both myself and others. However, I also have to be prepared to accept the fact that, as a result of my research, my own preconceived notions will be shifted and expanded, and I will have to face even more undesirable truths about the nature of acceptance, shame, independence, and loss.

Postscript

Since writing this chapter, I have chosen to refer to myself as transabled. I resonate strongly with the narratives of some transgendered people, who state that their identity does not align with their assigned gender. I feel this way about blindness; I have never had sight, but I have always felt as if I were sighted. However, though "transability" is one of the few words that captures my experience, I use this term with caution, as I do not wish to appropriate trans narratives. In addition, I have shifted my career focus from therapy to teaching and am now investigating strategies for explaining visual concepts to myself and other congenitally blind people who wish to learn.

REFERENCES

Claire, Eli. 2015. *Exile and Pride: Disability, Queerness, and Liberation.* Durham, NC: Duke University Press.

Hughes, B. 1999. "The Constitution of Impairment: Modernity and the Aesthetic of Oppression. *Disability and Society* 14 (2): 155–172.

Lang, R. 2007. "The Development and Critique of the Social Model of Disability." Available at http://www.ucl.ac.uk/lc-ccr/centrepublications/workingpapers/WP03_Development_Critique.pdf.

Oliver, M. 1996. *Understanding Disability, from Theory to Practice.* New York: St. Martin's.

Swain, J., and S. French. 2000. "Towards an Affirmation Model of Disability." *Disability and Society* 15 (4): 569–582.

White, M. 2007. *Maps of Narrative Practice.* New York: Norton.

III.5

What I Wish You Would Ask

Conversations about Cerebral Palsy

LEIGH A. NEITHARDT

My first memories of going to the post office were of being six years old and taking turns with my younger sister to give the postal worker a quarter to get a single stamp for my mother, who presumably needed to mail a bill. I remember liking the precision of one quarter for one stamp. It was easy to remember and seemed like a logical exchange: one for one.

Years later, the college post office was one of my favorite places to go; the two women who ran it were like surrogate grandmothers to the entire student body. They remembered everyone's face—so it seemed—as well as snippets of stories students would share, and they would follow up with students' stories whenever they came in to check their mailboxes.

It was also at the college post office that I had one of the most unusual conversations I've ever had.

One of the questions I am asked routinely is a variation on "Are you okay?" It is always here that my memory fails me, in what I think is an act

Leigh A. Neithardt, a Ph.D. candidate in teaching and learning with a focus on literature for children and young adults at the Ohio State University, has also completed an interdisciplinary specialization in disability studies. She is the author of "The Problem of Identity in *Harry Potter and the Sorcerer's Stone*," in *Scholarly Studies in Harry Potter: Applying Academic Methods to a Popular Text*, edited by Cynthia Whitney Hallett, and "'Splinched': The Problem of Disability in the Harry Potter Series," in *The Harry Potter Series*, edited by Lana A. Whited and M. Katherine Grimes.

of self-preservation. If I had a penny for every time I've been asked that question, I would likely be one of the richest people in the country. I am always confused. I always look at my arms or down toward my legs to see if I've bruised myself (very possible, because I am prone to banging into things). Then the "light bulb" turns on. *Ah. Right.* I was born with cerebral palsy, the form known as spastic diplegia, which means that the muscles in both of my legs ("diplegia") are tight ("spastic"). To many people, I look like I'm limping. I admit, I can get internally defiant about it and argue with myself that I'm *not*; I'm just walking the way that I walk, which happens to be different from the way that most of the rest of the world walks. If I try to imitate *that* movement, it feels awkward and stilted. I have spent countless hours repeating *heel, toe, heel, toe* in my head while walking up and down hallways for my physical therapist, my surgeon, the orthopedists who made my orthotics, and, then, most maddeningly, the shoe salesmen who very quickly morphed from being experts on shoes to Experts on Physical Disabilities when they realized that I was a Special Customer. Much the way models are taught how to walk on runways, I've spent a lot of time learning how to walk "normally," period.

When I got to college, likely because of the supportive nature of the all-female student body and staff, I began to feel comfortable enough to respond to "Are you okay?" with "Yes, thank you. I'm fine." I would wait a beat until confusion furrowed eyebrows or a person persisted with "Did you hurt yourself? You look like you're limping," before responding, "I have cerebral palsy." That usually elicited one of several responses, many of which were frustrating in their own ways, but which I became used to hearing and thus tried to respond to as politely as possible.

However, it becomes more and more difficult to be polite while being pressured to volunteer complex personal information. In this regard, my experiences echo those of Nancy Mairs, who writes of her experiences related to living with multiple sclerosis:

> I routinely encounter familiarity I find inappropriate, and I try to accept it as though the person were merely a curious two-year-old to my furious one. One of us just has to grow up. I don't think it's the normals' own fault that they lack disabilities to deepen and complicate their understanding of the world. (1996, 72)

Though it is comforting to know that I'm not the only one who has these experiences, it doesn't immediately solve the problem of how people who don't have disabilities may make careless remarks. Perhaps when a person realizes that he or she has overstepped, he or she will try to be more polite the next time. But perhaps not.

Most common is the "Oh, I'm sorry!" Faces flush, and people become very interested in their shoes. I'm never sure if it's an apology because I have cerebral palsy (*Don't be sorry—I'm not*) or an apology because they think I've been offended (*As long as you are asking about me out of concern, why would I be offended?*). I always say, "Don't worry about it," assuming that this covers any possible intent. I also don't *want* them to worry.

It was in the college post office one afternoon that I nearly came up short. I must have been extra-tired that day, because when I am tired, I tend to drag my feet more than pick them up, which makes my walk more pronounced; it also means that I'm more likely to trip and stumble. (I *have* gotten exceptionally good at catching myself before I slam into the floor or ground.) One of the women asked me, "Are you okay?" and I responded with "Yes, thank you. I have cerebral palsy." Her face crumpled. My thoughts were a simultaneous *Well,* this *is new* and *Uh oh. What did I say?* as I tried to figure out what it was that would bring this woman to tears. She leaned in, put her hand on my shoulder and whispered, "Are you going to *die*?" I was stunned and tried to think fast, saying, in what I hope was a convincingly amused tone, "Well, like everybody else, eventually, yes," and smiled.

I will say, in this woman's defense, that she had known me for about three years and liked me, so I could understand—and was touched by—her sudden worry that I might not be okay. But it became clear to me that the nondisabled world has very little idea about the world that overlaps theirs yet is filled with a "different" group of people. As Tobin Siebers puts it, "Able-bodiedness is a temporary identity at best, while being human guarantees that all other identities will eventually come into contact with some form of disability identity" (2008, 5). Disability is upsetting to those who are currently nondisabled because our bodies will, as we get older, not function as "well" as they used to when we were younger. Understandably, many able-bodied people don't want to think about that. I am not sure that *I* want to think about that.

The most common response that I get to my disability declaration is an "I had no idea!" from a friend. I realize now that, in many cases, this response is an attempt to apologize for not "noticing" earlier. People feel silly for what they assume is their own obliviousness to this Really Important Facet of their friend's identity. The level of their amazement—and the exuberance with which they express it—seems to be directly proportional to their embarrassment.

But this is the response that I always find to be a bit awkward; their view of me has shifted in some way—they are astounded—while I actually haven't changed a bit and am not sure how to embrace this new projection of myself. The exclamation is followed by the quick up-and-down glance that is a variation on checking out someone. I am being checked out, all right: looked over for signs that some part of me is odd.

There is, I admit, a part of me that is slightly annoyed. I want to say, "I didn't tell you, so of *course* you wouldn't have known." Disability is, quite obviously, personal, affecting a person's body in myriad ways. As someone who has a disability, I like to be in charge of when, where, and how I discuss it, because I am not talking about a nebulous entity that hovers over me or nearby, something separate that I can put away or ignore whenever I feel like it, but about something that is ever-present and yet selectively visible, unable to be completely separated from my body, and yet something that I can never precisely touch.

But I have realized that we like difference to be public, to be noticeable so we can be sensitive to it, but, maybe in a more selfish way, so we can *not* be surprised by it, especially if it is something that we might be discomfited by. As Rosemarie Garland-Thomson stresses, we have culturally "accepted hierarchies of embodiment. Corporeal departures from dominant expectations never go uninterpreted or unpunished, and conformities are almost always rewarded" (1997, 7). This insight might explain the occasional accusatory note that I sense in someone's voice with the follow-up question: "You *do*? How come you never told me?" I sense that I am being blamed for keeping something personal to myself and accused of purposefully trying to deceive the questioner, even if ever so slightly. The simple truth would be a benign, "I didn't tell you because it hadn't come up." The more complicated truth might be, "I didn't tell you because I wasn't obligated to do so."

Occasionally, if I do have the energy or the desire to share my story, people will be interested when they find out that I have cerebral palsy and will want more specific, medical information. I'm happy that I can expand their worldview, but then I run into another problem: I only know about my experience of cerebral palsy; for years, I didn't bother to look at a medical description because I don't think of cerebral palsy as a medical problem that can be fixed, though this is the prevailing disability narrative—a disability is something "wrong" with a person's body that must be treated and, if possible, "cured." And, indeed, cerebral palsy can't be "cured."

Cerebral palsy is an inability to walk on frozen snow, so people who don't shovel their sidewalks, or who block the wheelchair cutouts to the street (and crosswalks) by "helpfully" pushing all the snow to the curb and off the sidewalk, aren't helping me or people in wheelchairs or anybody else who isn't quite so agile. If I could have any superpower, it would be the ability to teleport. If I could have any so-called normal ability, it would probably be the ability not to always need even, flat, nonslick ground to walk on.

Cerebral palsy was the weekly physical therapy visits with Renée, my wonderful therapist, from the time I was eighteen months old (when I was diagnosed with cerebral palsy) until I was thirteen. Renée and I did repetitive activities to stretch my muscles: stretches, lunges, dives, climbing stairs, walking across rooms and up and down halls, jumping rope. Unlike the foolish professionals I've encountered more recently, Renée was never condescending; she explained everything to me just as she talked to my mother after my sessions, and she was always happy to help me practice whatever sport we were playing in gym.

Cerebral palsy was the four surgeries I had at three, five, ten, and eleven, to stretch my heel cords ("Achilles tendons!" a doctor sneered at me a few years ago because I wasn't using the clinical term), and Dr. Root, my amazing, gentle surgeon, smiling at me when he arrived in the operating room. Even though he was wearing a mask by that time, I knew he was smiling because his eyes crinkled, and I would relax a bit.

Cerebral palsy was the hell of participating in gym class. Most of my nursery school years were spent in programs with children who were "like me" in that we were "different" from other people. My memories of those few years are vague now, but they are infused with a sense of being happy. In gym, I especially loved when we all played with the rainbow-colored parachute. I don't ever remember feeling, or being made to feel, slow or uncoordinated. That quickly changed when I went to a public school.

From the time I was about seven, sitting on one of the taped lines that outlined one side of the center aisle (our gym was actually an open space at the front of the auditorium), I can remember picking at the cracked yellowing finish that protected the wood floor, wishing that I could somehow shrink and either fall into the floor or disappear entirely. If I didn't look at the two team captains, I didn't see them avoiding my eyes. After routinely not being picked last—I wasn't picked at all, and one of the teams ended up with me by default—I was at first confused: Why weren't my friends picking me to be on their teams? I very quickly realized that I was the weak link: the fact that I couldn't run fast, that I ran "oddly," that I couldn't always catch or hit or block balls, was a problem, and I understood why no one wanted me on their team. The object was to win the game; I was a liability. I would try not to mess up, pray that I wouldn't be left alone "covering" an area of the field or up at bat or to kick when we already had two outs.

Middle school and high school grew even more torturous, as we had gym multiple times per week. One of the happiest moments of my life was the morning in high school that I had my final gym class and could walk out of the girls' locker room for the last time, relieved that I'd never have to go back in; never again would I have to play an organized sport against my will.

Having cerebral palsy is, for me, for lack of a better word, "normal." I don't know life without it, just as I don't remember life without my glasses, which I've been wearing since I was three. We didn't (and don't) talk about cerebral palsy in my family, not because it was a secret but because it wasn't something that needed to be discussed. Other than the fights I would get into with my mother about whether I was doing my required stretches (not usually) or discussions of my four surgeries, it was a nonissue.

I always hope that every time I tell someone I have cerebral palsy, the reaction isn't going to be discomfort or pity or gawking but instead the very rare "Oh, I don't know much about cerebral palsy. Can you tell me about it?" Invariably, my response now includes a story about a certain trip to the post office.

REFERENCES

Garland-Thomson, R. 1997. *Extraordinary Bodies: Figuring Physical Disability in American Culture and Literature.* New York: Columbia University Press.

Mairs, N. 1996. *Waist-High in the World: A Life among the Nondisabled.* Boston: Beacon.

Siebers, T. 2008. *Disability Theory.* Ann Arbor: University of Michigan Press.

III.6

Take a Second Look

LESLIE JOHNSON ELLIOTT

G roucho Marx is thought to have once said, "Life lives, life dies. Life laughs, life cries. Life gives up and life tries. Life looks different through everyone's eyes." In the twenty-seven years I've been on this earth, I've done plenty of every one of these things; only recently, however, have I realized why my life looks different through the eyes of outsiders. If I were to describe my life without explaining the invisible disabilities with which I live, my story wouldn't make sense.

There are reasons why outsiders and even people who know me don't understand the progression of my life. If someone looks at me or even interacts with me, they may never guess that I deal with overwhelming pain. My illnesses are, in essence, invisible. I have spent most of my life steadily improving an act to present myself as "well" to those around me. I've never wanted pity or to engage with the negative connotations associated with my illnesses. In order to negate this misfortune, I've rarely discussed some events that I relay in this chapter. I put on a sort of mask when I am

Leslie Johnson Elliott lives outside Chicago, Illinois, and continues to pursue different avenues to alleviate and work through chronic pain and depression. She hopes to complete a master of arts degree in museum studies or anthropology. When she is not pursuing education, she loves to travel. Her most recent trip was to Peru, and she has plans for more on the horizon. She enjoys spending time with loved ones, watching TED Talks, and rooting for the Chicago Cubs.

experiencing an illness. I do this so that what's going on inside me won't be brought to the surface or provoke questions from others. It's an act I perform very well. I laugh, make jokes, and participate in conversation, but this act can be exhausting, so it can only be held up to a certain point.

Disabilities come in many varieties, and some might consider mine more benign than others. People with more visible disabilities have become the symbol of what disability might look like. Designated parking spots for the disabled are often painted with the symbol of a person in a wheelchair. Many ask how I can identify myself as someone with a disability when I look healthy on the outside. Confronting my illnesses as a disability can detail the extreme to which they affect my life. Even with an explanation, the fact that I try to appear healthier than I feel can often hurt the argument that I am ill.

My health problems began with migraines, which were diagnosed when I was five. During the day, my eyes would begin to hurt, and shortly afterward I would experience intense pain focused on the top and inside portion of my right eye socket. I would feel nauseated, and after an hour or so I would vomit and fall asleep. After a varied amount of rest, I would wake feeling much better. My elementary school nurse grew to know me quite well because I spent so much time on the cot in her office. I didn't like that I missed so much time in class, as well as time with my friends, when I was sick. These episodes occurred approximately three times a week until middle school. My health problems escalated in my teens, and the accruing absences often exceeded a quarter of the school year—and that time doesn't include when I attended school with intense pain or spent time in the nurse's office.

When I first began experiencing childhood migraines, my primary care physician began to worry about how the experience affected me emotionally. In fourth grade, I was sent to a therapist for evaluation. Looking back, my parents remember that I was a serious and quiet child; I wasn't silly like the other girls with whom I was friends. They now question whether this was simply my personality or the beginning signs of the anxiety and severe depression that have been a ruling factor in much of my life.

In high school, my migraines began to change. They began at any time of the day; did not include pain within my eyes, nausea, or vomiting; and could last for days and even weeks on end. The best way I know to describe my pain to someone is to ask if they have ever experienced "brain freeze," the intense pain in the head when one consumes a cold drink too quickly. Imagine for a moment that the concentrated pain caused by brain freeze (which lasts for only moments) simply doesn't leave, no matter what one does to combat it. This pain has paralyzed my life.

I have always been a well-performing student, and the more intimate atmosphere of my high school meant that I was able to make up assignments and tests with the help of my teachers. I had disability accommodations,

which emphasized these allowances, but because classmates didn't understand the reasons for my absences, I heard them ask if it was fair that I had
additional time to complete assignments.

It was during my junior year of high school that I again missed a quarter
of the school year. My migraines gave me little reprieve. However, I did manage to participate in different clubs, as well as sports, every year. Despite my
migraines making my academic performance more difficult, I was accepted
into the National Honor Society and performed well on the standardized
college entrance exams. I wanted to go to a good school and make something
of myself. Other than a general desire to thrive, I wanted to show my family
and everyone around me that their efforts to help me succeed weren't being
wasted. College was an exciting opportunity to strike out on my own and
attempt to take care of myself.

I was lucky enough to be able to choose from universities across the
country. Independence was on the horizon, and despite the immense impact that being sick had on my life, I excitedly looked ahead to making new
friends, having new experiences, and learning new things. Before graduation, a beloved teacher suggested that it might take longer for me to complete
my college education. Naively, I couldn't fathom such a thing. I only wished
that my health wouldn't continue to have such a strong hold on my life.

A few months into freshman year, it became apparent to me that going
to college hours from home, while experiencing debilitating illnesses, was
not going to be as easy as I had hoped. Pain and anxiety have proved to be
a vicious circle in my life, as problems that develop from being sick cause
my depression to escalate. I was sick and missed classes more often than I
was comfortable with. My grades suffered, which fed into an overwhelming
increase in the depression I had started to experience more acutely in high
school. Depression and migraines combine to become a vicious cycle.

After being in and out of school for four years and seeing all my friends
receive their diplomas, I resolved to continue at the same university. Over
a span of four years, I had acquired approximately two years of academic
credit. I continued to miss most of my classes once my fifth year of college
began. My boyfriend, whom I had met at college and had been seeing for
about two and a half years, would visit in an effort to help with the loneliness
that loomed over me each day. He, along with all my friends, was beginning
an adult life with a job and new responsibilities. It wasn't too long after a visit
that the years of chronic illness and major depression finally came to a head;
after the idea had been present in my mind for at least two years, I finally
confessed to my parents that I often thought about committing suicide and
had gone to the extent of planning how to end my life.

After that, my life became a whirlwind. I was swept off to a highly respected rehabilitation center across the country, which treated, among other

things, chronic depression. The center also claimed to work with chronic pain issues. My five weeks at this establishment were horrible. I feel that the center's treatment of my chronic migraines was a joke. My parents flew out for a weeklong family program, which they recall as being markedly emotionally difficult, and all the while, there was little improvement in my depression. I returned home feeling I had done something wrong. I felt I was in some way responsible for my health problems, as if I had some control over the chemistry inside my brain. These ideas had developed while I was at the rehabilitation center. My parents had spent so much of their own money to help alleviate my pain, but I came back no better than when I had left. I saw myself sinking deeper into a hole and had no knowledge of how to escape.

Many months later, I transferred schools and began to commute into the city to attend another university. It was closer to my family's home, so I could go to school and they could help take care of me. I never felt proud of switching schools. I felt like a failure. The usual pattern of starting a semester, being sick, and missing classes continued. I would withdraw mid-semester and my parents would lose all the money they had paid. This was yet another thing to pile onto my ever-growing mountain of guilt.

My personal guilt is only exacerbated by the long list of failed medical treatments and therapies I have tried over the years. While filling out the paperwork for my most recent neurologist, I had to check off all the medications I have taken in my lifetime. Since the beginning of elementary school until today, I have taken sixty to seventy different medications aimed at treating my chronic migraines or major depression. This reality feeds into my guilt with regard to how much time, love, and effort my parents have put toward helping alleviate my disabilities. My emotions cascade: I feel angry, guilty, sad, and disappointed that I have taken so many medications and still suffer from illnesses that are changing my life in ways I am unable to control.

I have experienced a diverse range of side effects from these medications, as one might expect. The more benign have included hair loss, shakiness in my hands and jaw, and tachycardia, which is a rapid heartbeat. More serious side effects include extreme weight loss and weight gain, an oculogyric crisis, pulmonary edema, and a grand mal seizure during high school. Although the seizure was induced as a side effect from a medication, not epilepsy, afterward, I wasn't allowed to drive for six months or work at my after-school job teaching swimming lessons.

People, even professionals, have never consistently related well to the idea that I am disabled, as they're unable to readily see it. During the last semester of my undergraduate career, I took a wonderful class titled "Sexuality and the Community," offered by the gender and women's studies department at my university. One week was devoted to relating lesbian, gay, bisexual, transgender, and queer (LGBTQ) issues with those of people with disabilities. An article by Ellen Samuels we had read that week resonated with me powerfully. In her article, Samuels discusses invisible disabilities, a concept I had never thought about before, even with my long personal history with chronic illness and pain. At one point, Samuels reflects on a conversation with a student regarding her thoughts about disabilities: she writes of "the shifting and contested meanings of disability; the uneasy, often self-destroying tension between appearance and identify; the social scrutiny that refuses to accept statements of identity without 'proof'" (2003, 233). In addition, in the most poignant part of the article, she writes that "people with nonvisible disabilities 'are in a sense forced to pass, and the same time assumed to be liars'" (242). This was exactly how I felt with regard to my friends, family, schoolteachers, medical providers, and many other individuals.

Reading this article was a catalyst that caused me to conceptualize a plethora of events in my life—events I now attribute to the fact that I have an invisible disability. If I hadn't become so proficient at presenting myself as healthy when I was with my family, friends, doctors, and so many other people, they would have had no reason to question whether I was really sick. There has been a repetitious set of questions I have begrudgingly attempted to answer for much of my life: "Are you sure that you're not feeling well?" and "Are you certain that it hurts as much as you say?" and "Are you trying to get out of doing something by saying you are sick?" I would truly never wish the pain I experience on my worst enemy, but my own descriptions of the pain I endure have been questioned by everyone. It always hurts more when these questions come from people who have been with me through everything. They know how serious my illnesses are, and yet they still feel compelled to question the validity of a pain they can't easily see.

I can now reconceive instances and experiences of my life as a pattern of treatment based on the invisibleness of my disability. A teacher in high school talked badly about me to my class in relation to my absences. I had disability accommodations that should have addressed his concerns, but I'm sure he thought I was a lazy senior. When friends told me what this teacher was saying about me, I confronted him. I'm extremely anticonfrontational, and addressing this authority figure was very difficult. Despite the fact that multiple people told me about his comments, my teacher denied speaking ill of me.

Even leading into my twenties, abortive pain medications never worked in a reliable manner. My constant pain has led me to the local emergency room (ER) on more occasions than I'd like to admit. On one occasion, the doctor approached my case in a vastly different manner than any other doctor in the past had. With tears streaming down my face from the acute pain I was experiencing and my mother sitting at my side, the doctor proceeded to accuse me of coming to the ER to feed an addiction to narcotics and not to alleviate my pain. If anyone should understand my illness, I would have thought it would be a doctor. I have never been addicted or nearly addicted to narcotics or any other kind of drug. While I understand that chronic pain sufferers can often become addicted to medication, being accused of such a thing was insulting and demeaning. It made me further question why my pain was so hard for others to conceive of.

Doctors have left me feeling bitter at other times, as well. I have changed neurologists throughout my life, usually when they felt they had run out of options or I felt they had grown complacent in my treatment. There was, however, one time I left my neurologic specialist because I felt confusion, anger, and abandonment. For students to receive disability accommodations in college, a doctor needs to write and justify that patients need aspects of their education modified. As an example, two of my accommodations were that I would have opportunities to make up class work and reschedule quizzes and tests missed due to illness. The neurologist I had been seeing, who specialized in migraine treatment, refused to write the required letter. He told me that using accommodations of this sort were like using a crutch. This argument displayed a deep misunderstanding of accommodation and disability. As someone might need a crutch to be as mobile as possible, I need my accommodations to help me perform as well academically as those who don't need them. His comment left me looking for a new doctor.

I enrolled in school every semester during my nine years of college, but more times than I can count, I had to withdraw when absences caused by physical and emotional pain kept me from leaving my bed. The transition from being a straight-A student to a C student caused an overwhelming amount of hate and disappointment, which I directed at myself. It also created a consuming depression, with which I still grapple. I often view my future as in jeopardy and feel extreme guilt associated with how my problems affect my family, especially in the seemingly wasted effort that has been put forth by so many people to help me.

Having a child who is chronically ill has taken a toll on my family from the very beginning. I have memories of my father literally pulling me out of bed in an effort to make me go to school when I felt too ill to go. My mother would drive me to school while I cried from the pain, second-guess herself once we arrived, and then take me home again. They have always wanted the best for me, but having a daughter who was sick all the time wasn't what they had planned. I've seen the effort my entire family and other loved ones have put forth to support me the best way they can. Sometimes one of them would say just the right thing to help me press on, but many other times they unintentionally did just the opposite. They would point out a prominent person on television who had survived a terrible event, illness, or accident and come out on the other side with a positive attitude. This only made me feel worse because I wasn't able to do the same.

Although I detail here many of the negative experiences that I've had, I've also had many positive experiences and interactions. So many doctors and practitioners are kind and supportive, as are my loved ones, and I'm forever indebted to all of them. While a rehabilitation center may not have worked for me, it can greatly aid others. A certain medication might not help me, though it can help many, many people. I'm thankful for any helpful suggestions that others might offer.

After nine years and being enrolled in classes every semester, I've finally received my college degree. Obtaining and keeping a job while dealing with chronic pain has proved to be difficult, but I am currently managing my illnesses as best I can with the help of a wonderful support system of friends, family, and medical professionals. Just as when I started college, I'm excited at what graduation might bring. Years of therapy have taught me that I can achieve and accomplish the things I desire, but it may not be in the way that other people do. Though I continue to feel embarrassed, guilty, dejected, and worried when I think about my past and future, I try to reason that if today is a good day, there is every possibility that tomorrow will be a good day, too.

It is obvious to me now that others do not see my life as it is. Part of this is because I don't want them to see my reality; the other part is that they are truly unable to think beyond what is visible to them. My experiences have taught me that we cannot rely solely on what our eyes reveal to us. Although life may indeed look different from every individual's perspective, we all benefit from taking a step back and looking again.

REFERENCE

Samuels, E. 2003. "My Body, My Closet: Invisible Disability and the Limits of Coming-Out Discourse." *GLQ: A Journal of Lesbian and Gay Studies* 9 (1–2): 233–255.

PART IV

MAPPING COMPLEX RELATIONS

B UILDING ON THE NECESSITY and difficulty of mutual communication, **complex relations** refer to the ways disability informs,
impedes, and enlivens relationships. Straightforward models of
disability can be helpful in guiding us to recognize major themes
and outlines of disability issues, but these models often obscure the many
nuances of specific individuals' ties to the world. In examining individual
adjustment and orientation to disability, authors in this part consider how
disability has affected or altered friendships, families, and broader social
relations. Contributors explore the real **vulnerabilities** caused by impairment, while still asserting **personal strength** and **in(ter)dependence**. A
few contributors describe instances in which people display **stereotyped
(mis)understandings** of specific markers of disability; they trace the ways
such attitudes produce partial conversations and hinder more meaningful
relationships. In addition, two military veterans describe combat injuries,
trauma, and the emotional bonds crucial to rehabilitation. Through negotiating disability, all these writers find themselves at times perplexed by their
changed relationships with friends and family, as well as with military and
civilian communities. Ultimately, these narratives invite readers to engage
critically with their own relations to disability, to disabled people, and to the
belief systems and practices that shape contemporary perspectives.

The first chapter in this part (IV.1), by Anna Roach, addresses the imposed social isolation that many people with intellectual or developmental

disabilities experience. Anna attends college in a rural setting with typical peers, but she is well aware that her visible markers of Down syndrome cause people to shy away from her—to not take time to get to know her and potentially build friendships. Roach experiences this as personal rejection but also reminds readers that her exclusion is a product of others' ableist attitudes, not her Down syndrome. In Chapter IV.2, Caitlin Hernandez reflects on how her disability has shaped friendships—not in ways that are inherently positive or negative but in material ways that should be discussed and acknowledged. Hernandez recounts a traumatic incident in college in which her blindness rendered her uniquely vulnerable. While the imagined vulnerabilities of blind women have been seductively exploited in films—the beautiful blind woman unable to see her attacker, to perceive the looming danger clearly visible to viewers—real blind people, as Hernandez points out, are often taught to be fiercely independent and resourceful. After experiencing an intense betrayal by a person she considered a friend, Hernandez begins to reassess what blindness means to her—how it shapes her experience of vulnerability and independence and complicates the process of forging new relationships.

Emily K. Michael, in Chapter IV.3, and Garrett R. Cruzan, in Chapter IV.4, address the conflicts between internal and external responses to highly apparent markers of disability. Michael recounts the dramatic reactions people have when she transitions to wearing dark glasses to mitigate her visual impairment. These are not the "cool" shades everyone wears; instead, they seem to signify blindness. Because people begin to notice and comment on her glasses—and her vision—more often, Michael ponders the social meanings of her shades in relation to the benefit they provide. As a wheelchair user, Cruzan describes encounters with strangers who invasively demand an origin story of his impairment. Like Leigh Neithardt (Chapter III.5), Cruzan is not averse to discussing disability, but he wants to engage in such conversations on his own terms. Specifically, Cruzan wants people to believe him when he describes his spinal-cord injury as a gift that has provided rare insight and a positive political identity. However, his chapter highlights the difficulty of translating a "crip" (Kafer 2013; McRuer 2006) orientation to people steeped in a worldview of ableism. Even after a robust history of disability rights in the United States, acquiring a disability is still predominantly viewed as a tragedy—as a profound limit to one's opportunities, abilities, and chances for success. Cruzan runs headlong into this mind-set, not only with strangers but even with family members, when he tries to share his newfound embrace of disability politics and theory.

Afghanistan combat veteran Michael T. Salter describes in Chapter IV.5 the impact that his invisible disability, post-traumatic stress disorder (PTSD), has had on his familial relationships. For Salter, reintegration back into his family, his community, and daily civilian life has been deeply complicated. Even as cultural awareness of PTSD has increased, and as the military has attempted to offer more support to returning veterans, the sense of isolation, anxiety, and fear of being different from one's former self remain intense challenges. Rachel Anderson describes in Chapter IV.6 another powerful dimension of veteran experience: the intense support that comes from relationships forged in combat environments. Her chapter describes the roadside explosion that significantly injured Anderson and her good friend Sam. Anderson weaves together their journeys through the complicated web of rehabilitation, contrasting their injuries, official military disability labels, and the bureaucratic medical processes they struggle to navigate. Anderson also highlights the ways in which being African American informs their adjustments to disability, capturing a cultural story with expansive ripple effects. As a group, these narratives push toward more nuanced discussions of the ways in which vulnerability, trauma, injury, and reorientation toward disability shape personal and social relations.

Reference the boldface terms as themes for discussion, and consider the following questions as you read the chapters in Part IV:

1. Anna Roach's chapter (IV.1) begins this part with a provocative open letter to peers, neighbors, and strangers, challenging them to reflect on their (in)actions and assumptions that result in social isolation for many people with disabilities. How does this chapter connect to others in this part and elsewhere in the book—especially in relation to themes of isolation, ableist attitudes, misperceptions based on apparent markers of disability, and friendship?
2. How do these writers recognize the very real vulnerabilities caused by disability and still assert personal power, independence, and interdependence?
3. How do veteran narratives compare and contrast with other narratives of disability? Think of traumatic war injuries, military culture, and PTSD in relation to acquired disability, nonapparent disability, and the experiences of people born with disabilities.

Suggestions for Related Readings

- Explore Michael T. Salter's narrative of PTSD in Chapter IV.5 in relation to other narratives of psychiatric and emotional disability by pairing it with chapters by Shayda Kafai (I.2), Megan L. Coggins (V.3), Susan Macri (V.4), or Rebekah Moras (VI.5).

- Consider the chapters by Emily K. Michael (IV.3) and Garrett R. Cruzan (IV.4) in conversation with any of the chapters in Part III. How do these authors also engage in complicating familial and social conversations about disability?

REFERENCES

Kafer, A. 2013. *Feminist, Queer, Crip.* Bloomington: Indiana University Press.
McRuer, R. 2006. *Crip Theory: Cultural Signs of Queerness and Disability.* New York: New York University Press.

IV.1

My Name Is Anna

ANNA ROACH

My name is Anna Roach. I was diagnosed with Down syndrome when I was born, and I would like people to read this. You might have seen me in town walking or at the YMCA, the library, basketball games, movies, or Sheridan College.

I think people are embarrassed of me because I'm different. But don't leave me out. Try putting yourself in my shoes. I do think about your feelings, but you don't think about my feelings. People don't give me much attention, but don't be afraid to ask me about myself. I will try my best to answer all your questions. The hard part of having a disability is that it's hard to talk to other people and make new friends. Give me a chance to be a friend. I'm just like you, so treat me like I'm a person.

Treat me like an adult, not a kid. I know I'm small, but I have an open mind about the world around me.

Do you?

Once I told my mom, "I wish I was normal." She said, "What do you mean 'normal'?" I said, "Like my friend Caty. I wish I didn't have a disability." My

---

Anna Roach is twenty-four years old and is an active and visible member of her community in northeastern Wyoming. She has two older brothers who are the inspiration and the motivators for her drive to be included and to follow her dreams fearlessly. She works, volunteers, and contributes to society.

mom said, "The way you were born, it's nothing you can change." I said, "Yes, I can! I will go back to the hospital and tell them to take my Down syndrome off!"

I was just joking.

Thank you for reading this. And remember to just give love to all people who are different.

IV.2

Living Blind

CAITLIN HERNANDEZ

"**F**riends aren't going to come to you, baby. You have to make them."
My mom said this to me when I came home after the first
day of kindergarten, whining about having no one to play with at
recess. Alone in the sandbox, I had pushed and pushed my shovel, digging a
hole to China and sensing the unwavering, protective gaze of my teacher as
clearly as I could hear her anxious voice asking me if I was all right.

On the second day of kindergarten, as my class filed outside for recess,
I grabbed the first kid I could reach. "What are you gonna play today?" I
demanded.

He didn't know, so I seized his hand and trailed him into the playground.
He showed me how to climb the parallel bars and told me that they were
blue, and when we went back into class, he guided me over to sit with him
for circle time. I learned that his name was Jesse Brown and that he had a

Caitlin Hernandez is currently pursuing her master's degree in special education from San Francisco State University. She aspires to teach elementary or middle school students with mild to moderate disabilities. As an undergraduate at the University of California, Santa Cruz, she mentored other students with disabilities and was copresident of the school's disability alliance. In her spare time, she enjoys various forms of creative expression, including writing songs and stories and singing in a cappella groups. Currently, she is writing a young-adult, LGBT-themed novel and putting the final touches on her third play for CRE Outreach, a nonprofit organization that hosts the only all-blind acting troupe in the country.

big sister the same age as mine, and maybe they knew each other, because they were both in fifth grade at this school and were in Girl Scouts. He was my first friend.

Jesse Brown and I moved through elementary school together, separated for middle school, and then came back together in high school. We both had third-period advanced English in tenth grade. He didn't say a word to me all year—he acted like we were strangers—and because his voice had changed, I didn't even know he was in the class at all until a substitute called roll one day in the middle of the second quarter.

Many people, like Jesse Brown, make it only halfway along the spectrum of seeing, grasping, and knowing what it's like to be me, and that's okay.

Kindergarten was filled with lessons. Besides the art of making friends, I learned to answer questions, fight my own battles, and be patient when people didn't understand what I did and didn't need. Feeling like any other kid, like I belonged, was a harder skill to master. I began to hate bringing my cane anywhere, since it immediately singled me out as "different." I resented having to miss recess to practice crossing streets; none of my friends had to do that. Almost as a defense mechanism, I withdrew into sulky silence when my classmates moved my things, or disguised their voices, or yanked down my sunglasses, or asked in obnoxious, grating singsong, "How many fingers am I holding up?" Not until years later would I know enough to retort, "How many fingers am *I* holding up?" while flipping them the bird.

From a young age, I hesitated to bring my problems to adults. I didn't want their sympathy, and I didn't need their interventions. I could hit culprits with my cane or employ friends to assist me in carrying out revenge. Most often, I'd overlook the bad things. The good things were much more interesting.

Kindergarten segued into first grade and beyond, and I strove to find an identity outside of blindness. Color-coordinating clothes, shopping, and deciding which boys were "cute" were concepts as complicated and unappealing as math. Getting blisters on my hands from the monkey bars, collecting scrapes on my knees and elbows, playing tackle football—I could understand those things. I could compete with the other kids.

Teachers nicknamed me "Speedy Gonzales" way back in kindergarten; they would watch, cringing, as I tore around the blacktop unassisted, smashing into poles and falling headlong down steps. Every once in a while, my big sister would call to me from where the big fifth graders played. I'd follow the sound of her voice, and we'd touch hands through the diamond-shaped wires of the fence between our playgrounds.

I didn't want to be "the blind girl who plays rough." I wanted people to forget that I was totally blind. Back then, I forgot about my blindness, and more often than not, others forgot it, too, or neglected to mention it. Blindness, I found, could hide in the background if I worked at it.

Sometimes people ask me, "How do you do it?"

How do I do *what*?

It isn't as though I wake up each morning, throw off the bedcovers, put my feet on the floor, and think, *Day six million of living blind.*

I don't think about it nearly that much. I just coast along like anyone else does—at least on the good days.

Fast-forward to college. Everyone said that I was ready, that I'd be great, that I'd have the time of my life. I would be a perfect role model for other blind kids.

After years of being flanked and chased by the shadows of others' hopes and dreams of my future, I was used to, if not happy about, the subtle pressure. I'd always been competent at wearing multiple hats: those of the Student, the Singer, the Sister, the Daughter, the Friend, the Girl with Perfect Pitch, the Writer—and the Blind Girl. Admittedly, I still balked at that last hat just a little. The others I wore happily, with pride, flaunting them from every angle. I wore the last lopsided, with the elastic not quite adjusted under my chin, maybe because the chip on my shoulder was getting in the way.

In many ways, starting college was a lot like starting kindergarten: new school, new people, new challenges. More than anything, I longed to move into my dorm and be seen as just another student. I hoped my blindness wouldn't supersede the rest of who I was. Maybe, if I worked hard, I could exceed everyone's expectations. Maybe I'd have hundreds of friends, and everyone would want to hang out with me all the time, and my schedule would be so busy that I wouldn't have time for homework. Everyone back home would be so proud of me, and that last hat would fit a little better.

Everything started out deceptively smoothly, falling seamlessly into place with almost disturbing ease. I didn't know a soul, and yet, somehow, I was surviving. I went to the dining hall, to class, and to random events as though I'd done it all before. I hadn't.

I kept the door to my dorm room open, memorized the voices of my hall mates, and shamelessly insinuated myself into their outings whenever I could. I never thought twice about wandering off with people I barely knew, or even on my own. Gleefully, even arrogantly, I basked in the thrill of independence, of knowing I had no safety net and was still skating along just fine.

My first college friend was the perfect gentleman. He ate countless dining-hall dinners with me, never treated me like a creature from another planet, laughed at my jokes, and learned about blindness by osmosis. He explained how the settings on my mini-fridge worked and helped me decorate my bulletin board. He read the stories I'd written and claimed to like them. He told me I was pretty.

He needed a close friend as much as I did. I, especially, needed his closeness. The effort of migrating from point to point, seeking accommodation after accommodation, and simply existing day by day in this still-new environment was beginning to take its toll on me. His friendship and understanding was my sole lifeline: an invaluable respite from the constant scramble to find and maintain my footing.

There was no blood, no physical pain. When he left, I could still think, I still had my clothes on, I was still intact. I knew I'd be late to a cappella rehearsal, but I stripped out of the jacket he'd unzipped, the T-shirt he'd touched without warning, the skinny jeans he'd forced his hands onto. I showered, then immediately threw my shampoo in the trash because I knew its scent would always remind me of what had happened.

I pulled on high-rise jeans, a baggy, button-up shirt, and a pullover sweatshirt that was three sizes too big. I ran out the door with my hair hanging in wet strings, scared he was just around the side of my dorm building, watching.

Sitting on a cement slab with the girls as we practiced, I squeezed between the two who knew me best. Tears pricked the backs of my eyes as I sang "Lean on Me" past the lump in my throat. The biting wind whipped my hair into my face and gnawed at my fingertips. One of the girls gently tied my hair back in a ponytail, while the other occasionally clasped my icy hands between hers to warm them. Nevertheless, the frozen concrete seeped relentlessly through my jeans, matching the numbness in my soul. Their well-meaning, affectionate touches couldn't reach me.

The overwhelming betrayal of my so-called friend left me devastated and frightened. And all those feelings, in turn, made me feel ashamed. It could have been so much worse. Still, he didn't even ask, and his hands were just there, and I hadn't liked it. I hadn't wanted it.

And he might not have done it at all if I could see.

I hadn't seen it coming. I'd only sat there, unsuspecting, with my eyes closed.

As the weeks passed, I attended class and a cappella rehearsal on autopilot and then immediately retreated to the safety of my room. I was paranoid, jumpy, on edge. I wouldn't go anywhere alone; if an outing necessitated walking by myself, I skipped it. Sleep rarely came, and when it did, I had nightmares.

Abruptly, and seemingly for no reason, the silence and darkness of my tiny dorm room would frighten me, and I'd rush to the bathroom. At least the strident hum of the fluorescent lights and the chill of the chipped countertop beneath my shaking palms were real, even if the entire floor of dorm rooms was deserted.

An unfortunate side effect of being a blind woman who looks considerably younger than her age is that strangers are forever rushing in to "help."

Being a hands-on person by nature, I'd never been fazed when well-meaning passersby wordlessly tugged my arm to pull me out of harm's way or steered me up stairs by the shoulders without warning. But now, in the wake of what he'd done, being touched unexpectedly caused me to lash out in instinctive self-defense. I clung to the older girls in a cappella like a second skin, hoping their hugs and gentleness could bring me back.

I still had a class with my former friend, but I couldn't drop it, and I couldn't tell the teacher about something so trivial. The words of the lectures flew over my head while I concentrated on hiding my spiking heart rate, hoping I didn't look as sick as I felt and that he wouldn't hold a door or pause to try to fix things or even to look at me.

Despite the friendships that I was slowly, tentatively building within my a cappella group, I acknowledged that I was falling apart. I hardly ate, rarely laughed, and constantly felt close to tears. If this darker side of blindness was too much for me to cope with gracefully, I knew it would alienate other people. And all I wanted was to make friends—*real* friends.

In desperation, I went to an unbiased source, hoping that her degrees and professionalism and understanding might work magic. But to my own surprise, I couldn't speak it.

Blindness.

The one word that meant everything: the word that was, in a sense, the source of all this suffering wouldn't pass my lips.

All my life, I'd been able to hide and gloss over all the ways in which blindness made me different. Now, I had stumbled and fallen. I didn't know how to speak the truth. What he'd done was making me hate my blindness— and hate myself, too, for allowing blindness-related insecurity to overtake my life.

Christmas vacation brought me none of the joy it once had. One night, I went to dinner with my dad, just the two of us, and as we drove home, he suggested that I come home and go to school somewhere closer, or take a break from school altogether. He said I didn't seem happy anymore.

I remember it as though it were yesterday: hearing his concern and squinting my eyes to hold back the tears I'd been warring against for months. It hurt so badly to grasp it all and keep it sequestered deep inside. It was like trying to hold water in my cupped hands, only to have it squiggle out between the cracks at the sides and junctions of my fingers.

I never cried in front of my dad—I hadn't for years—and even though it went against the part of me that was terrified that something similar, or worse, might happen again, I told him that I would go back. I told him that I *wanted* to go back, that I'd be fine. I believed in that. Or, at least, I wanted to.

I returned to school and found ways to mend the empty, aching places inside myself. On fair days, if I felt brave, I'd pick out a tank top and summer shorts, and I'd walk to class alone, cane swishing ahead of me and face tipped up toward the sun. Wrapped in birdsong and with my long, loose hair dancing in the breeze, I'd feel, suddenly and inexplicably, beautiful. Even on darker days, when clouds persisted in blocking out the sunshine, I still had those memories to go back to.

We live in a society where, rather than being outfitted with a permission slip to seek support when necessary, people with disabilities are saddled with the challenge of remaining steadfast, indestructible, and self-sufficient. Too often, I hear children with special needs being scolded by parents and teachers: "Do this yourself," "Don't let her help you," "Don't complain," "Try harder," "Your friends can do this on their own: Why can't you?"

But it's different. *We're* different.

The disability community has become so wary of being judged and making mistakes that putting our best foot forward requires significantly more gumption than it should. Too often, we feel burdened, responsible, tasked with eradicating misconceptions about and being a worthy member of a group for which we never signed up. We're rarely taught how to reach out for help, how to forgive ourselves when we fail, or how to break when breaking might be beneficial. When and if we do learn these things—when and if we are allowed to struggle—the reprieve is typically long overdue.

So much of blindness is tied to trust. Trust that the next footfall won't cave in. Trust that you can be strong, for yourself and for others, even when the odds seem like they're stacked against you. Trust that the clothes you're wearing look good, because your best friend says so.

As children wandering our way toward adulthood, we disabled people become wise in the ways of selecting friends. We have to. Above all else, our friends must be genuine. We have to believe that they're not standing beside us to enhance their own image, or to shatter our faith in and closeness to them in ways we can't bear to think about. We have to be secure in the knowledge that they won't mind carrying us if our bones grow tired or our spirit feels fragile.

My true friends, my allies, share everything with me: the good and the bad. Because there are good things about blindness—lots of them. There's hearing smiles, and teaching sighted friends braille, and holding hands with that person I have a crush on because I absolutely, positively cannot remember the way to the class that we've walked to a thousand times. I can get away with being a little more loud and expansive in my happiness for each time I'm a little sadder than everyone else but can't vocalize it.

One day, those positives intersected with the often-unspoken negatives. The scale recalibrated, and when I measured with my hands, I could tell that they were just about even.

IV.3

Shades of Shame

EMILY K. MICHAEL

O n a hot, sunny morning in August, my mother and I drive up to the Low Vision Center, a building whose design does not match its title. The doctor's office is located in a historic district of Jacksonville, Florida, in an old house with wood floors and charming white railings. As we get out of the car, Mom dryly remarks, "This place was hard to find—you'd think the sign would be bigger or easier to read!"

It has been a few years since my last low-vision evaluation. These appointments differ from my yearly visits to the eye doctor, because the center's implements for measuring vision are tailored to folks like me. Unlike a conventional visit to the eye doctor, a low-vision evaluation focuses on how the patient lives with low vision. An ophthalmologist will dilate my pupils, shine a loathsome bright light into my already sensitive eyes, and scribble something on my chart. A low-vision specialist will suggest new methods

---

Emily K. Michael is a blind poet, musician, and writing instructor who lives in Jacksonville, Florida. Her poetry and essays have appeared in *Wordgathering, Artemis Journal, Compose Journal, Breath and Shadow, Bridge Eight, Narrative Inquiry in Bioethics*, and *I Am Subject Stories: Women Awakening*. She writes for Classical Minnesota Public Radio and develops grammar workshops for multilingual learners. She also participates in local writing festivals, giving readings and workshops on grammar and poetics. More of her work is available at her website, *On the Blink*, at https://areyouseeingthis.word press.com.

for labeling household appliances or the use of yellow light bulbs to ease my eyestrain while reading.

Today, the doctor is friendly, helpful, and delightfully verbal, readily accommodating my requests for dimmer lighting in the examining room and always directing her questions and comments to me. She does not talk around me as if I were not present; she acknowledges that I am the expert on my own vision. She writes a new prescription for my glasses, designed to minimize the effects of nystagmus—the muscle weakness that makes my left eye dance unpredictable jigs. When she asks me to describe the most challenging aspects of my low vision, I explain that my light sensitivity causes most of my visual struggles. She asks if I've tried sunglasses, and I recount the ineffectual pairs I've worn, their lenses too dark or not dark enough. The doctor assures me that new styles and colors are available, so I decide to give sunglasses another chance.

One of the center's employees and I venture outside with a big bag of sunglasses to try. We stand on the sunny porch, and she hands me one pair after another, describing the color of the lenses and the shape of the frames. I try amber, black, gray, brown, and countless other lens colors. Finding the perfect pair of shades proves difficult. Because of my extreme sensitivity to light, I need glasses that cut the glare of our Florida sun. But I can't simply choose the darkest lenses—I need a high-contrast environment in order to make the best use of my vision. The glasses must eliminate a significant amount of sunlight, but they can't leave me staring into an abyss of muddy, indistinct colors.

I choose a black pair with reflective black lenses. Far from slim or stylish, the shades offer full coverage, fitting over my regular glasses to give me peripheral protection. They work beautifully, omitting the glare without destroying the palette of my surroundings. When I put them on, I feel ready to tackle the sunniest environments. I start to fantasize about spending more time outside—working in my parents' garden, exploring the extensive nature trails at my university, and planning picnics on the beach.

Like the white cane I have been using since high school, the sunglasses now claim a permanent place with me any time I leave my house. Out of necessity, I wear them in the car, and I am amazed at all the things that the glare rendered invisible. Passing cars, trees, buildings, and street signs come into focus as I stare out of the car window. I cannot read the signs, identify the types of cars or trees, or recognize the buildings, but I move closer to a visual understanding of my surroundings.

Though I dislike the look of the shades, they become part of my personal image. When I enter a bright, low-contrast environment, like a public restroom, I pop the sunglasses on, and my confidence rises. The space before me clarifies, and I can travel with greater ease. Then I catch a glimpse of myself in the mirror above the sink, and my confidence plummets. The image in the mirror doesn't resemble a face. It's a quasi-human mouth and barely distinguishable nose leading into a void of black. When I'm behind the sunglasses, I can't recognize myself.

Friends try to soothe my insecurities; they insist that the shades are stylish, something Audrey Hepburn might wear. But I know that the sunglasses do not match my personal style. Since their function necessitates their bulky, cumbersome form, the comparison to Audrey's sunglasses elicits a twinge of resentment. While Audrey could wear whatever style she wanted, I must depend on shades so large that they won't fit in a conventional glasses case. Yet leaving them at home is unthinkable—I shudder to imagine myself in a bright environment without them.

Because I cannot easily hide them unless I bring a large purse, the shades feel like an inescapable stigma, a sign of difference I must acknowledge each time I face my distorted reflection. When I need to use the shades, I do so with a mixture of relief and resignation. Wearing the shades alleviates the discomfort caused by glare and sunshine, but, as I slide them on, I feel awkward and embarrassed—convinced that I embody the blind stereotype.

From behind the shades, I notice an unprecedented reticence coloring my social interactions. Servers, manicurists, sales assistants, librarians, and even nurses seem discomfited by the dark glasses. While wearing the shades, I find myself surrounded by people who direct their remarks to my companions to avoid communicating with me. Within a few words, I can recognize their awkward hesitation. In one case, a waitress whispers to a friend at the table, "Would she like a braille menu?" and I lean toward the sound of her voice to answer with an emphatic "No!" I sense that the shades create an indomitable barrier between me and the world—that the strength of this barrier symbolizes the intensity of my own deficit. Clearly, I will not find acceptance among a sighted majority that is so uncomfortable with my dark glasses.

My brother offers me a more appealing perspective by making me laugh at myself. When we walk together and I use my shades, he calls me Stevie or Ray. Since I sing and play the piano, I welcome these associations. His comments remind me that others have worn the shades and created powerful identities. His affectionate teasing helps me accept the sunglasses as a natural part of my apparel. He insists that the sunglasses do not change who I am; they don't make him uncomfortable. They provide protection, relief, and—as we catalogue the awkward vocal stumbling they elicit from others—an opportunity for endless joking.

Still, when I put on the sunglasses, I cannot avoid thoughts of hapless blind beggars and awkward blind girls. These negative associations accrue more force as those around me voice disfavor with the glasses. When people ask pointedly, "Do you *really* need your sunglasses in here?" they convey the sense that the shades are only acceptable within specific parameters. Though I seldom hear objections when I wear the shades at the pool or the beach, my indoor use of the shades unnerves people around me. I wonder if people feel marked by association—perhaps even labeled as handlers or caregivers because they travel with me. In this view, removing a pair of sunglasses is more feasible than correcting a series of hasty, inappropriate labels.

Acceptance and disapproval aside, the shades remind people of how little they know about my vision. When others ask whether I really need to wear them, they are deliberately not asking, "How bad is your vision that you need those dark glasses in a room with average lighting?" If people think they have my vision figured out, my unpredictable use of the sunglasses destabilizes their theories. Suddenly they can't calculate what I can see—and, by extension, what I can do.

Despite my struggle to understand what they signify for others, I cannot fight the shades: they are too practical. Slowly, the sunglasses find their way into most areas of my life. No longer confined to outside wear, they creep into bright classrooms, coffee shops, restaurants, even bookstores.

Months after getting the shades, I stand onstage with my university chorale as we rehearse our pieces for the night's performance: a choral festival at a local community college. We're singing on unfamiliar turf—a stage with lights I have never experienced before. In our campus theater where I usually perform, the soft red and blue stage lights don't bother me; I don't even carry my sunglasses onstage. However, this new venue uses harsh white lights. Their oppressive glare settles into my eyes with heat and heaviness. The sensation reminds me of the achy fatigue of dilated eyes—with pain superbly amplified. I feel like I've had my pupils dilated and spent several hours under direct sunlight. I manage to make it through the rehearsal with my eyes closed, my fists clenched at my sides. Knowing I'm the only one who can't stand the lights, I feel foolish, weak, and embarrassed.

Seeing my discomfort, our conductor advises me to wear my sunglasses onstage. Since she assiduously monitors our performance attire for signs of difference, I am surprised that she will allow me to wear them. I grab the shades out of my purse and pop them on. When we return to the stage, the lights no longer distress me. My eyes feel soothed by the protective darkness of the shades. Now I can see our conductor standing before us—the black velvet folds of her outfit and the glint of her blond hair. I can distinguish the white keys of the piano and the bright rectangle of the sheet music on its stand. As the soreness fades from my eyes, I regain my confidence.

Unaccustomed to performing in sunglasses, I discover new challenges. Singing behind sunglasses feels drastically different from singing behind my normal glasses. When I breathe as a singer, I imagine air filling my whole body, entering through my mouth or nose and the tiny space above my eyeballs. Behind the sunglasses, this stream of air, so necessary to producing a vivid, resonant tone, is imperceptible—blocked by a wall of plastic that outstrips my regular glasses. It's also hotter behind the shades, and I worry that my face will be less expressive.

The concert continues without incident until the other performing groups join us onstage for the finale. To accommodate the extra singers, I unfold my cane—which typically rests folded at my feet—and step to the right. While my fellow performers hold their binders of sheet music, I stand with the cane unfolded at my side. A singer from the other group leans toward me to hiss, "You're blind, and you know your music so well!" This unsolicited attempt at praise reminds me that my shades and cane aren't ambivalent props; I can't pass for a musician among musicians.

I wonder why this singer, a stranger to me, uses the emblems of my blindness to evaluate my talent. Why should my musical skills be more impressive within the context of a white cane and dark glasses? I struggle to disarm these negative connotations and focus on how the cane and sunglasses facilitate my independence onstage.

I try to reconcile my vision of the shades and cane with what others see when I use these tools. For others, I think the shades especially mark an undesirable difference, because they seem to hide more than they reveal. Unlike an unconventional hair color, tattoo, or piercing that might inspire curiosity and promote conversation, the shades obscure my eyes and force others to stretch their communicating muscles. For some relatives and friends who have grown up with me, the shades distort my identity; they hide "the real me" from view. These people cannot see the world that the sunglasses give me. They see only a barrier between me and my environment.

My sunglasses are especially unwelcome in photographs, because photography helps to supplement our memories of a particular event. If I wear my shades in photos taken at important events, I taunt the viewer by refusing the camera visual access to my face. On the sunny afternoon of my first college graduation, my family members hold up their cameras, saying, "We want one of you without your sunglasses." Similar sentiments arise during the rehearsal for my brother's wedding. As the wedding coordinator helps us line up outside the church doors, a relative comments, "I'm sure you won't need your sunglasses in the church." If I won't need the shades in the church, then they won't appear in photographs. With a few camera clicks, we can erase the shades—and the disability that creates my need for them.

When people encourage me to take off the sunglasses, their voices full of concern or reassurance, I sense a powerful subtext: "Don't you want to look like someone else?" Perhaps they think they are offering me a reprieve, an opportunity to set my disability aside. Maybe they imagine they are handing me the keys to normalcy. Why wouldn't I want to take off the shades and adopt the look of a sighted woman?

Now that I have come to accept the sunglasses for what they are, a tool that augments my independence, removing them to appear normal seems absurd. To those who think that the dark glasses should be cast aside, I want to convey the world that comes to me from behind the shades. It is a space where I have exchanged fatigue, eyestrain, and an inability to visually understand my surroundings for relief, confidence, and a crisper visual reality. The sunglasses don't eliminate all my visual frustrations, but they help me make the best use of the vision I possess.

These shades invite me into the world. They make previously unthinkable situations accessible. Wearing them, I feel confident venturing across any stage, under any lights. When I graduated with my bachelor's degree two years ago, I walked across the stage with my white cane and dark glasses. I will graduate with my master's in a few days, and the shades will be an essential part of my regalia.

Once the sunglasses became a fixture of my performance attire, my entire chorus started calling me Stevie, a nickname I readily accepted. When I sang with a jazz combo last semester, the alto saxophone player confessed, "I see a cane and dark glasses on a girl in the pit, and I immediately think, Diane Schuur!" I am excited to hear these comparisons, to think that the shades could be an emblem of blindness without deficit. Maybe the shades hold the power to bridge the associative space between disability and talent. Maybe one day, someone will see the shades and think, *I wonder if that (blind) girl sings jazz.*

I am learning that the tradition of dark glasses and white canes can work for me, that it's my prerogative to wear and use what I need. I offer others a new perspective of me as I accept a different vision of myself. Reluctance and resignation have passed. I don't love the look of sunglasses, but I love how the world looks when I wear them.

IV.4

Abandoning Normalcy

GARRETT R. CRUZAN

I find it interesting that people are so concerned with how I became disabled—as if this narrative would explain who I am. Random people ask, "So what happened?" They assume I will intuitively know that they're asking about my chair and not a convenience-store robbery down the street or something. It's as if, for these people, that specific curiosity—the origin of my impairment—needs to be satisfied in order to understand and engage with the person sitting before them. I want to say, "Look, I'm just a guy who gets around a little differently than you do; being a person with a disability has helped shape my character, sure, but I am not some living manifestation of tragedy or misfortune." Does what happened really matter? The fact that strangers ask such things is of no surprise, though. I know some people go through life without ever *really thinking* about disability—despite the fact that all of us exist somewhere on a continuum of ability. I know, because I used to be one of those people, and there is a great sense of shame

---

Garrett R. Cruzan is a student at the University of Wyoming pursuing a bachelor of fine arts degree with a minor in disability studies. He is originally from Billings, Montana, but has been a resident of Wyoming for the past ten years. He began college as a music major but transitioned to a visual art concentration to more acutely engage with people on subject matter important to him. Through his writing, advocacy, and artwork, he addresses disability studies subject matter, as well as intersecting social justice themes, hoping to spread awareness and inspire change.

in that confession for me. If we return to the first question, though, and you're wondering whether *what happened* could ever be a welcomed inquiry, it's contextual. If it's part of a conversation having to do with how I've come to think about disability, we can talk.

My understanding of disability has been years in the making, which stands in stark contrast to how quickly I became acquainted with impairment. One minute I was able-bodied, and the next I was lying in an ambulance unable to move anything below my chest. I spent six months as a recovering inpatient and am one of the few who can say my mailing address has been a hospital—one of a few who understands what that feels like. I had sustained a spinal-cord injury (SCI), two broken ribs, two fractured wrists, and a punctured lung, so to say I was in need of repair at the time would be more than fair. That people have the same perception of me today, however, is entirely wrong.

Coming Home

Coming back to the agrarian community I lived in (reentry, as it is known in the rehab hospital) was perhaps just as difficult as enduring the pain of my injuries, although it wasn't because people had bad intentions. I was given a welcome-home party by my friends and neighbors; a benefit auction was held to alleviate my financial burdens; and my father organized the building of a ramp that made my new house accessible. But as time went on, it seemed I was fighting people's convictions; they weren't sure where I fit regarding ability and disability, religion, work, and their ideas of labor capital. Disability was supposed to be an unfortunate state that left someone bitter, angry, pitiful, and useless (in varying degrees). To make matters worse for me, my friends' beliefs were reinforced by the few disabled members of the community who seemed to exemplify such negative stereotypes.

They had hope for me, though. The doctors said that they could not predict how much my spinal cord would heal, and research showed that on average, about 5 percent of incomplete paraplegic SCI patients recovered enough to walk again. I hoped for recovery, too. That statistic became the life raft I clung to as the ship that was my previous life sank before my eyes. I was convinced that if I could just walk again, everything would be fine. Community members were helping to keep that raft afloat, insisting that God would heal me so I would walk again. *He* wouldn't let this happen to such a good person. *He* would make it right. They could feel it. Though I found no personal solace in religion, I still thought that the only way for things to get better was for me to be able-bodied—to regain all the sensation and functionality I had lost, to be healed. After all, it was no one's fault that the doorways were too narrow, the barnyards weren't paved, and everyone's houses had steps leading into them. I was the one with a problem. I was the one who couldn't walk.

When it became apparent that I probably was not going to walk again, exclusion and isolation became increasingly common. The physical demands and mobility that ranching required proved to be enough to segregate me from everyone else. Furthermore, since I never owned a ranch and was never employed by one (and didn't have the desire to be), federal funding for accessibility modifications wasn't available or appropriate. That being the case, I remained excluded from the majority of daily activities around me. Two years after my impairment, my home remained the only accessible building for thirty miles in any direction. I had received a few invitations to participate in seasonal undertakings—sheepshearing, for example. But when I showed up to help, no consideration had been given to my accessibility needs, and I was stuck watching everyone else do the work. I was someone who grew up idolizing the hard-laboring loggers, mechanics, and carpenters in my family; I had been a heavy-equipment technician myself. For someone who held manual laborers in such high regard, sitting next to the wall of the barn that day, just watching, was devastating. I was beginning to feel as though I didn't fit anywhere.

Then I was introduced to vocational rehabilitation (VR). I was fortunate enough to have been put in touch with my local VR office before I left the hospital, having no idea how much it would help transform my life. One of the most immediate things that came from my communications with the VR staff was adaptive driving equipment—VR covered the cost of a wheelchair crane, hydraulic lift, and hand controls that allowed me to operate my truck and get a driver's license again. In a world that had become so foreign and new, driving, as I figured out, was comfortably familiar. I could still roll down the window and feel the wind on my face, feel the sun on my arm, and play the same songs on my radio, and my dashboard was still there to listen when I sang along. Driving brought a great deal of comfort and independence to me because I could come and go as I pleased, and though there weren't many accessible places to go, I could leave home whenever I felt inclined. It was kind of funny how much bigger the world got when I looked beyond the county line. I took trips to see long-distance friends, drove myself to therapy reevaluations, and saw a couple of my favorite bands at Red Rocks Amphitheatre outside Denver.

When my counselor asked me what I wanted to do with my life, it was difficult thinking about anything outside what I had known. I, like so many people, had gotten comfortable with where I was in life, and it was hard to imagine doing something entirely different—it was almost as if I had just graduated from high school and had to make those big decisions all over again. I was trying to come up with a business plan for a welding shop or a small engine repair shop, anything I was familiar with, when my counselor, away on vacation, sent her assistant to meet with me instead. The assistant sensed that I was struggling to reach any solid conclusion, and asked, "What have you always *wanted* to do? I'm not asking what you think you need to do, but what have you always *wanted* to do?" I was so surprised, and taken aback at the absurdity of the question, that I couldn't answer. After a month's worth of soul-searching, though, I told my counselor I had decided to go to college for music.

College: Revealing a Bigger Picture

The first few months I spent away from home were especially liberating. The campus was bestrewn with sidewalks that I could roll on with ease I was in a place where people appreciated my eagerness to learn instead of my ability to perform physical labor, and I was meeting people who weren't preoccupied with the way I used to be. That's not to say that all was copacetic, however. Elevators don't work during fire drills, a foot of snow renders the smoothest sidewalks useless if they aren't plowed, and it's hard to find an accessible bathroom on campus after dark. Still, college was something exciting and new.

My big transition in mind-set occurred about a year and a half into that education. By chance, I was introduced to an instructor of disability studies who invited me to take a few of her courses. I thought little of it, except that it would provide a way to fulfill some requirements for my degree, and moved on. When the next registration period rolled around, I signed up for the online introductory class and her disability studies theory class. I can't recall what it was I expected to get out of the two classes, and maybe that says I didn't expect much. I can say that at that point in my life, I was content getting around on wheels. I probably wouldn't have ever pushed myself to understand ableism, disability studies theories, or the stigmas that permeate our culture and are so harmful to people with disabilities. It is no small wonder, then, that it took me awhile to adopt such a new point of view.

When I was first confronted with the social model of disability, I remember how ridiculous it sounded—how backward that kind of thinking seemed. Upon reflection, I suppose this was because I still lived by and unknowingly supported what Tobin Siebers calls the "ideology of ability" (2013, 279). Somewhere deep down, I still thought that able-bodiedness was superior to disability, that it was natural for me to have preferred able-bodiedness to impairment. To say that disability was a condition created by society went against everything I was raised to think. The moment I really started to consider such a notion, at least in part, was the moment I began to entertain several other theories. By the end of the semester, I was surrounded by people who were starting to think differently, and I felt confident in my understanding of what I was being presented with. Disability studies was providing a new language for the new life I was experiencing, and it was a language that made a whole lot more sense than the one I was used to. Maybe it wasn't my fault, after all, that I couldn't get into some buildings or use just any bathroom.

Negotiating Existing Family Beliefs and Culture

At the end of that school year, I gave a presentation to my theory class on ableist rhetoric in American pop music and music videos. Weeks of preparation and research led up to what some of my classmates said was the best presentation they had ever seen, and I was very proud of the work I had done. A corresponding essay followed, and when I learned I had passed the class with good marks, I was ecstatic. Riding high on all the positive feedback I had received from my peers and instructor, I traveled to Montana to spend a week with my family and decided to give the presentation to them.

Maybe I had been overly proud of my work, or maybe it was altogether unreasonable to expect a reaction like the one I got from my classmates, but I was crushed when I faced a great deal of criticism. I couldn't believe *my family* didn't understand, especially after the week full of conversations that followed. I was frustrated, in part, because in me they now had a family member with such a different perspective on life, which I thought would be enough to encourage them to entertain new ideas. I also saw evidence every day that reinforced the theories I learned. I could accept, for example, different meanings for the words *disability* and *impairment*. My body had been physically impaired, yet I felt disabled by society on a regular basis—it wasn't just a petty game of semantics. I also knew from daily interactions that popular opinion meant disability was synonymous with a lesser quality of life. I met people all the time who told me how sorry they were that I was in a wheelchair.

I needed to be fair, though. If I imagined myself giving the same presentation to a younger version of me, I could understand taking a defensive stance at the mention of ableism, as if someone was accusing me of doing something wrong just by adopting the cultural values I was taught. I had learned disability studies theory over the course of many months, not in one day, and even I didn't agree with a lot of the material at first. I knew how hard it was trying to understand issues that seemed contradictory to values I grew up believing without question. The big reality was that no matter how close my ties were to my family, we were living different lives. As it took time for me to gain a better understanding of disability, it would, too, for them.

Concluding Thoughts

Understanding and open-mindedness are important issues when critically reexamining our culture. I struggle to maintain my composure when confronted by strangers who ask intimate questions about my impairment. I know that if I am belligerent about it, it closes a door on dialogue altogether, and that's not good. I also know that if I give a short and simple response, they may not even recognize how presumptuous and rude they are being. Changing the way people think about disability begins one conversation at a time, so I have decided to be careful with that responsibility.

I tell people that my impairment has been a gift; I am very lucky to have been given such a unique perspective on life. Without my SCI or my wheelchair, I would be missing too many of life's most important lessons, so I can't really say I am worse off. But a proclamation like that defies most people's understanding of disability, and I don't think very many of them believe me. I do my best to convince them anyway; I just don't know how much I really change the way they feel. I wonder how the world would be if everyone realized that normal didn't exist, and that trying to achieve normalcy was futile. What if disability didn't always need a cure? What if everyone equated disability with difference, not deficiency? What if, when a stranger walked up to me, it was to make small talk instead of quiz me about my apparent physical difference?

My path to understanding disability as I do now has been one of ignorance, hardship, frustration, and great reward. I feel as though I cannot express enough gratitude for the opportunities I have been given and for the work of disability rights activists—without whom I would not have had those opportunities. I am learning to embrace my place in spreading awareness, and I know how important that is. As I continue to learn and grow, I will be more mindful than ever of my role in the future of disability (however you define the word). I am continuing on with a narrative, not of recovery but of embracing disability, and deserting the notion of normalcy that I once thought existed.

REFERENCE

Siebers, T. 2013. "Disability and the Theory of Complex Embodiment—for Identity Politics in a New Register." In *The Disability Studies Reader*, 4th ed., edited by L. J. Davis, 278–297. New York: Routledge.

IV.5

A Quiet Conflict

Post-traumatic Stress Disorder

MICHAEL T. SALTER

The journey began in 2005, upon receiving orders to deploy to Afghanistan for twelve months. A hard-core soldier was determined to be part of something bigger and aid a country that was in shambles. He took all his skills, core beliefs, instincts, and determination to a foreign country to perform a job and had every intention of returning home safely to his family. A lifetime of training culminated in that one short period of time. Yet sometime during those twelve months, he changed. He arrived home, with all his body parts attached, to the joy of a beautiful wife and two sons, but he found himself scared to leave home and started shutting people out of his life. What happened?

This story is repeated again and again as service members redeploy to the United States. They serve with honor and pride as ambassadors for their nation, only to return to a society that seems different from the one before their deployment. The change appears to them as people thank them for their service or discuss how great it is to see them home in one piece. The "one piece" is a myth because, mentally, they are in many pieces. They lock their doors, do a security check at night, put kids to bed during daylight, and

Michael T. Salter wrote this chapter as part of a project for a college disability studies class. In the past five years, he has completed a bachelor's degree in social science and earned a master's degree in education.

insist that their spouse let them be in charge. Trash on the road, holes in the asphalt, sudden movements, smells, aggressive drivers, and other situations send them mentally back to the war zone.

This is my story. I deployed to Afghanistan in 2005 with a range of normal emotions. As always, I found myself deploying with people from various backgrounds and building the bonds needed to cope with what lay ahead. A "Band of Brothers" (and sisters), based on sharing common situations and events, boarded a plane, laughing, joking, and enjoying our moments. This group would be my family for the next twelve months. The first three months passed in a flurry of operations and missions. Days were long, and nights were longer. We worked every day with the passion and dedication of warriors. Everything was normal in an abnormal world, or so I thought. In reality, I was changing.

I started to notice a slight change in late January, after returning home for a bone-marrow donation. I received the request to give bone marrow while in Afghanistan, and my chain of command allowed me to return to the United States for the process. The notice came via the Department of Defense (DOD) Bone Marrow Program. The process is similar to a blood transfusion, except that bone marrow is extracted. The timing could not have been any better. Our house was built and my dear wife, Steffi, and the boys were moved in, and there were boxes everywhere. I was given six days at home in South Carolina after completing my physical, while waiting for the doctors' clearance to perform the marrow transplant in Washington, D.C.

I went to work on the moving boxes with the goal of emptying every one of them before flying back to Washington. On the final day, I was working on the last forty boxes when Steffi called. It was a simple phone call. She needed some information for paperwork that was being filed. I lost control of my emotions and told her, quite loudly, that she could handle it and I needed to get the boxes unloaded so she wouldn't have to worry about them after I left. We hung up and I remember asking myself, "What was all that about?"

I rationalized it as stress and called her and apologized. This behavior would become a pattern, something I only now understand, as the pieces are coming back together. I completed my trip and woke up back in Afghanistan, unaware of the change that was taking place. Six months passed, and I found myself home again, for some rest and relaxation. Steffi and I hooked up the travel trailer and went to the beach for ten days. It was paradise. For me, it was the perfect fantasy: playing with the boys on the beach, enjoying quiet moments with my wife, and just relaxing. I rationalized that this was what life would be like upon my return in a few months. This thought, I would find out, was far from the truth. I returned to Afghanistan to complete my tour of duty.

Two weeks before returning to the United States, I found myself on high alert. My only desire was to leave Afghanistan and return to a safe environment. I began to distance myself from my fellow service members and was at times a little snappy. I just wanted to leave before something bad happened to me. When I was younger, I read about this situation with Vietnam veterans. I now understood it firsthand. I was scared, and safety was anywhere but Afghanistan. I flew out of Afghanistan a week earlier than expected, and I was excited. I thought I would be able to return to my true self once back in the United States.

My first stop on the journey home was a transit center in Manas, Kyrgyzstan. I found myself trying to look in all directions at all times. I trusted nothing and no one and kept waiting for something bad to happen. I was surrounded by a large group of airmen who were friendly and engaging. They assisted me at the gym, sat and talked at the cafeteria, and were thankful for my service. Although the camaraderie was great, I felt alone. I could not wait to return to my room. My biggest desire was to leave base and return to my home in South Carolina. It would be better there, right?

Steffi picked me up from the airport. As we were driving away from the airport, I noticed a brown United Parcel Service truck traveling at a high rate of speed on a road perpendicular to us. Fear gripped me as I reached behind my back only to find no weapon to use for defense. Steffi asked if I was okay, and I explained that I had been spooked and was reaching for my 9 mm pistol. At the house, I settled in. The boys returned from school and were happy to see me. I was so happy to see them, and I just hugged them as tears grew in my eyes. I remember thinking, "Why am I so soft and at the point of tears?"

In a combat environment, you take chances. When you survive it, you feel a high resulting from the rush of adrenaline, but you feel down once the high wears off. Thoughts like *I could have died, Am I really safe?* or *Can I trust the local workers around me?* enter your head. It is scary, and you mentally fight the depression of the situation.

Returning to the States, there was no place to experience that adrenaline high of the abnormal experiences I had gone through. In a combat environment, I felt like I was making a difference. At home, I felt like I was misunderstood and no longer made a difference. I attempted to enjoy my family, but they went on with their lives. I felt confused. They had gotten over my return home and gone back to their daily routines; I wasn't ready to move on. But the world turns, and I was left standing there knowing that something wasn't right. I gave Steffi the keys to the gun closet and instructed her to never give them to me until I was stable. I called the hospital and made a medical appointment with my doctor. He referred me to a civilian psychiatrist.

The doctor was professional, but he just sat there. I felt like Freud was interviewing me. He asked some questions and then rendered his decision. I was given the drug Zoloft (sertraline) and sent to a family counselor. I did ten sessions with the counselor over the next few months, and then she included my wife. That got us eight more sessions. Steffi expressed her frustration because I would not talk to her about what was going on. I talked, but I was numb. The first year passed, and I was unsure where it went.

Sleep was minimal because my dreams would wake me in a cold sweat. I started to eat a lot and always felt that nobody understood what I was going through. I was a little bitter toward everything and felt that danger was around every corner. I spent a lot of time at home, as my wife would go shopping or out with the girls. Public places, and any type of crowd, were a nightmare for me, because I felt trapped. Walmart was the worst, because I felt locked in a maze without a way out. I would find my survival instincts kicking in, and I had to get out. I left many times without the items I had come to buy there.

Steffi would then go to the store to buy what I had failed to get. My depression worsened, and I was sure she was going to leave me. I had no self-confidence, and each day added to my downward spiral. Steffi and the boys talked me into going to see the movie *Transformers* at a local theater, and a combat scene in the desert at the beginning of the movie sent me into the back of my chair—I almost got up and ran out of the theater. This happened with many movies. The movie *Ironman* was one of the worst, because the story was based in Afghanistan.

During the next nine months, I retired from active duty, started a new job, and found myself being treated for my PTSD for the second time. Some positive events were happening, and I saw a psychiatrist at the Veterans Administration (VA). It was the same treatment plan: take some Zoloft and have sessions with a social worker. Eventually, I talked my doctor into stopping the Zoloft because I felt strong enough to make it on my own. Steffi started my best treatment. She got us enrolled in ballroom-dancing classes. It was different, but the people were friendly, and I was getting out of my comfort zone. Between having someone to discuss PTSD with and the dance classes, I started to realize that this is who I am, and I am okay. I still do not consider myself disabled, but I will tell you up front that I am challenged. Life, as I knew it before Afghanistan, has changed, although I do not feel like a victim. In fact, I look at this change as positive, because of the joy I have when I realize how blessed I am with my family. Then there are the times when I must retreat and rebuild.

I am still seeing the VA psychiatrist, taking some new drugs and sleeping pills, and losing weight, but I no longer see the social worker. Sometimes I feel that the VA is just trying to cure PTSD, not help me as an individual. It seems, at times, that I am just a research project to support some statistics they require. I am completing my bachelor's degree in social science and, thanks to my disability studies class, I am proud to be me.

Through the disability studies class, I changed my view of my PTSD. I recognize that I am a person with a disability and not a disabled person. I refuse to be the victim, and I embrace this change. The class gave me courage to tell my story to others, which, in return, makes me more confident of who I am. I acknowledge that people with a disability are more than what society ascribes to them. We are not helpless beings needing to be rescued. We are people who desire to achieve, live, and love. With a new perspective and accepting that PTSD is part of who I am, I know that I am normal and I still have challenges to overcome.

I still have nightmares and keep track of my surroundings. I focus by listening to music and blocking out distractions. For example, Steffi asked me the other day if I remember what happened around 1:00 A.M. I only remember going to sleep and waking up. She described how I was thrashing in the bed and how she gained the courage to touch my arm. She said that after she touched my arm, my breathing returned to normal.

I have spells when driving and another car flies by or cuts me off. My foot hits the gas, and I am gone. Steffi is my honest broker in this matter and sternly reminds me that there are others in the car. Our unaware boys think it is cool and tell me what a great move that was, as I weave through traffic. My stress tolerance is low to medium, and I still snap at my coworkers at times, although this happens a lot less now. They joke by blaming the medications, or the lack of medications. I still jump at unexpected events and cry for no reason at all. I know the cycle, and we work through it. Although my hands shake as I type this, I found working on this chapter to be therapeutic. Writing about my journey lets me know that I am better than I was yesterday. My motto is "Never quit," but I do allow myself to stop for a while.

In this chapter of my life, I have learned that PTSD affects not only the returning service members but also their families. My family wants to help, but they are wary because they do not understand, or they fear setting me off. I am more aware of the effect of my behavior on others now than I was right after my return. I have found that my early detection and treatment were keys to recovery. The longer you wait to ask for help for PTSD, the worse you will get. I still check the perimeter, lock the doors, and turn on the alarm before going to bed. It is a sense of control that calms me, knowing that we are secured in our house. We adopted a dog, and she gives me unconditional love. When I get anxious, she will come over to me and cuddle. Her awareness alerts me to the fact that I am getting worked up and need to relax. It is reassuring for me when the boys and my wife are not home.

The pieces of my life are coming together, but the puzzle is different from the portrait of me before Afghanistan. I still have to work on identifying and placing other parts of PTSD to fit me. PTSD is like fighting a battle every day. It is a quiet conflict, which, left untreated, will become a raging fire that society never sees, because you look normal to them. People with PTSD, like me, must journey forward with the hope that one day we will be normal; sometimes abnormal is normal. My hopes for people with PTSD are as follows: seek out hope, recognize yourself, understand that limits exist (for now), and make a difference in your community while helping others with PTSD.

I completed a sixteen-week program with a social worker using cognitive behavior therapy (CBT) and was discharged from the VA mental health department. Cognitive behavior therapy was effective for me and gave me a different way to deal with anxiety-driven events. Since writing this chapter in 2010, I now slow down when people cut me off in traffic, and I move away from them calmly. There are still some tense moments in crowds and at Walmart, but I think about the worst and best possible scenarios and then recognize what is really happening. Realizing that no harm is around me, I can calm down and enjoy life. My journey with PTSD is better, but there are miles to walk. I know I can make it, and when I start thinking I can't, I ask for help.

RESOURCES FOR PTSD

Dryden-Edwards, R. 2015. "Posttraumatic Stress Disorder (PTSD)." *MedicineNet*, November 11. Available at http://www.medicinenet.com/posttraumatic_stress_disor der/article.htm.

Mayo Clinic. 2014. "Post-traumatic Stress Disorder (PTSD)." Available at http://www .mayoclinic.com/health/post-traumatic-stress-disorder/ds00246.

National Institute of Mental Health. 2016. "Post-traumatic Stress Disorder." Available at http://www.nimh.nih.gov/health/topics/post-traumatic-stress-disorder-ptsd/index .shtml.

Porterfield, K. M. 1996. *Straight Talk about Post-traumatic Stress Disorder*. New York: Facts on File.

Roberts, C. A. 2003. *Coping with Post-traumatic Stress Disorder*. Jefferson, NC: McFarland.

U.S. Department of Veterans Affairs. 2016. "PTSD: National Center for PTSD." Available at http://www.ptsd.va.gov.

IV.6

Brother and Sister in Arms

RACHEL ANDERSON

It was a normal, hot day at Balad Air Base about an hour north of Baghdad. Sam and I were headed out with a group of other medics to do a run. Our runs consisted of collecting and delivering medical supplies to some of the outlying camps. I had three deployments under my belt, and Sam was a virgin to the desert. I was a "plaque slayer"—a dental technician—and Sam was a medical technician. In the desert, all medical professionals have to have experience in all areas. Since Sam was new to the war, I considered myself his personal tour guide. I found that a great sense of humor can get people through hardships. Sam had just left his wife and newborn son, so he was down in the dumps. We started the day at the "pool" with a few "cool drinks"; in reality, it was a kiddie pool, which someone's wife had sent us, and a warm canteen full of water. Imagination is everything in the desert.

Sam was nervous about the upcoming convoy because the news always told stories of soldiers being injured or killed by roadside bombs. These

Rachel Anderson is a wife, veteran, student, and advocate. She continues to assist disabled veterans in filing claims to receive services for themselves as well as their families. Through times of difficulty, she has always found that family and friends provided the support and encouragement to prevail. Since her separation from the military, she volunteers her time to provide street outreach to veterans.

Acknowledgment: I thank Sam for our deep friendship and his permission to share his story. At his request, his name has been changed. Sam is currently working as a vocational rehabilitation counselor with the U.S. Department of Veterans Affairs.

bombs are usually in debris from buildings, soda bottles, cars, or even dead bodies on the side of the road. The Iraqi insurgents know that Americans are unable to resist helping someone who is lying on the side of the road. In the late afternoon, we set out on the convoy as the caboose, and everyone was joking around at first, but we settled down to say a prayer of thanks before we set out. Prayer was always a part of our day. We were family and loved each other, no matter what our cultural backgrounds were. We made it to two locations safely and were on the way to our last location when Sam and I were changed forever. All I remember is seeing the normal stones and debris that had been on the road on any other run. Sam was telling us about his son's birth, when suddenly everything was chaos.

I heard a loud ringing in my ears. I was dazed and looked around in an attempt to understand what was happening. The truck was on its side. One of my friends had been crushed by the vehicle. Sam was not even inside the truck. I tried to move and looked down toward where one side of my uniform had been. It looked as if my whole right side had been blown away. I was in shock. I saw Sam once I pulled myself across the ground only to see his right leg hanging off. I don't remember Sam again until we were on the helicopter headed out of Balad on our way to Germany. It was one of the most frightening times of my life. I might have felt better if I didn't know the process—that it's common for disabled veterans not to receive services or financial compensation upon return. My job in the war was to stabilize soldiers and then medically evacuate them to Germany. I looked over at Sam, and we both smiled at each other. It seemed like a strange thing to do at the time, but we realized that we were lucky to be on the plane alive and not dead, like the people who had been in the cargo hold.

Is it better to be alive with limitations or dead with none? This is the question that Sam and I asked ourselves over and over after we realized our situation. In Germany, the doctors, nurses, and technicians swarmed over us like bees. I now realize that Sam and I were being assessed to see if we would be fit for duty after our injuries. The providers used what Julie Smart refers to as "objective, clear-cut, standardized measures and . . . prognoses, and methods of treatment" to diagnose us (2008, 60). All military personnel, regardless of service, have to undergo a medical physical before they are able to enter the service. A medical assessment is also required on the way out of the service, to identify what medical issues were incurred while on active duty. Sam and I were at least a decade too early to have our separation physicals. One provider said, "Oh, he is definitely not going to be able to do his job missing his leg." Sam later told me that this was one of the lowest points of his life. Once we were both stabilized, we were taken to a large room full of other injured members who were separated by curtains, and Sam and I ended up across from one another. One of the doctors told Sam that he was no longer fit for military service because he had third-degree burns over 30 percent of his body and had lost his right leg above the knee. I was informed by the same provider that they were unable to save my uterus and had needed to perform a hysterectomy. I had lost over 50 percent of my abdominal wall and a portion of my intestines. I was told that there was a possibility that I could continue service in the military.

Sam was shipped off to Walter Reed National Military Medical Center, and I stayed behind for a month before heading to Johns Hopkins Hospital for reconstructive surgery. We both spent over a year in and out of hospitals in the Washington, D.C., area before we actually saw each other again at Walter Reed. Sam was no longer the happy twenty-one-year-old I had met a year earlier. He told me he hated the world and those people for what they did to him and his family. I told him that I was angry as well, but I also encouraged him to stay positive and keep his head up—as I sat there, at twenty-four years old and with a colostomy bag. I made him laugh when I showed him the leopard-print bag cover my mother-in-law had sewn for me. I told him she might just come out with a line of sexy covers for "poop bags." We understood that we were now members of a devalued group of people, those with disabilities. We smiled and made each other laugh every time we talked, but we also felt depressed, helpless, and uncertain about our lives after our accident.

The world is a truly different place when your body doesn't do what your mind tells it. In the beginning, Sam had more issues than I did with this new reality. Sam was given a wheelchair until his stump healed, with promises of a prosthetic leg later. I was given a walker to assist me to regain my independence. I was also informed that I would need assistance to sit and stand until my abdominal wall was reconstructed completely. Sam and I attended physical therapy, or "torture," as we called it, twice a week. At times, Sam and all the other amputees were given sympathy, while I was pushed around as if I had only sprained my ankle. Each week, the technicians would speak openly in front of me, informing the new people on duty about my injury in an objectifying and insensitive way. I got so angry! I quickly realized the difference between an invisible disability and a visible one.

Sam had other problems, including his frustration with the constant, repetitive questions of each counselor who interacted with us. "How do you feel? Are you angry? Are you thinking of hurting yourself or anyone else?" Sam joked that he wanted to say that he wanted to hurt *them* for asking him the same thing each week. We were both medical professionals and were aware that veterans sometimes came home with post-traumatic stress disorder (PTSD). Sam hated counseling because the counselors seemed focused only on ensuring that he was not suicidal or homicidal as a result of his injuries. The counselors maintained focus on our new functions in society.

They asked us about our activity levels prior to our injuries and tried to give us alternatives that we might enjoy in our new bodies. Veterans Affairs (VA) offers programs such as vocational rehabilitation, which assists veterans with education, counseling, job placement, and on-the-job training, as long as the chosen career does not aggravate their service-connected injuries.

This phase of rehabilitation deals with not just employment but personal issues as well. Fortunately, both Sam and I were married and did not have to concern ourselves with dating. We still had the need, however, to be accepted by our society. Sam and I are African American, and disability has a special stigma in our culture. For example, men are seen as the head of the household and strength of the black family. Sam told me of his struggle with the idea that he would not be able to provide for his family, play sports with his son, or be sexually attractive to his wife. I mostly struggled with my ability to take care of my children, but I also had some issues with my sexuality. Disability and sexuality are not usually displayed in any way in our society. The onset of a disability does not decrease the sexual desire or need to be touched by a partner (Yarber, Sayad, and Strong 2010, 410). We both discussed this area more with one another than with our counselors, because our counselors did not seem comfortable discussing different options for sexual activity with us. After this phase in our transition, Sam and I were ready to integrate back into society as functioning civilians.

The services lead veterans to believe that our benefits are guaranteed. Sam and I have had different experiences with the VA and the Air Force. Sam was medically retired with 50 percent of his basic pay. I was medically separated with 10 percent disability for pain and a lump sum. We were both outraged. We couldn't believe that we didn't get more from the Air Force. Currently, there is an investigation into the small percentages of veterans who are receiving low disability rates from the armed services. The advisory board that reviews disability ratings explains:

> The military assigns disability ratings to injured veterans based on injury severity and long-term impact. Veterans . . . less than 30% disabled with fewer than 20 years of service are given a one-time lump sum and are provided veterans affairs medical assistance. . . . [V]eterans above 30% receive a monthly income payment and retain military-provided care. ("Board to Review Disability Ratings" 2008, 21)

I fought my rating. Sam accepted his once he learned that he would be retired and would retain some benefits of military life. I met my board but, unfortunately, was still rated at 10 percent because even though I lost muscle, my abdominal wall seemed to be intact. Sam and I have both been struggling with obtaining education, medical, and financial benefits from the VA. We have both been told that the VA is currently experiencing a backlog due to the number of injured veterans and the new education benefits. Neither of us wants to be a burden to society, but we agree that we are entitled to the benefits for which we are eligible.

Six years later, Sam and I are still recovering from our injuries. We have both gotten used to our new bodies, but we are struggling to gain our new places in society. We have not quite been integrated back into society. We are both currently unemployed and can't wait to get back into the workforce. Our need for independence reminds me of Simi Linton's discussion in her memoir, *My Body Politic* (2007): after she began recovering from the accident that cost her the use of her legs, she needed to go to Berkeley to attend school alone, without her mother and her family hovering around. Sam is currently reading Linton's memoir, as well. We both agree that we love our families and the support that they provide, but we just want to accomplish one goal by ourselves without their assistance. Disability studies perspectives and my relationship with Sam have helped me appreciate the tribulations that I have experienced. I gained a brother, and I see the world in an entirely new way. I have gained a passion to assist people with disabilities, especially veterans. So watch out, world; here we come!

REFERENCES

"Board to Review Disability Ratings." 2008. *National Guard* 62 (8): 21.
Linton, S. 2007. *My Body Politic: A Memoir.* Ann Arbor: University of Michigan Press.
Smart, J. 2008. *Disability, Society, and the Individual.* 2nd ed. Austin, TX: Pro-Ed.
Yarber, W., B. Sayad, and B. Strong., eds. 2010. *Human Sexuality: Diversity in Contemporary America.* 7th ed. New York: McGraw-Hill.

PART V

IDENTITY, RESISTANCE,
and COMMUNITY

T HE PRESENCE OF DISABILITY studies programs and scholars on university campuses, coupled with the ongoing work and increasing visibility of disability advocacy and activism, informs many contemporary students' sense of self and their political commitments. Building on the previous part, the chapters in this part continue to map complex relations, this time both at the level of **personal identity** and in the context of the larger **institutions** that affect our lives. Many of the contributors detail personal **resistance** to stigma or prejudice. At the same time, they highlight the fluid nature of and differing approaches toward identity and community. Specifically, these narratives explore questions of fitting and misfitting into **disability communities** and consider the ways diverse groups engage both in **enforcing their own boundaries** and in **expanding notions of belonging**.

The first two chapters explore **disability identity, academic expectations**, and **learning disability**. Allegra Heath-Stout engages in disability activism on her college campus but sees her efforts to promote disability rights, community, and access in terms of others' claims for justice, not through her own experience with learning disability. She confronts her own internalized distinctions between apparent and nonapparent disability in her personal movement toward "**disabled and proud**"—a well-known mantra within disability rights. In Chapter V.1, Heath-Stout examines her friends' resistance to her public claims of disability: some friends try to "reassure" her that she does not have a disability, while others do not understand her desire to proudly claim a disabled identity.

In Chapter V.2, Nancy La Monica reflects on the stigma of learning disability, especially among a group of preservice teachers in her graduate cohort. La Monica describes her frustrations with others' discriminatory beliefs about learning disabilities, and the **pressure to pass as nondisabled**. While disability diagnoses often benefit students with special education support, La Monica also witnesses how diagnoses sometimes become negative **labels** that limit teachers' perceptions of certain students' potential. She argues for challenging preservice teachers' **ableist biases** in order to truly **accommodate** and welcome students with learning disabilities in educational environments.

Megan L. Coggins, in Chapter V.3, and Susan Macri, in Chapter V.4, explore personal identity and a search for belonging in relation to mental and emotional distress. Coggins describes a period of feeling so isolated and emotionally distraught that she considered suicide and had to withdraw from school. In the process of regaining emotional equilibrium, she depended on familial relationships and her faith community for support. Macri's narrative provides an insightful depiction of anxiety by connecting her experience to larger cultural meanings and the pervasive stigma of mental distress. She traces the way in which anxiety has shaped her sense of self, from childhood into her evolving identity as an adult. Her personal path also involves navigating multiple medications and managing their myriad effects. Coggins and Macri share with readers deeply internalized and often silenced elements of emotional pain in an effort to encourage more open dialogue about anxiety, depression, and other forms of **psychosocial disabilities** (Marks 1999; Price 2011), a term some scholars use to refer to psychological or neuroatypical conditions that are deeply affected by social context, norms, and expectations.

The chapters by Suzanne Walker (V.5) and Denton Mallas (V.6) explore the links and tensions between **social isolation** and finding **community**. Walker examines her personal resistance to **self-disclosure**, or sharing one's disability status, to receive accommodations, in contrast to the "lure of escapism" she experiences in online communities, where she is able to construct an ideal virtual self. Ultimately, however, she realizes that she is suffering from the efforts involved in **masking her disability** in both actual and virtual environments. Mallas, born deaf within a hearing family, uses video games as a form of escapism and communication. Before going to a Deaf school where he could fully participate in the Deaf community, Mallas used video games as a way to relate to peers and develop friendships. Reflecting on their use of technology and virtual worlds, both Mallas and Walker come to realize that disclosure and openness about their experiences with access, stigma, and barriers (including the social pressure to be silent) actually clear pathways for them to more fully engage with both campus and online communities.

Taken as a group, the chapters in this part reveal the intricate connections between resisting externally imposed impairment labels, disability identity, and the deep yearning for sustaining—and sustainable—communities.

Reference the boldface terms as themes for discussion, and consider the following questions as you read the chapters in Part V:

1. How are you coming to understand disability communities? How do specific groups enforce their own boundaries, and what does this demonstrate about disability exclusion and belonging on a broader social level?
2. Although identity is increasingly understood as fluid and changing, it remains powerful as an element of personal self-definition. Identity is also shaped by resistance, often borne out of a sense of anger in the face of ableist ideas, practices, and systems of power. Referencing specific narratives, discuss the relationship between identity and resistance.
3. As you think about these chapters together, what specific ideas come to mind for making classrooms and university campuses more accessible and welcoming? The opening narratives by Allegra Heath-Stout and Nancy La Monica discuss college environments explicitly, but all of the contributors offer insight into socially imposed isolation. What strategies can be culled from this section for creating spaces where a wide variety of disabilities are seen as integral—as offering perspectives that enhance learning?

Suggestions for Related Readings

- Read Allegra Heath-Stout's chapter (V.1) with those by Alyse Ritvo (I.1), Zachary A. Richter (I.6), Adena Rottenstein (VI.1), and Lydia X. Z. Brown (VI.6) to discuss disability studies and its relationship to activism and identity.
- How do the chapters by Megan L. Coggins (V.3) and Susan Macri (V.4) compare and contrast with other narratives about mental illness and distress? Consider some key themes such as stigma, access, appearance, disclosure, shame, silencing, personal identity, and pride. Specifically, consider these chapters in relation

to those by Shayda Kafai (I.2), Michael T. Salter (IV.5), Cindee Calton (VI.2), and Rebekah Moras (VI.5).

REFERENCES

Marks, D. 1999. *Disability: Controversial Debates and Psychosocial Perspectives.* New York: Routledge.

Price, M. 2011. *Mad at School: Rhetorics of Mental Disability and Academic Life.* Ann Arbor: University of Michigan Press.

V.1

Disability, Belonging, Pride

ALLEGRA HEATH-STOUT

"But you're not disabled!"

I stare at my friend from just inside his front door on our college campus, watching as he takes in the sight of my bright purple T-shirt emblazoned with "Disabled and Proud." I am taken aback by his declaration. Finally I respond, "Yes, I am. I have learning disabilities."

He answers, "Oh, I didn't know that. I was going to offer to kick you in the shin, to help out. I try to enforce accuracy in T-shirts."

Later, I walk away feeling unsettled. What just happened? What led my friend to see my shirt and express not surprise, not curiosity, but a flat-out denial of my identity?

Moments like this punctuate my life and the lives of others with non-apparent disabilities. My learning disabilities, processing-speed disorder and dyscalculia, are an important part of how I understand myself, and I

Allegra Heath-Stout is the fellowship director and trainer at Jewish Organizing Institute and Network (JOIN) for Justice in Boston, Massachusetts. In this role, she trains and mentors young Jewish community organizers. Previously, she was a community organizer at the Boston Center for Independent Living for four years. In that role, she organized people with disabilities to create change in areas such as affordable housing, health care, and transportation. She has also served on the Boston Commission for Persons with Disabilities and is a founding member of the Massachusetts chapter of ADAPT, a national grassroots disability rights direct-action group. She graduated from Wesleyan University in 2012. She can be reached at allegra.stout@gmail.com.

continually chafe against others' expectations of what disability "looks like." Whether it's a classmate saying, "Oh, but you don't seem like you have a disability!" (intended as a compliment) or a roommate asking what it's like to be a nondisabled person working in an organization run by disabled people, someone is always ready to tell me that my appearance unequivocally conveys a nondisabled status.

I don't blame others for not knowing that I'm disabled before I tell them. What bothers me is the assumption that everyone is nondisabled until proven otherwise. Outside of a few precious communities, people tend to forget that not all disabilities are written in obvious ways on the body. Even worse, ableism, or oppression of disabled people, leads to such a stigma that most people regard any implication of disability as an insult.

My friend's reaction to my purple shirt was particularly striking because of the context in which I had acquired it in the first place. I first saw a crowd of people wearing "Disabled and Proud" shirts at the second annual West Coast Disability Pride Parade. I immediately declared that I wanted one. When I wear other disability-related shirts, whether focused on fundraising or disability rights, people comment that it's nice that I support people with disabilities. This new shirt would declare my identity to the world. I knew that many people would probably see it and continue to assume that I was an ally, but I yearned to make my appearance match my self-understanding.

I wore the shirt to my internship at a disability community organization the next day and was gratified by my coworkers' compliments. In a community in which so many people's disabilities are made visible through their nonnormative bodies and their wheelchairs or other assistive devices, it felt good to outwardly assert my identity. Yet, as I already knew but experienced all over again when visiting my nondisabled friend back at school, markers of identity are rarely foolproof and are read anew in every context, by every perceiver.

My desire to express my disability identity sometimes surprises those who have known me for a long time, because it's only in the past few years that I have begun to consider myself disabled, let alone wanted to broadcast this to the world. My experiences with what I now consider disability began at age nine, when I developed stomach ulcers. Even though the ulcers were soon cured with a dreadful course of antibiotics, it took a decade, until I started college, for my stomach to calm down. I missed dozens of days of school each year because of pain that made it hard to get out of bed, and none of my doctors could help much or even identify an exact cause. I received several diagnoses, none of which seemed quite right to me, and I took various medications. No one ever suggested that this chronic illness might be a disability, even though it limited my participation in major life activities like school, family events, and extracurricular activities.

Starting in middle school, I received accommodations through a 504 plan, mandated by the Rehabilitation Act of 1973, a law protecting the civil rights of people with disabilities. I was granted modifications to my school's attendance policy so that my teachers couldn't fail me for missing class so frequently.

I also received extended time on in-class tests and assignments, with the rationale that timed assessments provoked anxiety that made my stomach worse. In high school, my parents and I realized that there was more to it than this and also that my doctors' notes were not likely to convince the College Board to grant me extended time on the SATs. Accordingly, I missed two more days of school to go through a battery of neuropsychological tests.

The results showed that I had dyscalculia and a processing-speed disorder. Dyscalculia, a math-related learning disability, helped explain why I could do calculus but needed a calculator for simple multiplication, as well as some of my other quirks, like the fact that reading analog clocks has never been automatic for me. My rock-bottom processing speed finally explained my need for extended testing time, my need to have certain types of information repeated, and more.

These diagnoses gave me the tools to advocate for myself in bureaucratic systems. I received extended time on the SATs and in college. At least as importantly, the labels helped, and continue to help, me understand why I struggle with certain tasks and what support I might need. Even after being diagnosed with two learning disabilities, though, I did not really think of myself as disabled. The term "disability" seemed to imply a level of daily challenges far beyond mine. Throughout middle and high school, I worked with children with developmental disabilities, including my younger sister, who has Down syndrome, and their disabilities seemed to permeate their daily lives and how others perceived them much more than mine did for me.

At some point in high school, my understanding of disability began to shift. I credit one dear friend, my boyfriend for most of high school, with introducing me to the concepts of disability as a social and political issue and of disabled people as an oppressed minority group. Through his passionate involvement in the autistic rights movement, my boyfriend exposed me to a world of disability beyond what I had ever imagined. I started reading blogs by autistic writers and following disability issues in the media. Eventually, I became critical of the structure of my volunteer group for creating a sharp division between children with disabilities and their mostly nondisabled mentors. I talked an English teacher into supervising an independent study on disability literature.

These growing connections to the disability rights movement and the field of disability studies had a profound impact on my self-understanding. I began questioning my own identity and struggling with how exactly I fit into the world of disability politics and the community where I was starting to feel at home. My boyfriend was endlessly patient in supporting me through my frequent confusion about my ability status, as well as my ignorance of disability politics and my occasional unintentionally offensive comments.

When I started college, I still did not consistently identify as disabled, but I was passionate about disability issues. My university did not have any disability studies classes, but I found courses with related content and asked the professors for extra reading. Still, I felt disappointed and isolated upon finding that no one talked about disability, at least not out in the open. Not only were there no activist groups or cultural events, but I never heard my college classmates chatting about accommodations or campus accessibility, or comparing notes on professors' openness to students with disabilities.

I was disconcerted enough by this silence that I started a campus disability rights group during my first semester. I needed a disability community both for social reasons and as a base for activism. When people inevitably asked why I cared so much about disability issues, I had a lot to say about my sister and my volunteer experiences. At the end, I usually tacked on a comment about how I sort of had a mild learning disability, and I got accommodations for it, so I had some direct experience, too. But I never said, "I'm disabled" or "I have a disability."

The group grew slowly that first year. A few members came and went as their schedules permitted. I met another student who shared my passion for disability activism and has shared leadership ever since. Still, I worried. The disability rights movement lives by the motto "Nothing about us without us," meaning that discussions and work about disability need to be led by disabled people. Nondisabled allies can play important roles, but disabled people must set the agenda for matters concerning them (now, "us").

Where did I fit in as a pretty-much-nondisabled person who had a little experience with a sort-of disability? How could *I* legitimately run a disability rights group? On the other hand, no one else was going to do it, and I felt fervently that it needed to happen. Even as I considered these questions, I was beginning to lean more toward identifying as disabled, but I was terrified of doing so with the underlying motivation of added political legitimacy within the disability community. For a long time, I worried that I wasn't "disabled enough." Even though I felt a strong affinity with the disability community and had official disability diagnoses, I feared that claiming a disability identity would be claiming an experience that wasn't mine and asserting more similarity than I truly had with people who faced much more significant barriers.

I can't pinpoint the moment at which I finally stopped worrying and claimed my disability identity. Really, there was no key moment, because I went back and forth for years before settling into my current identity. My ongoing exploration of disability studies helped, as I encountered theories and personal accounts that helped me see the vast variety of disability experiences. It became clearer to me that there is no universal disability experience, and that disabled people are united instead by having bodies and minds that fall outside society's norms and by their (our) shared struggle against societal barriers.

I was lucky enough to have the support of friends, including my high-school boyfriend, who were more secure in their status as people with disabilities and whose work in the disability rights movement I respected. Each time I broached the subject of my own budding disability identity with politically conscious disabled friends, they assured me that whatever identity choice I made would be respected, as long as I remained conscious of and forthright about the differences between my own experiences and those of people with different needs and abilities. As I began to participate in disability conferences and other disability community events, I found this to be true; no one scorned me as "not disabled enough."

Finally, I realized that separating myself from the disability community wasn't helping anyone. On a certain level, society had long identified me as disabled. After all, I was getting *disability* accommodations for a reason. Additionally, I realized that mass disability movements can reach their full potential to transform society only when people with diverse disabilities recognize our common struggle. For me, identifying as disabled is a way to unite with people with all kinds of disabilities.

Identifying as disabled, as I began to do consistently at some point during my sophomore year of college, does not mean that I can speak for other disabled people. I strive to be an ally to people who face different and greater societal barriers than I do. Although others' assumptions that I am non-disabled are often uncomfortable, they also grant me power and privilege. Unlike people with readily apparent disabilities, I have the choice to remain silent and let others see me as nondisabled, thereby protecting myself from ableist attitudes. My teachers, for example, do not know that I am disabled until I tell them, so they never doubt my intelligence or capability. It is my responsibility to ensure that I do not use my many layers of privilege—including my ability to pass as nondisabled, the ease with which my disability has been accommodated, and my race, class, and education—to overshadow others' perspectives. The same lesson from disability studies about the vast variety of disability experiences that helped me identify as disabled in the first place serves as a reminder that I must affirm and support the vast diversity within disability communities.

My identity as a disabled person shapes the way I live my life. Most of my disability-focused work—in summer internships, in campus and online activism, and in classes—would be possible for me as a nondisabled ally, but embracing my disability identity has widened my perspective on disability issues. Viewing my own experiences through the lens of disability gives me a framework to understand myself better, as well as a point of commonality with other disabled people.

Additionally, the unique contours of my disability story motivate me to strive for a better understanding of disability in our society. Having taken years to adopt a disability identity, I am intrigued by the borders of identities and the factors that determine how individuals conceive of themselves. I am deeply aware that disability is not an inherent characteristic of individuals but rather a socially constructed and continuously negotiated category. My vantage point as a disabled person who passes as nondisabled, as well as a queer person who passes as straight, motivated my senior research project in my school's feminist, gender, and sexuality studies program. I interviewed disabled and queer students and analyzed their perspectives and experiences in light of theoretical literature in order to better understand how identity operates on our campus and in our society. By opening the doors to disability culture and disability studies, my disabilities have enriched my life immeasurably.

In the summer before my senior year of college, just weeks before my friend's unsettling reaction to my "Disabled and Proud" shirt, I attended a conference in Syracuse, New York, with other disabled college students from across the country. We came together to connect, share experiences, and strategize toward social change. I felt a deep sense of ease at being surrounded by disabled people, with the expectation of nondisabledness flipped on its head. Upon first meeting one another, the question on all the students' lips—or their signing hands, or their communication devices—was "What disability do you have?" The assumption embedded in this question was a far cry from the reactions of denial and surprise I regularly face when I disclose my disabilities, and it was a relief. I felt at home.

V.2

Deconstructing "Accessible" Education in Academia

Prologue: The Classroom

Seven weeks passed before I broke my silence. My friend described my performance as playing the "passing" game in a class I attended that included a group of education students.

"Isn't it fun?" my friend exclaimed.

"Fun. Really. Are you kidding?" I continued without waiting for a response. "All they do is say the most stupid remarks, and you know I don't use 'stupid' loosely. They sit there and joke about accessibility as though there is something to laugh about. One had an epiphany while watching

Nancy La Monica holds a Ph.D. from McMaster University. She advocates on behalf of students who face social, institutional, and economic barriers. In her doctoral research, she explored the lived experiences of non–visibly disabled graduate students as they negotiated academic and workplace accommodations. Her aim is to better understand non–visibly disabled graduate students' everyday embodied experience of academia as a place of both academic learning and paid work. An integral part of this work includes exploring the emotion work and emotional labor that students engage in as they contend with processes of disablement in the academy. Currently, she teaches at Seneca College.

Acknowledgments: I express my sincere gratitude to my mentor and friend, Dr. Nancy Viva Davis Halifax (York University), who encouraged me to find my creative genre in all spaces of academia. Much appreciation goes to Fady Shanouda for his valuable input. This research is supported by the Social Sciences and Humanities Research Council (grant number 766-2009-0897).

a comical presentation about physical space and accessibility issues. The presenter made observations from an able-bodied perspective when trying to access the information desk at a shopping mall, laughing while describing images of inaccessible doors and minimal space to physically move between aisles. Oh, and the best part: I remember the counters described as 'suited for everyone—that is, unless you're only three feet tall; then you'll have a problem.' Another student agreed and pointed out how hard it is for him to order specialty coffee at a local coffee shop without a learning disability [LD], suggesting that he couldn't imagine how LD folks place these complex orders. What could I say to all of this? I am tired of educating everyone, especially *the educators*. I know these comments are not directed toward me. How could they be, as I didn't disclose my nonvisible disability? I am sure they are not intended to be malicious either, but I am just sick to my stomach with the assumptions being made about disability. Would they have been so open about their assumptions about learning disabilities if I had disclosed to the class?"

"Well, Nancy, I wonder if you just hit the nail on its head. It seems like, from what you are describing, these education students have a misconception about what disability is, which is understandable if they are not trained in disability studies. Perhaps these students assume that you are nondisabled along with the rest of your peers in the classroom because you don't look disabled. In 'passing,' you perform the role of the assumed nondisabled university student; you're only disabled when you disclose—that is, when you follow the bureaucratic rules of registering with disability services to access accommodations [Hibbs and Pothier 2006; Jung 2003; Olkin 2002]. Your disability is not evident until you say otherwise, by 'coming out.' As a non-visibly disabled person, you have a privilege in playing this game, whereas others with evident impairments, like students who use wheelchairs, cannot conceal their disability as easily. Of course, this is not to assume that people with visible disabilities do not experience other types of impairment, like mental health or learning disabilities. Just imagine the look on your class-mates' faces if you disclosed your nonvisible disabilities to them one day."

"You're right! That's it! I'm going to come out of the 'able-bodied closet' for my presentation next week," I said.

"The 'able-bodied closet'?" my friend probed.

"Yes, Linda Kornasky [2009] uses the notion of coming out of the 'able-bodied closet' to describe the process of disclosing disability to others."

"I'd love to be a fly on the wall for this. Should be fun," my friend laughed.

I nodded my head and agreed.

The following week, I was due to present. I was ready to move forward in the passing game. I wanted to get to the finish line.

Here goes nothing, I thought.

I stood before my peers. My presentation notes were shaking in my hands. Deep breath in. I stared at one of my peers in the class as the phrase rolled off my tongue:

"I have a learning disability!"

Silence.

"Why would you want to pass?" one student asked. Feeling interrogated, I froze. It had been only a few minutes since I came out of my able-bodied closet. Before this day, I had sat silently in class for seven weeks. I rarely contributed to the discussion because I didn't know how to actively participate in a space where I didn't feel like I belonged (Ryan 2007; Price 2011). Instead of choosing to address the student's question, I curled back into my protective "passing" shell, like a turtle in a fight-or-flight response, the way I had done for the past few weeks. Then another student responded, "But if you choose to pass, then aren't you contributing to the stigma that is attached to learning disabilities?" As I tried to make sense of my choice to pass, the other students began to self-doubt their own methods and strategies toward teaching self-advocacy, questioning whether they were doing something wrong by teaching their students to self-advocate.

In an obviously distraught state of uncertainty, I tried to be empathetic to this student who was trying to conceptualize the notion of passing in an effort to understand why I would choose to pass. Trying to hold my emotions together—partly because not doing so could embarrass the student for asking—I thought but didn't say out loud, *Do I really have a choice when I pass?*

Learning disabilities might affect a student's perceived academic ability, which might influence her or his academic performance. Therefore, this discrepancy between academic performance and ability makes it hard for "outsiders," like professors and peers, to understand how LDs affect a student in the classroom. Instead, outsiders misjudge LD students "as lazy or not trying hard enough as indicated in Lock and Layton's (2001) findings where some professors believed students use learning disabilities as an excuse to get out of work" (Denhart 2008, 485; see also Griffin and Pollak 2009, 34; Titchkosky 2003, 130). When professors and peers believe these assumptions to be true, disabled students lose their equal opportunity for higher education. Research indicates that at the postsecondary level, the "availability of reasonable accommodations and appropriate support through a combination of individual and systemic resources are the keys to improving academic outcome and achievement" (Wolf 2001, 390) of disabled students. To avoid potential stigmatization, LD students within academia make difficult decisions about passing as nondisabled rather than bear these negative labels of misconceptions of disability (Hibbs and Pothier 2006; Ho 2004; La Monica and Chouinard 2013; Olney and Brockelman 2003).

Coming Out as "Learning Disabled"

Learning disabilities are commonly referred to as nonvisible or invisible disabilities. Unlike students with visible disabilities, such as those who use wheelchairs for mobility, LD students do not have signifiers that indicate disability is present (Lingsom 2008, 3; Walling 1996). The stigma attached to the label of nonvisible disability has implications for students in the classroom when professors and classmates do not understand how a learning disability that is not visible to the observer may hinder these students' ability to process information and thereby mean that they require extra time for completing an assignment (Mullins and Preyde 2013). Simply put, these students are perceived as lazy because the social barriers they face in navigating their education programming are not easily understood. Barriers in built environments are noticeable, and respondents may (presumably) open the inaccessible doors so that blind people can navigate to their destination in the same way that other people can. These barriers, such as missing automatic door openers, are evident to an observer who takes access to space for granted. Disabilities constituted by an inaccessible physical environment are conceptualized as visible disabilities because a signifier exists to identify an impairment. Learning disabilities often lack such signifiers and remain hidden unless explicitly disclosed. Thus, not all persons identified with an impairment are disabled (in the sense of being structurally and socially unable to do what they want to do) and sometimes neither impairment nor disability marks a person in a way that would be noticeable to observers (Denhart 2008, 484).

Differences Within

I do not presume to demonstrate a hierarchy in differences that exist in impairments and disability. Rather, I highlight that "invisible disability" is an ambiguous term when we explore issues of passing—a person's right to disclose and negotiate a disability identity. Susan Lingsom demonstrates that persons with invisible disabilities "are in a position where they may continually reflect upon whether or not, when, how, and to whom they should attempt to conceal or reveal their impairments" (2008, 3). In stark contrast, persons with visible disabilities may not be in the same position to move in and out of their disabled (invisible) identity. Thus, as a disabled graduate student with the ambiguous privilege of moving in and out of my disabled identity, because of invisibility (Lingsom 2008), I argue that this privilege is achieved with extra work in the form of emotional work, or labor, in order to conceal the characteristics of my disability through management techniques (see, for example, Goode 2007). Sociologist Arlie Hochschild introduced the concept of emotional labor to explore how employees manage their emotions in particular employment settings involving face-to-face interactions with customers. She describes the notion of emotional labor as the work involved "to induce or suppress feelings in others to sustain the outward countenance that produces the proper state of mind in others" (1983, 7). Passing techniques, which are learned behaviors and negotiations of invisible disabilities, involve "self monitoring and self surveillance" to ensure that they conceal attributes of disability (Lingsom 2008, 4).

In reflecting on the implications of passing, I ponder Audre Lorde's 1977 work "The Transformation of Silence into Language and Action," which is useful in understanding these negotiations more critically. Lorde explains, "I have come to believe over and over again that what is most important to me must be spoken, made verbal and shared, even at the risk of having it bruised or misunderstood" (2007, 225). The fear of being "bruised" or misunderstood as the disabled "other" silenced me into passing as I listened to my classmates' stereotypical attitudes that stigmatize people like me.

What gives anyone the right to ask about impairment or disability in the first place? As I begin to mull over my peer's accusation that, by passing, I will contribute to the stigma that is attached to learning disabilities, I realize that the real issue we need to address is the social responsibility that we, as educators, have to ensure that all students have access to equal opportunity in places of education. That is, we must ensure a barrier-free learning environment.

Accessible Education

Disabled students are entitled to, and have a human right to participate in, higher learning spaces that encompass an inclusive, discrimination-free learning environment (Ontario Human Rights Commission, n.d.). "The [Ontario Human Rights] Code guarantees the right to equal treatment in education, without discrimination on the ground of disability, as part of the protection for equal treatment in services" (Ontario Human Rights Commission 2003, 5). For disabled persons, I argue that the fundamental right to access education is contingent on whether or not they are provided with academic accommodations that suit their educational needs. When students do not have access to needed accommodations, they do not have an opportunity to a level playing field or the same rights to education as those without disabilities. Unlike their nondisabled peers, disabled students must fight to achieve equal education rights.

Disabled students' right to an education is fulfilled when accommodations are met with dignity and respect. Their right to dignity and respect is not met when students have to disclose their disabilities. For example, for a disabled student to access higher education on an "equal playing field," students must disclose their impairment, first and foremost, in order to be "eligible" for any type of academic accommodation. It is then that students meet with disability services counselors at their institution to establish what reasonable accommodations they will need to ensure that their educational needs are met.

This class was predominantly made up of education students who questioned the concept of passing. Placed in a position in which I felt cornered, like a child being bullied, I imagined shouting, *"But that's tokenism!* Why should I have to disclose my impairment, time and time again, so that you can understand my impairment? Why should I have to bear the stigma of being associated with characteristics such as weak, lazy, or using the disability card? Why am I not entitled to the same privacy and autonomy of not having to share my personal life as you are? Why is it up to me to eradicate discrimination of disabled persons or any social group that is considered to be a deviation from whatever you think of as normal?"

As all these thoughts run through my head, the frustration of it all makes me wish that I had a pause button that would shut down my body or just turn my feelings off, like a light switch. On the other hand, if I remain silent, then I, too, contribute to the social injustice around me, as echoed earlier by my peer's accusation. To remain silent means that I cannot criticize my peers for the ableist assumptions they make about the justifications of passing. They are working from a misconceived notion that disabled students in university are able to access higher learning without any barriers, per our constitutional right. Prior to my disclosure, they had little or no understanding, and not by any fault of their own, that only when disabled students legitimatize their status of being disabled can they exercise their right to barrier-free learning spaces (through, for example, academic accommodations). Without my voice, and those of others who embody the same oppressed experience, how could they understand?

How can I pass judgment?

Discussion

Educators need to deconstruct assumptions of accessible education in academia. As Douglas Biklen highlights, "The key lesson for inclusion would be for teachers and students to have opportunities to learn from the insider's perspective, from autobiographical accounts" (2000, 348). Here, my aim is to illustrate that accessible education is only accessible for nondisabled students. For disabled students, the experience of accessible education involves an ongoing fight in order to be eligible for accommodations that level the playing field.

If academic culture were more inclusive—if it met the needs of LD students by implementing inclusive teaching practices—then accommodations would no longer be needed. Accommodations could be normalized if they were embedded in the curriculum and institutional policies. If this option were made available to disabled students, disclosing to their institution would be necessary only in extreme cases when teaching practices were not enough to meet the needs of students with learning disabilities. Thus, all students would have the opportunity to experience accessible education.

Postscript

After I announced my impairment, everyone's gaze was on me.

Was I the only one who felt like everyone stopped typing on their laptop computers? Or did I just imagine this? Clearly I was uncomfortable, *again*.

I continued with my contribution to the discussion: "I am part of the group of persons who identify as being disabled by an educational system that caters to the dominant learner, the nondisabled student. I stopped identifying as a 'student with a learning disability' when I recognized that my learning style is 'different' from the 'norm' and that this is not my 'problem'; rather, it is the problem of the educational institution. Hence, I identify as a student disabled by an educational system that fails to recognize my strengths and focuses on my weaknesses because of the pathologized label of 'learning disability.' I am one of your students whom you teach in your class every day, of whom you speak badly when they are not around. You know, the one whom you label as having a 'severe learning disability'! Is it any wonder I feel so uncomfortable when I listen to these experiences about your students, whom I fit into the same category as? Can you blame me for feeling labeled as 'socially deviant,' abnormal, or dysfunctional when I am exposed to your disruptive complaining about your students with 'severe learning disabilities'? You speak of these students as though they purposely want to be a 'burden' to your teaching load, as if they enjoy feeling socially isolated and unable to learn the material that you teach. Do you really think that these students, students like me, I should add, premeditate ways in which we'll make you want to hate your job—a teaching job you thought you could never hate?"

The only problem with my contribution that day is that these thoughts were all in my head, and my attempt to vocalize them as I had intended to was just that, an (unsuccessful) attempt. I failed to move my player closer to the finish line at the roll of the dice. I blanked out, the way I always do when I get uncomfortable. I stood there in silence as I collected my thoughts about what to do next. I couldn't find it in me to tell my classmates that some of the comments they had made had discouraged me from contributing to the collaborative learning space that the professor had attempted to organize. I didn't have it in me. The last thing I wanted to be perceived as was a bitter disabled student looking to blame my classmates for not understanding my perspective. After all, isn't that what learning is all about—learning from each other so we can move forward?

But where do these notions of accessible (higher) education come from? I thought. Obviously, they are learned through institutional discourse, social structures, and social interaction. What does this all mean? Do I need to be more patient with people who just don't know? I turned the conversation in my head and thought about the "r-word" debate that I continue to have with others outside of the disability studies community. I vividly remember writing about it in a paper for my master's program:

> Prior to my own understanding of "retarded" as a derogatory term, I too used it in a pejorative manner. I did not understand the implications of my language. Living with a disability and coming to an understanding of the negative consequences attached to the meaning of "retarded," along with reflecting on where I was and where I have come to in my understanding, have made me aware of my opportunity to teach, rather than verbally punish others for "not getting it." (La Monica 2009, 5–6)

But what was different for me now, as I sat in this class with a group of teachers? Did I assume that, as education students, they should know better, in comparison with other learners? When did I lose the patience and understanding that I enter every class with, whether I am in the role of an instructor or a student? Had the frustration with this unjust educational system—which I feel has failed me so much, as a young learner and then into my adult years, that every day feels like one more battle—turned me into a cynical educator? Had it made me feel that anyone who assumes that disabled students have access and rights to the same types of education as those without are just completely arrogant and need to wake up? Or was I the one who needed to wake up and remember where I came from prior to my own understanding of disability?

There. Is it over? I thought to myself.

No. It has only just begun.

REFERENCES

Biklen, D. 2000. "Constructing Inclusion: Lessons from Critical Disability Narratives." *International Journal of Inclusive Education* 4 (4): 337–353.

Denhart, H. 2008. "Deconstructing Barriers: Perceptions of Students Labeled with Learning Disabilities in Higher Education." *Journal of Learning Disabilities* 41 (6): 483–497.

Goode, J. 2007. "'Managing' Disability: Early Experiences of University Students with Disabilities." *Disability and Society* 22 (1): 35–48.

Griffin, E., and D. Pollak. 2009. "Student Experiences of Neurodiversity in Higher Education: Insights from the BRAINE Project." *Dyslexia* 15:23–41.

Hibbs, T., and D. Pothier. 2006. "Post-secondary Education and Disabled Students: Mining a Level Playing Field or Playing in a Minefield?" In *Critical Disability Theory: Essays in Philosophy, Politics, Policy, and Law*, edited by D. Pothier and R. Devlin, 195–219. Vancouver: University of British Columbia.

Ho, A. 2004. "To Be Labelled, or Not to Be Labelled: That Is the Question." *British Journal of Learning Disabilities* 32 (2): 86–92.

Hochschild, A. R. 1983. *The Managed Heart: Commercialization of Human Feeling.* Berkeley: University of California Press.

Jung, K. E. 2003. "Chronic Illness and Academic Accommodation: Meeting Disabled Students' 'Unique Needs' and Preserving the Institutional Order of the University." *Journal of Sociology and Social Welfare* 30 (1): 91–112.

Kornasky, L. 2009. "Identity Politics and Invisible Disability in the Classroom." *Inside Higher Ed*, March 17. Available at http://www.insidehighered.com/views/2009/03/17/kornasky.

La Monica, N. 2009. "That's So 'Retarded.'" Unpublished manuscript, York University, Toronto.

La Monica, N., and V. Chouinard. 2013. "Warning: Labels May Cause Serious Side Effects for Learning Disabled Students." In *Youth: Responding to Lives: An International Reader*, edited by A. Azzopardi, 193–209. Rotterdam, Netherlands: Sense.

Lingsom, S. 2008. "Invisible Impairments: Dilemmas of Concealment and Disclose." *Norwegian Social Research* 10 (1): 2–16.

Lorde, A. 2007. "The Transformation of Silence into Language and Action." In *Feminist Literary Theory and Criticism: A Norton Reader*, edited by S. Gilbert and S. Gubar, 222–228. New York: W. W. Norton.

Mullins, L., and M. Preyde. 2013. "The Lived Experience of Students with an Invisible Disability at a Canadian University." *Disability and Society* 28 (2): 147–160.

Olkin, R. 2002. "The Rights of Graduate Psychology Students with Disabilities." *Journal of Social Work in Disability and Rehabilitation* 1 (1): 67–80.

Olney, M. F., and K. F. Brockelman. 2003. "Out of the Disability Closet: Strategic Use of Perception Management by Select University Students with Disabilities." *Disability and Society* 18 (1): 35–50.

Ontario Human Rights Commission. n.d. "Education and Disability: Human Rights Issues in Ontario's Education System." Available at http://www.ohrc.on.ca/sites/default/files/education_and_disability_human_rights_issues_in_ontario%27s_education_system.pdf (accessed September 8, 2016).

———. 2003. "The Opportunity to Succeed: Achieving Barrier-Free Education for Students with Disabilities." Available at http://www.ohrc.on.ca/sites/default/files/

attachments/The_opportunity_to_succeed%3A_Achieving_barrier-free_educa
tion_for_students_with_disabilities.pdf.

Price, M. 2011. *Mad at School: Rhetorics of Mental Disability and Academic Life*. Ann
Arbor: University of Michigan Press.

Reed, M. J., T. Lewis, and E. Lund-Lucas. 2006. "Access to Post-secondary Education
and Services for Students with Learning Disabilities: Student, Alumni and Parent
Perspectives from Two Ontario Universities." *Higher Education Perspectives* 2 (2).
Available at http://hep.oise.utoronto.ca/index.php/hep/article/view/617/673.

Ryan, J. 2007. "Learning Disabilities in Australian Universities: Hidden, Ignored, and
Unwelcome." *Journal of Learning Disabilities* 40 (5): 436–442.

Titchkosky, T. 2003. "Disability Studies: The Old and the New." In *Disability, Self, and
Society*, 129–169. Toronto: University of Toronto Press.

Walling, L. L. 1996. "Hidden Abilities—Visible Disabilities?" In *Hidden Abilities in
Higher Education: New College Students with Disabilities*, edited by L. L. Walling,
13–22. Columbia, SC: National Resource Center for the Freshman Year Experience
and Students in Transition.

Wolf, L. 2001. "College Students with ADHD and Other Hidden Disabilities: Outcomes
and Interventions." *Annals of the New York Academy of Sciences* 931:385–395.

V.3

Fake It until You Make It
(or until You Find Your Place)

MEGAN L. COGGINS

Throughout high school, I experienced mood swings and anxiety that had been written off by counselors, teachers, pastors, and others as normal teenage angst, although it felt anything but normal. At eighteen, I moved six hundred miles away from home for college. The mood swings and anxiety persisted, and I also began experiencing visual and auditory hallucinations. I took a medical withdrawal from college and fled home as fast as my Toyota would carry me, needing people and places I was familiar with in the midst of a psychological crisis. In December of that year, two days before Christmas, I was diagnosed with schizoaffective disorder, bipolar type, and panic disorder. I could not cope with the combination and severity of my symptoms, which led me to several hospitalizations and medical withdrawals from school. The symptoms alone were jarring enough, but for a girl who loves books and loves to learn and study, the inability to be in school was devastating to my morale.

Megan L. Coggins holds a bachelor's degree in religious studies and a master's degree in theological studies with a concentration in ethics, for which she primarily focused her research on issues relating to disability. She currently serves as the disability concerns representative for the North Georgia Conference of the United Methodist Church, where she is involved in providing forums for individuals to share their stories of disability and faith and provides training and resources for creating accessible congregations. Eventually, she hopes to pursue a Ph.D. in theological ethics.

At twenty, after countless medication changes and tweaks, my doctor determined that I am medication resistant (although we would continue to seek medication that would provide at least a modicum of relief from the ever-present symptoms). At twenty, I was at one of my lowest points. I was living in my parents' basement and barely able to manage a less-than-part-time job. I was in the midst of what was jokingly referred to as my "nocturnal hermit" phase. I had minimal contact with my family and even less with the world outside my house. I was hallucinating constantly and the medication I was on did very little, beyond provide unpleasant side effects. The prospect of trying to interact with the world while trying to deal with everything going on in my head and tell the difference between reality and hallucination was daunting. People terrified me, and the thought of making conversation and engaging with others was exhausting.

By this point, two years since my diagnosis, there had been countless medication changes and hours upon hours of therapy, and there had been hospitalizations. During stints in hospitals, I saw chaplains come in to pray with the patients and refuse to close their eyes—instead, they would pray out loud and keep their eyes on the other patients in the room. I was exhausted from the effort that it took to get out of bed, and there were plenty of days I simply stayed in bed. I barely recognized myself and didn't like what I saw in the mirror or in self-reflection.

As a pastor's daughter, I had grown up in the church, and I was active in my congregation in my own right; it was a huge part of my social life prior to being ill. My illnesses, however, took a toll on my relationship with that community. I could barely manage to get to church and, when I was there, I hid in the back. I felt so deeply and painfully alone and trapped in my own reality in my own mind. People in my church started drawing away from me because I needed too much attention, because I was always sad or too unpredictable. I made them uncomfortable if I spoke about my experiences of hospitalizations and hallucinations. The people who loved me did not know what to do to help me, so they offered and set up healing services and attempts to cast out the demons in my mind. These attempts were unsuccessful because it was never demons that caused my problems. I knew it was brain chemistry.

At that point, that moment, all I wanted was to simply be, to have a simple life and a simple faith—and from the bottom of the pit that I felt trapped in, the obvious answer was to stop existing. After one particularly frustrating week of doctor visits (psychiatrist and therapist) and a rough week with my brain, I attempted suicide. My reasoning was simple: I didn't want to keep living the way I was. If this was to be my new reality, I did not want it, and I was not interested. I wound up back in the hospital. Upon release, I went back to the basement and into being a nocturnal hermit.

I could not put my finger precisely on what began to change from that point, but somehow, with the help of my therapist, I began to seek a way out of my own madness. I wanted to be better so badly that it hurt. I threw myself into therapy. I had struggled to cope with the constant visual and auditory hallucinations, rapid mood swings, and intense anxiety. Now, I also had to learn how to manage my own struggle and how to make it work enough for me to be at least moderately functional.

The lessons I had learned during the earliest years of this experience were ugly truths about society, the church, and the ways that mental illness is perceived. I thought that if I masked it well enough, I could make it all go away. I was ashamed, and no one ever told me that I had no reason to be. I remember sitting in a church service one day and hearing the worship leader imploring the congregation to leave their concerns at the door, to come happily and without burden to worship God. I thought, at the time, that maybe that's why I couldn't feel close to God anymore—because I was incapable of leaving the burden of my brain at the door. I internalized the idea that if I just kept quiet about my pain, my struggles, and my anger with God, people would have an easier time dealing with me, and I would be able to worship again.

I started hiding as much of my illness as I could. What I could not mask, I turned into a joke. I laughed off "bad brain days" to make others feel more at ease. I began putting the pieces of my life back together enough to make it look like I had things together, and I was finally getting my life back on track (much to the relief of my family and congregation). Internally, however, I was still an angry, bitter, and hurting mess who could not accept this new reality, despite the fact that it had been three years. I was ashamed that I could not cope, so I fought harder to hide the symptoms. That fall, I returned to college at a school much closer to home—only about an hour and a half away. I was holding onto the façade of my functionality by a thread, and I was terrified. I had not lived away from home and doctors since my diagnosis. I wound up back in the hospital that first semester, but I refused to take another medical withdrawal.

Although my grade-point average suffered, I made a stand and decided that I would not let my brain limit my life—that I was tired of having to leave school. I found my way to the religion and philosophy departments inadvertently, by way of an elective class. These departments were headed by two of the most generous professors I have ever come across. They shared their spirit, humor, and knowledge, and each of them encouraged me to use my experiences with my illnesses to propel my intellect forward, to channel my energy into studying my own experience and the experiences of others.

It was this pair of mentors who introduced me to the field of disability studies. With their encouragement, I began to explore ways to articulate my hallucinations, my fears, and my mood swings. They provided and encouraged extracurricular research and reading opportunities, and I threw myself into those opportunities. I began to try to channel my energy less into masking my illnesses and more into embracing them as a part of my identity. Through all of the years that I have been in school and in all of the different schools I have attended, I have been lucky enough to have found a small handful of mentors who have encouraged me to learn, who have worked with me in the midst of struggles, and who have challenged me to be better at articulating my experience. I have been incredibly lucky to have mentors who have sought to learn from me even while teaching me. These professors gave me the courage to tell myself that I had no reason to be ashamed.

Perhaps more than anything else, my education has been the best tool for me to learn how to care for myself as well as to advocate for myself and others. Studying religion and ethics has allowed me to explore the way people think about issues such as healing and theodicy (reconciling the existence of evil with the idea of a god that is good). I have spent a considerable amount of time, both within and outside the classroom, studying the ways religion has been used to both subvert and enforce disability prejudices, paying particular attention to mental illness. As I continued to learn and read, the world of disability studies opened up to let me know that I was not alone. This new world let me know that it was okay to be angry with issues of stigma that I faced and that I was allowed to be angry with myself, with the world, and with God for the hand that I had been dealt.

One of the first books I read in the field of disability studies is Kathryn Greene-McCreight's *Darkness Is My Only Companion: A Christian Response to Mental Illness*. Greene-McCreight's experience as a pastor and an academic spoke to me, as did her experience with bipolar disorder. Her book helped me map out a way to start drawing together my faith, my illnesses, and my intellect, allowing me to knit together a more cohesive identity. More than that, it was the first time I had read about someone else struggling to make sense of stigma through the lens of faith. Greene-McCreight notes:

> With the darkness, I experience visions and voices. This is true of mental patients from time to time. But the stigma of mental illness, including the jokes made by the healthy about the ill, is worse than the visions and voices. At least the visions and voices teach me something about myself and about God. But the stigma teaches me nothing except about the proclivity of humanity to harm humanity. (2006, 56)

Greene-McCreight's book still sits on my bookshelf, dog-eared and highlighted. It has served as a constant companion through my studies, providing insight and comfort.

With each passing day, I become more comfortable asserting my voice, my experience, and my own place in the world. As much as I struggled to gain this confidence (and still struggle—it is two steps back for every step forward), I know there will continue to be incredibly difficult periods. I still hide most of my symptoms. I am extraordinarily careful about decisions I make, big and small. I still have to be hyperaware of my surroundings, and sometimes I still struggle to differentiate between reality and hallucination. Because I have been unmedicated for several years, I have worked with my therapist to focus on learning the tools and tricks that allow me to coexist in a world that I do not feel entirely at home in. I still struggle with prejudices and issues of stigma. I often hear, when I share my story, that I do not "look sick." I am aware that what people hear me say does not match what my actions and body tell—that I do not show the signs and symptoms one would expect, and that I do not manifest symptoms in necessarily standard ways. I know that there is a certain amount of dissonance here. It is challenging when I am faced with individuals who question the truth of my experience, who ask how much is "really real" and how much I make up, because the way they see me does not match their idea of how someone with a given mental illness should act or look.

One of the most maddening and marginalizing aspects of being functionally mentally ill is that society tells me that I should not be functional. I can be debilitated by mental illness, or I can be functional—but I cannot be both. The two do not coexist. I know, however, that this is a false dichotomy. I know that I can be both, and that I am both. I also understand that mental illness is a scary thing for many people. It is one of the next great frontiers for society to address in the continuing dialogue of human experience. The church has also begun those conversations and is beginning to realize that unity is not synonymous with uniformity, but there is still much work left to do.

As I began learning about and articulating my experience, I had to redefine how I understood God, myself, my disorders, and the world in general. I had to relearn my faith within the context of my disorders. I shifted my understanding of disability from a moral view—something that could be fixed by my behavior or by action on God's behalf—to a broader understanding that did not make me culpable for my brain chemistry. As I shifted my understanding of my illnesses to a blend of medical and biological models and social models, as well as a mix of some other underlying interpretations that engage other aspects of my life, my understanding of everything about the faith I had grown up in changed, too.

I had to learn, and teach others, that healing, for me, is as simple and as major as the fact that I can get up every morning. I had to redefine practically everything in my life, not only for myself but within my interpersonal relationships as well. However, as complicated and frustrating as living with my illnesses is (both in terms of personal and social experience), this is reality for me, and I cannot change it by willing it away; I cannot pray it away, and there is not a lack of faith that causes illness to remain in my life. I have fought to learn more, using many of my open-topic papers for my master's degree program to explore issues that relate disability to the coursework for the class at hand. Having mentors in my life who encouraged me to study my own experience, who validated my continued existence and pushed me to try to conquer my own limitations, has proven to be invaluable. If it were not for these mentors, I might never have found my way into disability studies or have found the courage to embrace my life. I know that on my bad days, I can turn to the stories of others who have had similar experiences. I can try to remember, in the depths of darkness, that I am not alone. But more than that, I can remind myself not to be ashamed of who I am. It has proven liberating for me to be able to say that I am different—and that difference is okay.

REFERENCE

Greene-McCreight, K. 2006. *Darkness Is My Only Companion: A Christian Response to Mental Illness*. Grand Rapids, MI: Brazos.

V.4

My Anxiety

SUSAN MACRI

I f I were to tell you the story of my life thus far, where would I start, what would I say, and how would I say it? What would I choose to share about myself? How far back in my memories would I travel? I could revisit times in my adolescence, or my childhood, or both. Who am I, and what makes me, *me*? It is necessary to include a discussion about my anxiety in order to provide an accurate representation of myself? The anxiety is very much a part of who I am, but it is not all of me—and this is an important distinction. Perhaps through telling my story, my experiences with anxiety can be an empowering narrative that others can understand, relate to, and use as a tool to start (or continue) a dialogue about anxiety and other mental health issues. Because mental health is an area in society that remains fraught with negative stereotypes and stigmas, one of the most constructive things people

Susan Macri is a scholar and an activist in the field of disability studies and has a master of arts degree in critical disability studies from York University in Toronto. As a lifelong learner, her research passions include women's mental health, women's sexual health, disability and inclusive education, and international disability rights. As a woman with an invisible disability, she has presented workshops on anxiety and is an advocate for women's mental health issues and awareness. Her current work is focused on inclusive higher education opportunities for persons with intellectual disabilities. Envisioning a world where inclusive living is everyone's right, she works with children and their families in her local community, promoting and teaching acceptance and equity for all members of society.

with invisible disabilities can do is share their stories of their own volition. This act of sharing and self-reflection educates others, humanizes mental health, and helps to dismantle the preconceived notions and attitudinal barriers that still exist in society. This is why I choose to share.

To give some context to my narrative, it should be noted that I write from a critical disability studies perspective. This means, on issues relating to disability (whether they be physical or invisible impairments and disabilities or issues of law, education, policy, and so on), I think critically about things like accessibility, language, meaning, power relations, social influences, identities, and the effects all these things have on people and society. It has been said that stories "are not simply personal. They are also social and cultural" (Smith and Sparkes 2007, 18). So while this story is of a personal nature, it also cannot be separated from the society and culture in which the author finds herself; my story is at once both a reflection on my lived reality and a reflection of my sociocultural existence.

My anxiety accompanies me wherever I go; it is personal to me, and I know it well. Sometimes it is an impairment, and other times it is all-out disabling—but it is *with* me, always. Perhaps, at times, it could be thought of as its own entity, an entity I am in a certain kind of (dys)functional relationship with—but that conceptualization may be giving it too much power. Yet it feels powerful during a panic attack when it takes over my body and I am shaking, feeling as though I cannot breathe, and completely overwhelmed. That is why I want to interrogate, deconstruct, and interpret the language and meaning of the words *my anxiety*. "My" is a possessive pronoun, implying ownership over something, something I own; I take ownership of my anxiety, it is mine, a personal belonging that I carry with me every day. "Anxiety" is a noun. A noun is a person, place, or thing. My anxiety has been all three at different times and places. My anxiety is a *person*: it *is* me, at least in part; the two cannot (and should not) be separated. My anxiety is a *place*: the places in my mind and body where it happens, especially when I am in the midst of a panic attack. My anxiety is a *thing*: sometimes it feels like a heavy object that I drag or carry, or something detached and impersonal; it is something I despise, something that is fluid and ethereal, and also something that I accept. It all depends. Depends on what? My mood, my state of being in a particular moment, whether I remember to take my medicine, timelines, deadlines, conversations, breathing and breath, change, sleep (whether I've had enough), music, stress, laughter, reassurance, stability—it depends on all of these.

Some people do not acknowledge that anxiety is a legitimate impairment, or disability, with which I, and many others, must deal on a daily basis. I am reminded every day on the news, subway ads, or Facebook posts that mental health issues still make people uncomfortable. This is why I cannot talk openly to everyone about my anxiety. When I read about anxiety or other invisible disabilities in medical journals or mass-media forums, the language used is either full of medical jargon and inaccessible to most readers or demonizing, through fear-mongering, to those with mental health issues. For example, the fact that one generally is referred to as having an anxiety "disorder" implies that order is lacking or missing within the person, be it in the body or the mind. To be in disorder also suggests a grand normative notion of how *orderly* should look, feel, or act, and those with the mental health impairment or disability are going against the normative grain. From a critical disability studies perspective, this creates a tension between those with the disability and those who do not understand it or fear it, simply because they do not know about it. And this is where I find myself: I have anxiety. It is a real thing. It links me to the medical world when it comes to my symptoms, medicine, doctors, and the science behind brain chemistry. But there is also a social component that is of equal value and importance: my anxiety affects the way I see myself, how I interact with others, and how I live in the world.

According to Robbie Woliver, generalized anxiety disorder (GAD) "is an illness characterized by chronic overworry and fear, occurring most days for a period of six months or more, that involves concern over a number of activities or events. The mean age for onset is around 8 years old" (2010, 245). From this one sentence I am told that I have an "illness," a sickness. Why am I ill? What part of me is ill—my mind? This must mean I am different, and I am automatically and anatomically labeled as a defect; my mind does not work as it should. I am also told that my anxiety has "characteristics"— perhaps it is an entity, after all. The word "chronic" implies forever; I know I will always have anxiety, even with medication. Apparently, scientists and doctors have even calculated the mean age when GAD typically first appears in people: eight years old—so young. But I was younger, I remember.

Woliver also lists symptoms of anxiety, of which I have experienced at least twenty-seven. The most significant ones for me are anticipatory anxiety, attention problems, breathing problems, heart palpitations, insomnia, lack of concentration, and obsessive-compulsive symptoms. He later goes on to say that "GAD, like all anxiety disorders, has several causes: biological, environmental, and family-based factors. It can be inherited, or it can be behaviour learned from an anxious household" (246). I am curious now. What is the cause of my anxiety? Is it part of my genetic makeup? Or did I learn how to be anxious from my family? At the end of the day, is the *cause* really what matters, or is the reality of having anxiety more important? This may be a good place to delve into exploring my lived experiences with anxiety, my narrative, my story.

This is the scary part, the part where I get personal, open up, and tell my story. I may not use the most politically correct language as I tell it, but my intent here is to express myself without apprehension or barriers. Whether you are able to relate or not, I am attempting to be as accurate and transparent as possible, and I hope you will see the value in sharing this narrative. I have always been an anxious person. For as long as I can remember, even as a young child, I had panic attacks, worried excessively, and was overwhelmed to the point of tears and hyperventilation. My earliest memories of being anxious go as far back as three or four years of age. I was a very clingy and nervous child. I remember being dropped off at my day care and kindergarten classes. Every day, I cried and clung to either my mother or father, and the teachers had to pry me away and bring me, with my tear-stained face, to the carpet with the other children. Why could I not simply join the others? The whole ordeal took about twenty minutes.

But the anxieties did not start the moment I got to school; that was just the emotional explosion being released. They actually started at home, from the moment I woke. Was I afraid to go to school? But I really liked kindergarten once I was there, and I settled down after the storm had passed. I recall kindergarten with much fondness: I liked my teacher, the room, the toys, and some of my classmates, too. Why, then, did I fear social situations? When I was in second grade, I turned down the lead role of Suzy Snowflake in the class Christmas play because I was worried about everyone looking at me. I remember my mother and teacher were very disappointed, and I felt awful for disappointing them. These sorts of moments flash into my mind when I think back to how my anxiety displayed itself during my childhood. I felt very inhibited by my worries, wishing I could do things other children seemed to do with ease—like make friends or socialize in groups. I worried about silly things, and not just in the school setting. For example, I worried about getting water on my face and up my nose when I rinsed my hair after washing it. I worried about taking medicine—I got sick often as a child and took antibiotics frequently. I would give my mother the hardest time when it came to swallowing the spoonful of banana- or cherry-flavored liquid. It was always a battle, and there was no way she could get me to swallow pills, because I was afraid of choking on them. Now I take a pill every day for my anxiety. I am a consumer, dependent on my meds; I can feel that warped, cloudy, dizzy feeling when I miss a dose. How ironic.

I do not wish to place blame on my mother, but I think my anxiety may be the result of a combination of genetics and learned behavior. My mother's side of the family has a lot of mental health issues, including anxiety, depression, and drug and alcohol addictions. I think I have been lucky in just dealing with my anxiety. My nana called it having "bad nerves." Both my late nana and my mother have dealt with anxiety and depression. They went untreated for years and did not have the resources to help them cope. I grew up close to both women, and so I am fairly certain I have internalized and learned a lot of their behaviors. Sometimes I feel resentment toward my mother for not helping me sooner (with "early intervention" as it is called), but how could she know what to do for me if she did not know and recognize it within herself? The resentment fades to understanding.

When I was thirteen years old, I wrote a note to a boy telling him that I liked him. I stuck it in his desk for him to find, but he did not find it; someone else in the class did, and it soon became everybody's business. It was quite the shy kid's nightmare: I was mortified and endured the expected taunts and teasing. Most kids might have just laughed it off, but the incident stayed with me long after it had blown over for everyone else. I internalized it and made myself sick with worry. It got to the point where I could not keep my food down, my stomach was so nervous. I began to lose weight rapidly, so my mother brought me to our family doctor, who thought I was anorexic. It never occurred to anyone to ask me if things were all right at school. And, of course, I could not bring myself to say anything about it because just the thought of talking about it made me anxious, too—such a vicious cycle it was.

My teen years during high school were a turbulent blur. The panic attacks became more intense and more frequent. My obsessive-compulsive behaviors also occurred more regularly. My mother suggested that I take medication—she had been taking meds for a few years by this point for her own anxiety and depression. I staunchly opposed the idea and denied having any problems. I was aware of what it would mean to have a "head problem," even though I was not able to articulate my thoughts about the negative stigmas associated with mental health. *I* did not need to be medicated, no way. But I did realize how unhappy I was; on top of dealing with anxiety on a daily basis, I also faced bouts of depression. All this had a negative effect on my grades and my relationships with family members and peers at school.

I remember when I first went on them, the meds: Effexor (venlafaxine) to be exact. I still recall feeling the change that took place in my brain. My brain chemistry was being altered. The transition felt weird. I felt strange, as though I was drugged (which, I guess, I was), but eventually my body got used to the daily dose. After a while, I did see an improvement in myself, as did my family. My overall attitude and outlook on life changed, becoming more positive. The anxiety and depression were under control, and my panic attacks became less frequent and less severe. It is because of these changes and improvements that I believe my anxiety is, in fact, part of my genetic makeup. I took Effexor for seven years, and in that time I put on a lot of weight, which is one of the drug's side effects. My mother kept telling me to lose the weight by changing my medication, so I eventually caved in and switched to Celexa (citalopram). The drug was not the right fit for me, and my anxiety became worse, so from that drug I switched to Cipralex (escitalopram). This one was definitely not right for me: I had the worst panic attack I have ever had in my life—I honestly believed that I was dying while it was happening—while taking Cipralex. So back to my doctor I went. This time she prescribed Pristiq (desvenlafaxine), a drug in the same family as Effexor. I have been taking it now for about four years, and I think my mind and body are now fully used to it. Sometimes I wish I had never stopped taking Effexor, because it seemed to have worked for me and I was comfortable with it, despite the weight gain. The frustrating part is that I have not noticed a significant difference in my weight since switching meds. My doctor said I should watch my weight for other reasons: diabetes and heart problems also run in my family. Now, at twenty-nine years old, I am still dealing with my anxiety. I have often thought about what it would be like if I went off my meds—how liberating the idea is! I imagine what it would be like to not have to remember to take something every day. Sometimes I forget to take them, but then I am reminded of why I am on them—they help control what I cannot control by myself. I think of my situation with meds as similar to that of asthmatics, who need to use inhalers for their lungs to be working at their best.

The anxiety will never fully go away; the medication just helps me to manage it. Still, there are days when I cannot leave the house, even though I need to go to work or to class, because of my anxiety. This is something that most people do not understand, especially employers. This is when my impairment becomes a disability—when society does not appreciate what I deal with and I am treated differently because of it. I went to a psychiatrist for the first time a few years ago. I had put off going for a long time because only "crazy" people go to psychiatrists, right? (See, even people with disabilities have to unlearn social prescripts and prejudices.) He said I might be agoraphobic, which makes a lot of sense to me: I like to stay home most of the time, and when I do go out, I do not like to go out alone. Also, I do not open the front door when someone knocks unless I know who it is, and I tend not to answer the phone until it goes to voicemail so that I can scan the call first. Although I got my full driver's license when I was eighteen, I drive only when I have to, never on the highway, and I stick to routes with which I am familiar. Although I would like to, I do not go for walks alone, even during the day, because I worry about all the bad things that could happen. I get anxious when I have to eat meals alone because I am afraid of choking by myself without anyone around to help. I get insomnia from time to time, and when I am sleeping I am tense and I grind my teeth; I had to get a night guard for my mouth because I am wearing my teeth down from the grinding. There are days when I am too anxious and overcome with worry to even leave my bed. Also, I have these obsessive-compulsive thoughts of irrational worries that play on repeat in my head that I am constantly trying to turn down or mute. For example, I could be out with friends having dinner and drinks, enjoying myself, but constantly in the back of my mind I am worrying about having an allergic reaction to something and fearing that I won't be able to breathe, even though I know I do not have an anaphylactic allergy to anything in my surroundings. It can be really quite exhausting to have to try to suppress these thoughts constantly.

This is a snippet of what I live with every day. It sometimes leads to social isolation (self-induced at times) because I am unable to "get over" my anxiety. I realize that it may not be easily understood for those who have never experienced it and are looking at my situation from the outside. I have been told countless times to "just relax" and "don't worry so much." Try telling someone in the grip of a full-blown panic attack to "just relax." Unfortunately, it is not that easy; everyone with anxiety would be instantly cured if it were. I have educated myself by reading literature on the topic of anxiety and coping strategies, which has helped. Talking about it with my partner and my mother also helps a great deal. It is a very good feeling when you can tell someone you trust what you are going through and they understand, without judgment. But from time to time, I still question why I am like this.

This has been a deeply personal extension of an ongoing conversation I have with myself, and with those understanding individuals who are willing to listen with empathy and openness. I have chosen to share my story and expose my experiences with anxiety. There is an empowering element of agency and self-advocacy in being able to make that choice. Being afraid to show yourself does no one any good, and it deprives the world of the true you. Everyone's story has value. Narrative (as a process and as an educational tool) has an important place in our society as well as in the field of disability studies, because of its ability to start conversations and convey novel understandings of everyday life: "narratives are both a way of telling about our lives and a means of knowing" (Smith and Sparkes 2007, 17–18). I hope to convey the importance of sharing experiences, as I have done with mine. With this in mind, I realize that each day presents its own set of challenges; some days, weeks, months, and years are better than others. Having anxiety means I will always have to consciously negotiate my life around it, and with it. This is *my* anxiety. This is *my* "normal."

REFERENCES

Smith, B., and A. C. Sparkes. 2007. "Narrative and Its Potential Contribution to Disability Studies." *Disability and Society* 23 (1): 17–28.
Woliver, R. 2010. "Generalized Anxiety Disorder (GAD)." In *Alphabet Kids: From ADD to Zellweger Syndrome*, 244–248. London: Jessica Kingsley.

V.5

Disability, the Lure of Escapism, and Making the Invisible Visible

SUZANNE WALKER

A s the former president of the Columbia University Science Fiction
Society, I am no stranger to the lure of escapism. A disproportionate
amount of my college career has been spent playing in imagined
worlds, whether I'm baking a cake for Frodo and Bilbo Baggins' birthday,
running a world-building workshop, or, yes, conducting a blood sacrifice
to the Dread Lord Cthulhu. Even as we never forget to talk about the more
serious sides of science fiction, by, for example, leading discussions on how
dystopian futures in science-fiction works such as Suzanne Collins's *The
Hunger Games* offer critical commentaries on our own societies, there's no
denying that the primary purpose of our club is to offer *fun*. One of the
primary appeals of science fiction is its revelry in escapism, and we gleefully
indulge that to the best of our abilities.

Escapism is something that can be easily criticized as childish, idealistic,
or useless. I've made these criticisms myself on many occasions. Yet it would

Suzanne Walker graduated from Barnard College in 2012 with a degree in American
studies. Her primary academic work focuses on the history of government-sponsored
theater in the 1930s, and her article "'Now I Know Love': Hallie Flanagan and Euripides'
Hippolytus," appears in *Classical World*. Her academic interests also include disability studies and comics studies. She is actively involved in the science-fiction fandom
community and has presented on disability representation at multiple conferences and
conventions. She currently lives in Chicago and works as a manuscript editor for the
American Medical Association.

be foolish to discount the lure and power of escapism, especially as someone who has lived with bilateral hearing loss for most of her life. The technology of the future comes to life in science fiction, and it's tempting to imagine how my life might be different if I lived in a world where I could have better hearing aids or, better yet, a complete elimination of the hearing loss itself. In a world with cyborgs, jetpacks, and hyperspace, such things would likely be taken for granted. Escapism then becomes more than just a fun release. It allows us to imagine the possibility of a world where the obstacles we face on a daily basis no longer become problems.

Yet when I stop and think about it, I can never forget that other, more serious side of science fiction: the side that engages in dystopian, postapocalyptic worlds and that demonstrates how a reliance on technology comes with its own consequences. Science fiction can be such a useful tool to teach us about society's own flaws, and our obsession with "the norm" and perfection certainly can be counted among these flaws. So I look back at my own experiences over the past four years, as a college student with a disability, and I wonder how useful escapism becomes after all. The technology of the future has unlimited potential, but if I imagine a world where my hearing loss no longer exists, what then? All I've done is erase a part of my identity. My hearing loss doesn't define me, but it is a part of me, and I've spent so much of my life pretending that this is not true. My mother often asks why I get so touchy about dealing with my hearing loss, and why I could never really have a conversation about it. It was inexplicable to her that, until I started college, I never enjoyed talking about or even admitting that I had hearing loss. But the fact of the matter is that my environment makes it easy for me to do this. Because my disability is an invisible disability, one that requires very few accommodations, it is not that difficult to pretend it doesn't exist. And it is far easier to pretend this on a college campus when the basic assumption remains that everyone operates on a level playing field. Disability awareness is something that is improving every day at Barnard and Columbia, but it is far from perfect. There remains a lack of basic awareness throughout most of campus, and Barnard itself exists within a world that prefers to hide rather than acknowledge disability. In such a world, it is easier emotionally, if not practically, to keep my hearing loss invisible and attempt to pass as "normal."

Nevertheless, just because something is easy doesn't mean it is proper or right. Thus, my time at college has been a continual process of learning to move past pretending. Throughout my four years here, I have worked to acknowledge my hearing loss as an integral part of myself and treat it as something people can and should know about, rather than as something to hide. The office of disability services (ODS) at Barnard played a huge part in helping me work through and past this hiding, but it was a long process.

The act of self-identifying soon stood out as one of the hardest battles for me. The ODS tells all of their students to self-identify to professors early on in the semester, even if we think we won't need accommodations. As a first-year student, the idea of this seemed ludicrous to me. I needed accommodations in only some of my classes, and if I wasn't going to need a note taker or accommodations beyond sitting in the front row, why should I inform my professors about my hearing loss? The ODS stressed the need for professors to be aware, just in case something were ever to come up, but it took a long time for me to accept this idea. As the semesters went by, I grew more comfortable with self-identifying, and it was made easier by professors who would respond with "Thank you for telling me; let me know what I can do to be helpful." At the same time, it was made all the more difficult by professors who would meet my carefully rehearsed spiel with blank looks, wondering why I was telling them any of this at all. Disability continued to be something that existed on the periphery of my campus experience, and it was something that was never talked about in my social life or my academic life.

Indeed, until the fall semester of my junior year, I never imagined that questions of disability or disability studies would be addressed in an academic atmosphere. But in my American studies junior colloquium, there was a weeklong unit on "bodies and norms," for which we read a multitude of theoretical articles on disability studies. Reading these articles excited me and pushed me to think like nothing else in that class had. For the first time, I was reading theory about specific experiences with disability that were just like mine, and I could engage with the material on an academic level as well as on a personal level. I came to a number of realizations about myself and my own disability while reading these articles, particularly Mimi Nguyen's "Queer Cyborgs and New Mutants: Race, Sexuality, and Prosthetic Sociality in Digital Space," which discusses the Internet as a potential source of empowerment for those with disabilities. Again, the lure of escapism came into play, as the article "celebrate[ed] digital space as the denaturalization of gendered and sexual norms and the proliferation of multiplicity" (2003, 294), portraying it as a sort of "blank slate"—a form of escapism that mirrors the possibilities that the Internet represents to us today. I realized that my own use of the Internet reflected this, for in the numerous online communities I was involved with at the time, nobody knew that I was a twenty-year-old white female with a hearing impairment. I was—and still am—allowed to pick and choose which aspects of my identity to reveal online, and if I wish to abandon my own disability, there is nothing to stop me from doing so.

At the same time, though it feels safer to hide in the anonymity of the Internet, I realized that aspects of my identity had become lost in the shuffle and that the escapism of the Internet in some ways reinforced stigma—the notion that there is something to be ashamed of and to hide in the first place. I realized that I had never been truly comfortable with hiding my hearing loss from acquaintances on the Internet. In terms of the broader themes of Nguyen's argument, the science-fiction examples used in her argument became problematic to me, as they created a form of escapism that in many ways avoids the root causes of the problem, in some ways even contributing to marginalization and the stigma assigned to various groups.

Wrestling with these thoughts and realizations both frustrated and exited me, and I came to class that Tuesday with a lot to say. Of course, all of this also meant that in order for me to truly get across what I wanted to say in seminar discussion, I would have to talk about my hearing loss in class—a completely unprecedented experience. I will never forget my feeling of anxiety and nervousness when talking in seminar on that day. I had never before talked about my experiences in so public a forum, and, after a lifetime of keeping my hearing loss under the radar, I was terrified that I would be dismissed—for making a mountain out of a molehill, drawing unnecessary attention to myself, or something else. Even at age twenty, I still irrationally feared what had happened to me at age nine—that I would be ridiculed by my peers once they had knowledge of my disability. But none of those things happened. My classmates responded positively to what I had to say and provided thoughts of their own. I knew on a rational level that talking about my hearing loss would incur no negativity, but it took discussing it in an academic setting to realize this on an intuitive level. One of my roommates told me afterward that she had never really thought about how having a disability affected me on a daily basis, and my worries about talking about it in seminar had made her more aware of this.

It was this experience, more than anything else in college, that started me on the path toward realizing that my worries and fears about making my invisible disability "visible" were truly for naught. After that first conversation in seminar, talking about my disability in front of people became so much easier. Bringing it up in public spaces became something I grew more and more comfortable with, to the point where I allowed myself to be talked into speaking on a panel about it in the fall. It was easier for me to point out flaws in the system, such as assemblies or events where the use of microphones wasn't even considered. I finally have become comfortable with accepting my hearing loss as a part of myself, and while I still have the ingrained instinct not to speak up for fear of inconveniencing people, I now have a louder voice telling me to do it anyway.

At the close of my college career, I find myself more accepting and aware of my body, for all its flaws, than I ever have been before. But the promise of escapism and erasure looms in society and technology, particularly as I remain entrenched in the world of science fiction. Like everyone else in the young-adult science-fiction world, I jumped on *The Hunger Games* bandwagon in the weeks leading up to the movie's release. In the dystopian world of Panem, Suzanne Collins's protagonist, Katniss Everdeen, is thrown into a gladiatorial Battle Royale–esque arena in which ability is crucial to survival. A skilled archer and hunter, Katniss thus finds herself at a horrifying disadvantage when an explosion in the arena renders her deaf in one ear. Reading this for the first time, I realized that I had rarely, if ever, encountered a fictional character that shared my disability. Even as I feared for how this would affect Katniss's chances for survival, I identified with and deeply appreciated seeing a fictional protagonist deal, at least for a time, with a disability very similar to mine.

Yet when Katniss wins the games and leaves the arena, she wakes up in the hospital to discover that the Gamemakers have completely restored hearing in her ear, making it as if her deafness had never happened in the first place. Katniss briefly celebrates the return of her hearing, and the incident is rarely mentioned again throughout the trilogy. Her entire experience with hearing loss has been erased (though this is to say nothing of the other forms of disability that Collins addresses at later points in the trilogy).

As I finished the novel and thought about the implications of Katniss's magical cure, I thought back to how I would have reacted to this revelation four years ago versus how I react to it now. Even as the restoration of Katniss's hearing is the responsibility of the games' cruel arbiters, their ability to fix her hearing loss still has a tempting appeal. How many times in my life have I wished for the same thing? Four years ago, I likely would have only seen the appeal of this. Now, however, I can't help but think about how a cure at the hands of the Gamemakers only demonstrates the underlying sinister nature of such escapism. Katniss's entire experience with disability has been erased by an institution that promises "bread and circuses" to its people, eliminating imperfections and presenting Katniss only as a televised facsimile of herself. The nation never realizes that Katniss faced these experiences, and it becomes easy for Collins's readers to forget this as well.

But it is impossible for me to forget or, now, to even wish that I had access to the technology that the Gamemakers possess. The motivations behind their use of technology make it so that I would not want the full package that comes with their "cure." Instead, I would rather use this story as a lens to view the reality I live in now: one in which standards of an assumed "normality" still permeate our most basic structures. In this respect, science fiction should indeed be used as a way to interrogate our own society. Disability awareness is growing and stigma is fading, but it is a long, complex, multifaceted process that I can't even begin to address here. Nevertheless, if my time at college has taught me anything, it's that awareness is the first step toward making any sort of substantial change. And fostering that awareness is one of the most important things anyone can do.

REFERENCE

Nguyen, M. 2003. "Queer Cyborgs and New Mutants: Race, Sexuality, and Prosthetic Sociality in Digital Space." In *AsianAmerica.net: Ethnicity, Nationalism, and Cyberspace*, edited by R. C. Lee and S. C. Wong, 281–305. New York: Routledge.

V.6

Discovering My Deaf Identity

A door opened for me when I decided to go to a school for the Deaf[1] right after I graduated from middle school. When I enrolled at the Wisconsin School for the Deaf, I came to discover what being Deaf actually meant. I certainly struggled before that, in my years in mainstream schools, because I actually denied my Deaf identity during these years. I did not understand why it was so important for me to tell people that I'm Deaf. I did not want to "admit" my disability and that it interferes with my ability to communicate. It was one of the worst feelings in the world when someone I knew, such as my family, told another person without my permission or knowledge. The shame disappeared as I learned more about Deafness and my identity. I've learned to announce my identity as Deaf, not in a pathological way but in a cultural-linguistic way. I am no longer afraid to say, "Yes, I'm Deaf, and I sign." However, it took time to understand why my identity has changed over time. To understand my identity, you must also understand my place in the mainstream society.

Denton Mallas was born deaf as a result of sensorineural loss caused by cytomegalovirus (CMV). He was born and raised in South Milwaukee, Wisconsin. He graduated from the Wisconsin School for the Deaf in 2009 and graduated cum laude with a bachelor's degree in history at Gallaudet University. In December 2015, he graduated with a master's degree in secondary education and Deaf education, also from Gallaudet University. He teaches social studies at the Louisiana School for the Deaf.

At one point in my young life, I was looking for a way to make friends. To be specific, I was looking for a way to make friends with my hearing peers. At that point, I could lip-read fairly well, but my main mode of communication was sign language, not speech. When I say sign language, I do not mean American Sign Language (ASL). At that time, I was using contact signing, a mixture of ASL and Signed Exact English (SEE). I eventually found a way to "communicate" with my hearing peers, and it was through video games.

The birds were chirping, the grass was swaying back and forth, the sun was shining radiantly, and I was inside the house. I was sitting on my bed in my room with the TV on, and there were the sounds of clicking buttons repeatedly, with a few grunts at times. I was playing video games on a beautiful day, when I should have been outside playing with my friends. Is that what a normal teenager would have done? I guess I'm abnormal because I believe video games are more fun to play. Through video games, I was able to communicate with the hearing gamers online in our common language, written English. When I would play outdoor games with hearing peers, I would not have a clue what they were saying to me or other people, because it is not realistic to have an interpreter with me every minute of the day. In short, I had more access to language through online video gaming than I did through outdoor games. Like the rest of the world, video games have continued to evolve with technology. With technological advancements, video games started to become even more accessible for me, as they enable me to exchange information with other gamers at a quick rate. In the real world, language has also become more accessible for me and other deaf people; however, we still have several barriers we have to navigate through. Perhaps that is the reason why I was, and am still, an avid gamer, because playing gives me a sense of security.

In middle school, every time I got a new game, I immediately played it without breaks because I had the competitive urge to beat the game, no matter how difficult. I would not rest until I beat the game, but when I did, then I could be at peace. I can play any kind of video game: sports, first-person shooter, role-playing, or strategy. But how is this relevant to my identity? It certainly had a part in my Deaf identity, as it reveals how difficult it was for me to develop social skills without access to language. Even when I first entered into the Deaf World at the age of fourteen years, it was not easy for me to acquire social skills. Before I knew the concept of Deaf World or stepped into it, my social life was not so great. I probably said (through signing and writing) fewer than five hundred words per day, and I hung out with my hearing "friends" by playing video games. In short, video games allowed me to communicate with my hearing peers, yet at the same time it affected my social interaction skills, which were indeed delayed. When I transferred to the Wisconsin School for the Deaf and started interacting with my Deaf peers at the school, I still did not say many words, because I was always nodding as I was listening to what they were saying. It took me a while to break out of my shell, but my current identity finally began to form. During my junior year at the School for the Deaf, I began to participate in after-school clubs such as the Academic Bowl, the Drama Club, and the Student Body Government.

Like most Deaf people, I was born into a hearing world where I'm the only Deaf person in my family. Naturally, they sent me to public schools from kindergarten through eighth grade. I was the only deaf kid in school; in fact, as far as I know, I was the only deaf person in my hometown. Theoretically speaking, I was already stigmatized because I was the only person with an interpreter in class, and everyone knew my name just because I'm deaf. My family often claimed that they knew me because of who I am, not because I'm deaf. That may be true, but when they hear my name or see me, it would not be a surprise to me that the first thing that comes to mind for them is the fact that I cannot hear. My interpreter was my mark of stigma, but it was not my first mark. My first stigma had already started before I started school. In my early childhood years, I had to wear a hearing aid, and I started speech therapy when I was in preschool. However, my experience was a bit different from the common story of a lone deaf child having to grow up speaking, with no signing at all. I communicated with my family in contact signing from the beginning, as my parents thought it was vital for me to learn both ASL and English. When my parents learned that I was deaf, my father took an ASL class, and my mother bought an ASL dictionary. Their open-minded approach helped me to be exposed to both languages at an early age, even though it didn't help me much academically until fourth grade, which was the turning point of my academic career—the year I finally broke through. I was behind in English and reading until then, and I cannot count how many times my fourth-grade teacher had reading sessions with me throughout the school year. When I was reevaluated at the end of the year, my reading and English abilities were at the fifth-grade level. Thanks to this teacher, a door opened up for me, and I was able to bloom as my academic career took off.

I already hated my hearing aids by the time I was in first grade. In fact, I discarded them when I was in first grade and I never wore them again until eighth grade. Eighth grade was a turning point in my life; I was at a crossroad. I was not sure what the future had in store for me, and I was still trying to discover my identity. I did not want to be viewed as an odd person, and my hearing aids were, to use Erving Goffman's (1983) term, "giving off" my deafness. Everybody could tell I was deaf by just looking at my hearing aids. I felt that my hearing aids prevented people from viewing me as a human being. In reality, it wasn't possible to hide my deafness. Even when I took my hearing aids off, I still had my interpreter to accommodate me. My interpreter was another tool that "gave off" my deafness and stigmatized me as a deaf person. I thought I was the only deaf person in the world and that I would have to deal with that every day, but my parents would not allow that to happen. In fact, they encouraged me to meet other deaf people by sending me to summer camps. A typical deaf child would be ecstatic to realize that he or she was not alone in the world, but that was not the case with me.

I hated it, and I thought the kids at camp were weird even if they were deaf just like me. I was in denial, as I was not used to the Deaf World; I preferred to stay in the mainstream world. To use J. W. Berry's language (1997), I had acculturated to the mainstream society. I went to public schools, had hearing friends, and had rejected the Deaf World even though my parents encouraged me to join it. In addition, I didn't make lot of friends, because I was quiet all the time. Like my affinity for escaping into video games, my quietness is one of the habits I've developed from staying in the hearing world for too long. I became used to saying only a few words each day because I never really had much to say, or perhaps I couldn't express my opinion in complete sentences. Even if I tried, I'd just waste my time because people would not understand me and I was somewhat socially awkward.

I was awkward because I did not develop peer-interaction skills. I didn't have much access to language when I was among my hearing peers. Back in mainstream days, I would often say that I had hearing friends. But would you call someone a friend if they just talked to you expecting you to read their lips, instead of learning sign language to communicate with you? Real friends were those who actually made an effort to communicate with me in sign language. I can count on my fingers how many hearing friends I had in my childhood years who actually signed with me. Not many, right?

My negative view on deafness persisted when I enrolled at a public middle school and even into my first year at the Wisconsin School for the Deaf. One time when I was in middle school, my mother, being motherly, mentioned that she could not wait to see me get married and have kids. I merely laughed and replied, "Impossible. Why would anyone want to marry a Deaf guy?" When I said that, she was taken aback and could not give a response. My reply probably stemmed from the trauma of the stigma placed on me in public schools. It had gotten to me so much, to a point where I indeed thought deafness was a severe disability, that it limited my prospects in life. I tried to hide my deafness as much as possible because I knew people would looked at me differently once they found out I was deaf.

The stigma still lingers and haunts me to this day. Sometimes when I'm on Facebook, or when I get a chance to see my parents, I am told how my hearing peers remember me so clearly and that they wanted to know how I am doing. I also learn that they reminisce about the old times with me, and I wonder, "Was it really that fun?" To be honest, when they reminisce about the old times, I can't really remember them; nor can I remember what we did back then. I can only just nod or agree with whatever they say, because grade school and middle school have become a complete blur; it is like I simply drifted through the years without doing anything significant, besides playing sports. Basically, I felt as if I was completely invisible in elementary and middle school, even though I wasn't due to my deafness. However, I have one vivid memory: the eighth-grade graduation dance. I got to dance with the prettiest girl in our class, and everyone was envious of me. Next to sports, that dance was probably the only time I got an upper hand on my hearing peers at school.

Otherwise, I never really had a social life. The only time I went out after school was for athletic activities. I rarely had sleepovers, and when I did, we just played video games. That was probably the only way my friends and I communicated—through video games. That social life wasn't fulfilling; I wanted a fresh start somewhere else. That's why I decided to say good-bye to my "hearing" life and start a new life in the Deaf World at the Wisconsin School for the Deaf—and, ultimately, at Gallaudet University.

When I enrolled at the Wisconsin School for the Deaf, I finally got my Deaf "exposure." Everything was completely new. It took me a while to get used to the new environment I was thrown into. I started to acknowledge being Deaf in a cultural way, and I began my personal growth from there. Initially, however, I looked down on some Deaf students because of their poor grammar skills. I was still ignorant about Deaf culture and Deaf education, so I actually felt bad for them. When I caught myself saying that, I actually was shocked at myself and realized that I was stigmatizing them from an ableist and audist "hearing" perspective.

I was one of the top students at my school, and I was the valedictorian of my graduating class. As a student, I did not realize how my writing skills privileged me at my Deaf school. I did not understand at the time, but now, from within the Deaf community, I certainly can see differences between my peers and me, and skill in written English is one of them. I became aware that many Deaf and hard-of-hearing children struggle within their hearing or Deaf families to gain a full range of access to language from a young age, which affects written English skills. What was really important to me, however, was that I finally learned what ASL was, how it was different from contact signing, and how it was actually signed. I also was able to hang out with other Deaf people from other states. I finally found a community I could be a part of and in which I could communicate in my natural language, ASL. ASL allowed me to open my eyes to the world beyond the walls I was sheltered within. In fact, I will say that 70 percent of my learning in high school took place outside the classroom. Everywhere I went, I learned so much about life—dorms, video phones, other schools for the Deaf—and the teachers taught us life lessons not related to class. Ultimately, I also gained Deaf friends and peers.

To this day, I may be a little quiet, but I'm more comfortable with expressing myself than I was before I went to the Wisconsin School for the Deaf. I suddenly believed that I could do anything I put my mind to and that being Deaf is not a limitation. A valuable lesson I learned was that only I can stop myself from succeeding. In turn, it is one of the reasons why I want to become a teacher at a school for the Deaf. I want Deaf students to lead a better life than my generation has. I want them to continue to make a difference in the society we live in. I want my students to acknowledge their abilities and rights, not only as human beings but also as Deaf persons. During my high school years, I began to be proud of being Deaf, which led me to discover my identity.

Gallaudet University helped me further understand my Deaf identity. I am still a man of few words. Quietness seems to be a habit that will remain with me for the rest of my life. But I believe that when I say something, what I have to say is important and necessary. That's why I want to be a teacher, and a coach as well. I want to make a difference in other people's lives and guide them to the path they desire. I am Deaf, and I am determined to make a difference, no matter how small it is.

NOTE

1. There is a distinction within Deaf studies between being culturally Deaf and audiologically deaf. The use of the terms here tries to follow that distinction and reflects my own journey to becoming Deaf.

REFERENCES

Berry, J. W. 1997. "Immigration, Acculturation, and Adaptation." *Applied Psychology* 46 (1): 5–34.
Goffman, E. 1983. "The Presentation of Self in Everyday Life." In *Social Interaction: Readings in Sociology*, 2nd ed., edited by H. Robboy and C. Clark, 129–138. New York: St. Martin's.

PART VI

THEORIES AND LIVES

THIS FINAL PART FEATURES chapters by engaged student activists as well as graduate students working within the field of disability studies. Specifically, these contributors focus on how disability studies theories have influenced and transformed their self-perceptions, political commitments, and academic perspectives. Building on theoretical insights introduced by Shayda Kafai (Chapter I.2), Zachary A. Richter (Chapter I.6), Joshua St. Pierre (Chapter III.1), and Garrett R. Cruzan (Chapter IV.4), among others, these narratives delve into the enduring effects of structural ableism, the power (and complexity) of understanding sociocultural dimensions of disability, and the ongoing, pressing need for disability activism. From diverse perspectives, these authors trace the influence disability theory can have on individual lives, from reframing biocultural meanings of disability to developing self-identity and, ultimately, to shaping the direction of intellectual and professional pursuits.

Adena Rottenstein, in Chapter VI.1, and Cindee Calton, in Chapter VI.2, reflect on the intellectual struggles and emotional paradigm shifts they experienced by integrating social model perspectives into their understanding of disability. Rottenstein describes her initial resistance to shifting from a medical to a social approach to disability—arguing with classmates and struggling within herself. Over time, however, as she realized that much of her opposition stemmed from her own experience with chronic pain, she began to recognize an internalized bias against disability she could no longer support. Calton also reflects on the ways in which disability theory reshaped her thinking about mental illness. She admits that her oversimplified initial understanding of social construction caused her to question medical and psychiatric interventions that were actually beneficial to her. This narrative provides a pivotal course correction, from situating social theory and medical approaches as purely oppositional toward a more nuanced—and more accurate—understanding of disability studies theory. In Chapter VI.3, Rodney B. Hume-Dawson adds to this discussion by connecting disability theory to faith and spirituality. Hume-Dawson recounts his childhood with polio in Sierra Leone, bridging traditional West African beliefs about disability and the importance of faith and family with disability studies and his life in the United States.

Adam P. Newman, in Chapter VI.4, and Rebekah Moras, in Chapter VI.5, offer poignant glimpses into the power of disability theory to empower disabled students, to transform negative self-perceptions, and to engender new intellectual research. Newman recounts a childhood of seeing himself as the "sick kid" and being socially isolated as a result. After living through illness, surgery, and depression, he saw college as a chance to "pass" as nondisabled and enjoy a new start; however, the reemergence of a brain tumor forced him to "come out" in order to request accommodations. At this crucial juncture, Newman began reading disability studies scholarship, which allowed him to feel empowered as a disabled person—as someone with embodied insight of value to others.

Drawing on a growing body of research bridging disability and mad studies, Moras argues that more work needs to be done in disability studies to engage with the concerns of people with mental illness diagnoses. She recounts her own journey through the chaos of psychiatric symptoms to gaining more mental and emotional balance, part of which was coming to understand that she was not just a problem to be "fixed." Moras reflects on her introduction to disability studies, disability rights, and advocacy as she worked and studied at two University Centers of Excellence in Developmental Disabilities (UCEDDs) in Alaska and Illinois. As a person with a psychiatric diagnosis, she often felt excluded from the concerns of disability advocacy more broadly. Her chapter encourages scholars and students in disability studies to become more actively engaged with mad pride and to challenge able-minded privilege. Connecting madness and disability studies is an emergent area, and many new voices are contributing to the discussion of how these fields connect and inform each other. Indeed, the growing interest in the overlap and relationship between the two fields is reflected in the large number of narratives focused on anxiety, depression, mental illness diagnoses, and other forms of mental or emotional distress in this book.

Chapter VI.6, by Lydia X. Z. Brown, weaves snapshots of the personal into a larger story of political action. Autistic traits and ableist perceptions about the label of autism have caused people to misjudge Brown as unpredictable and potentially dangerous. Brown contrasts this presumption of violence with a reminder of the very real violence and abuse autistic people have suffered and continue to experience all too often—in educational settings, in institutions, and sometimes at the hands of caregivers, including parents. Further, Brown connects the mistreatment and violence against autistic people to the dominant public rhetoric around autism that has been shaped by the organization Autism Speaks. The urgency in this chapter serves as a stark reminder of the indignities and abuses many autistic people are made to suffer; at the same time, as a determined activist, blogger, and student organizer, Brown joins with other voices in this book to point toward, imagine, and build a future that is otherwise.

Reference the boldface terms as themes for discussion, and consider the following questions as you read the chapters in Part VI:

1. According to these writers, what intellectual, emotional, and material effects has disability studies had on their lives? How does this help you understand this relatively new academic field?
2. What is the relationship between disability activism, a politics of access, and disability studies? How do you see disabled and nondisabled people engaging in these activities and intellectual pursuits?
3. How do psychiatric disabilities expand and complicate understandings of disability in general?
4. How do all these narratives add texture to static understandings of the social model and social construction? How do these chapters expand your understanding of the interconnection between medical, social, cultural, and minority approaches to disability? How would you use these narratives to describe biocultural approaches to disability?

Suggestions for Related Readings

- Read Adena Rottenstein's chapter (VI.1) with those by Alyse Ritvo (I.1) and Allegra Heath-Stout (V.1) to discuss issues of campus access, peer dynamics, and disability identity.
- Cindee Calton's chapter (VI.2) and Rebekah Moras's chapter (VI.5) explore the hidden nature of and imposed silences around

psychiatric disabilities, which could be linked to a number of chapters, including those by Shayda Kafai (I.2), Megan L. Coggins (V.3), and Susan Macri (V.4).

- Pair Rodney B. Hume-Dawson's chapter (VI.3) with those of Anmol Bhatia (I.3) and Mycie Lubin (II.1) to discuss cross-cultural and immigrant perspectives on disability.
- Lydia X. Z. Brown's chapter (VI.6) details ongoing violence against autistic people and the importance of activism. Pair their[1] chapter with those by Zachary A. Richter (I.6) and Allegra Heath-Stout (V.1) to explore themes of autism and neurodiversity, radical disability communities, and activism.

NOTE

1. "They" and "their" are Brown's preferred pronouns.

VI.1

Taking Great Pains with Disability Theory

I n my second year of graduate school, I decided to engage in a small act of rebellion: I enrolled in a course called Topics in Disability Studies. While this might not seem like the most treasonous act one can engage in, it felt like a very real risk to me, as disability studies fell far outside the core curriculum of my psychology Ph.D. program, and I was already behind in my required classes. Looking back, I cannot help but smile at the mix of anxiety and joyful insolence I felt during course registration, for I did not know then what I know now: my small act of rebellion led to a large revolution in my life.

I should have known something was afoot when I started to notice the very strong, very visceral reactions I was having to the assigned readings for the class. The professor began with materials that reviewed the medical, social, and business models of disability (Albrecht 1992; Linton 1998; Wendell 1996; WHO 2002). The medical model was by far the most familiar

Adena Rottenstein completed her psychology Ph.D. at the University of Michigan in 2013. She takes an interdisciplinary approach to research and teaching, blending the methods and literatures of social, personality, and community psychology with disability, women's, and LGBT studies. She takes a special interest in approaching all projects from a social justice perspective. The dissertation mentioned in her chapter can be found via the University of Michigan's Deep Blue database (https://deepblue.lib.umich.edu) and is titled "Predicting Disability Self-Identification: A Mixed Methods Approach."

and intuitive viewpoint for me, as I had always considered disability to be a clear-cut category based on an individual's physical or mental limitations.

The social model, however, really threw me for a loop. I had trouble wrapping my head around the idea that disability is a socially constructed phenomenon in which the associated disadvantages stem not from physical or mental differences but from societal beliefs and practices that limit people with disabilities in a variety of ways. It seemed that the social model was saying that there was nothing inherently wrong in being disabled, but that there was something inherently wrong in the way society treats people with disabilities.

As a self-identified feminist and antiracist, it was easy for me to accept the idea that society was oppressing and marginalizing a group of people based on a socially constructed category. However, the idea that there was nothing inherently wrong with being disabled was a profound challenge to the way I saw the world. *How can not seeing, not walking, or not hearing be anything but a burden?* I thought. "I'm all for social justice," I said in class, "but these conditions are still disadvantages. They're limitations. How could anyone want a limitation in their life?"

Many of my classmates responded to my comments. Some of them said that they saw their own disabilities as just another part of who they were, similar to their gender or upbringing or taste in music. Others said that their disabilities were not disadvantages but advantages, helping them to perceive and navigate the world in unique and beautiful ways. Others still said that having a disability made them better, kinder, or more empathetic.

I quietly listened to their responses, head bent ever so slightly down, hands flat on my desk, but as each person spoke, I could feel my heart beat faster and faster. I felt my palms begin to sweat, my head start to ache, and my stomach muscles begin to tighten. Red faced, hands clenched, I started to challenge my classmates. "Listen," I said, my voice gradually rising, "I'm *not* a person with a disability, okay? But I know, *I know*, that some disabilities cause pain, severe, chronic pain, and I cannot see how any reasonable person could possibly want a condition that caused them pain." I raised my eyes and looked about the classroom for support. I only saw looks of pity. "Why would anyone want pain?" I shouted.

I don't remember the exact details after that, but our professor defused the situation and led the class conversation in a different direction. I left campus that afternoon in a daze. I felt angry and confused, ashamed of my behavior. *Why did I get so upset?* I wondered. *What the hell was my problem?*

The answer did not come immediately. It came slowly over time, over discussion after discussion in our disability studies course, over countless hours spent puzzling over my emotions, my opinions, and my beliefs. One day, several weeks after the class had ended, it dawned on me. *I* was a person with a disability. *I* was the one with chronic pain.

I was diagnosed with scoliosis when I was eight years old. My right shoulder slightly above the left, I remember having weekly visits with a friendly yet terrifying neighborhood chiropractor to help "straighten me out." Upon reflection, it is difficult for me to remember a time in my life when I wasn't seeing a chiropractor, a physical therapist, or someone in orthopedics to help with my musculoskeletal dysfunction and pain. When I got to graduate school, things only became worse. My pain, once an occasional annoyance, became a continuous hindrance. I woke up in pain, spent the day in pain, and went to sleep in pain. I was in such a state that when I started to experience numbness and partial paralysis in my left arm, I happily welcomed it as a reprieve.

Looking back, it is no wonder that I reacted so strongly to the social model. If it was true, then disability status was not the result of a concrete system of classification but rather the product of some nebulous, perhaps arbitrary, distinction made all the more complex by the interactions between individuals and society. And if that was true, there was the distinct possibility that I was a person with a disability, that the pain I felt was not a temporary inconvenience but, rather, a very real part of who I was and how I experienced the world.

I did not want to be a person with a disability. I did not want to be in pain. But as a person predisposed to self-reflection, I also did not want to ignore my rather disturbing knee-jerk reaction to the label. Fortunately for me, the realization that I may be a person with a disability was paired with the social model's insistence that there may not be anything inherently wrong with that identity. It was this combination of thoughts that freed me to explore my disability status medically, socially, and academically.

Medically, I became more active about my health care. I stopped passively following my doctor's recommendations and instead started to push for better treatment. Within six months, I had my answer: I had fibromyalgia, a medical disorder characterized by chronic and widespread musculoskeletal pain. This diagnosis radically changed my treatment plan, and I went from constant pain and partial paralysis to being able to play volleyball once a week with friends. (The treatment did not magically take the pain away, but it did make it a whole lot more manageable.)

Socially, I reached out to other people with disabilities and found quite a welcoming community. I became very close to a group of other graduate students at my university who, like me, experienced great conflict both internally and externally because of their disability status. The acceptance and understanding I felt around these individuals completely shifted my views of graduate school. No longer did I lament my inability to "fit" my program. Rather, I began to challenge my program for not fitting me.

It was this change in perspective that helped me to shift the focus of my academic studies. I switched mentors and began working on a project that ultimately became my dissertation. It was a large-scale survey of people with various medical conditions, and it asked, quite simply: "Do you identify as a person with a disability? Why or why not?" (My dissertation was a success; I was able to collect responses from a sample of almost three thousand people.)

With graduation now less than four months away, I cannot help but feel grateful for my turbulent exposure to the social model of disability. While it is by no means perfect, often ignoring the day-to-day realities of living with conditions, like mine, that can be unpleasant to experience (Barnes 2009; Crow 1996; Morris 1996; Thomas 2001), it does serve an important function. It helps us, people with disabilities, to understand that our experiences do not exist wholly inside ourselves; rather, they exist in a complex system, which we must actively work to navigate and challenge. Perhaps someday, I will teach my own course in disability studies and will see a struggling psychology student engage in a small act of rebellion by enrolling in my class. I can only hope that I will be able to influence this student in a fraction of the way that disability studies has influenced me.

REFERENCES

Albrecht, G. L. 1992. "The Social Meaning of Impairment and Interpretation of Disability." In *The Disability Business: Rehabilitation in America*, 67–90. Newbury Park, CA: Sage.

Barnes, E. 2009. "Disability, Minority, and Difference." *Journal of Applied Philosophy* 26 (4): 337–355.

Crow, L. 1996. "Including All of Our Lives: Renewing the Social Model of Disability." In *Exploring the Divide: Illness and Disability*, edited by C. Barnes and G. Mercer, 55–73. Leeds, UK: Disability Press.

Linton, S. 1998. "Reassigning Meaning." In *Claiming Disability: Knowledge and Identity*, 8–33. New York: New York University Press.

Morris, J. 1996. *Encounters with Strangers: Feminism and Disability*. London: Women's Press.

Thomas, C. 2001. "Feminism and Disability: The Theoretical and Political Significance of the Personal and the Experiential." In *Disability, Politics and the Struggle for Change*, edited by L. Barton, 45–58. London: David Fulton.

Wendell, S. 1996. "The Social Construction of Disability." In *The Rejected Body: Feminist Philosophical Reflections on Disability*, 35–56. New York: Routledge.

WHO (World Health Organization). 2002. "Towards a Common Language for Functioning, Disability and Health: ICF." In *The International Classification of Functioning, Disability and Health*, 1–19. Geneva, Switzerland: World Health Organization.

VI.2

Medicating My Socially Constructed Disability

CINDEE CALTON

This is a very personal story of my attempt to reconcile my personal life, in which I was being told to take medication for bipolar disorder, and my academic life, in which I was learning and arguing that things like bipolar disorder are socially constructed. It is common for people with bipolar disorder to go off their medications (Jamison 1995). I'm sure there are as many reasons for this as there are people with bipolar disorder: side effects, missing the "high," shame, and fear, to name a few. I'm sure those factors were a part of my own resistance to medication. However, there was an intellectual issue involved for me as well. As a graduate student in anthropology planning to do my research on Deaf people and American Sign Language (ASL), I was a new arrival in the field of disability studies. I was lucky enough to be on a campus where there was a faculty member with expertise in disability studies. The notion that disability is socially constructed made intuitive and intellectual sense to me, and it still does. What I would like to show via my personal story is the danger of not treating

Cindee Calton holds a Ph.D. and is an anthropologist and educator. Her 2013 dissertation, "Teaching Respect," examines the intersection of identity and language ideologies in American Sign Language classes. Her publications include a 2010 article in *Disability and Society* analyzing the role of socioeconomic class in parenting children with disabilities and a chapter on the history of sign language linguistics in the 2014 book *Deaf Gain*. She is an adjunct professor at McNally Smith College of Music.

the concept of disability as social construction as the complex and nuanced idea that it is. I say this not because I think disability studies scholars fail to approach the idea with complexity. I say it because I didn't, and it could have cost me my life.

Background: What Depression and Mania Look Like for Me

Like many mental illnesses, bipolar disorder is a personal disease. It manifests itself differently from person to person. In my experience, it is so much a part of my personality that no medication could ever truly get rid of it without altering my soul.

I have had long, difficult bouts of depression for as long as I can remember. For me, depression manifests itself in the form of crying fits, difficulty getting out of bed in the morning, a lack of interest in things and people that I love, feelings of overwhelming emptiness, and a general lack of vitality. These are, as I understand it, fairly typical symptoms of depression. I have also, like many other people with bipolar disorder, contemplated on many occasions that death would feel much less painful than life.

What is perhaps different with regard to my experiences with depression is that my depression is irrevocably linked to a general sense of despair about the horrible things that human beings do to each other. Even when I am not depressed, a newspaper story about a gay youth who took his or her life because of bullying or rejection can easily make me cry. When I am depressed, it is enough to make me feel like I simply cannot keep going when the world is such a cruel and horrible place. This is the place where my depression and my personality meet and blur together. This is where I cannot always tell them apart.

As for mania, I am fortunate enough that my mania is not accompanied by bouts of feeling invincible or maxing out my credit card. Rather, mania for me is a mix of mental and emotional hyperactivity. Thoughts spin in my head at the speed of light. Sleep seems impossible, but also unnecessary. It is difficult to explain how wonderful this can be to someone who has not experienced it. Just imagine, if you will, that the world is more lively, that colors are more vibrant, sounds more crisp, and *every* moment feels like an "aha" moment, the ones where suddenly the entire universe seems to make sense.

My mania meets my personality at the point of productivity. I am a productive person who enjoys feeling as though I accomplished many tasks in a timely manner. This is so much the case that my husband made a word to describe me: a "concrastinator." By swapping out "pro" in favor of "con," my husband's word aims to describe the fact that I am not just *not* a procrastinator—I am the complete opposite of a procrastinator. I am driven to high levels of agitation by work that is incomplete, even when there is plenty of time left to complete the task. This is heightened to extreme measures during mania. Much of the transcribing for my dissertation was done in the middle of the night, because I couldn't sleep. The interview tapes were sitting in another room waiting to be transcribed, and I couldn't stand it.

The best quotation I have ever encountered to describe this feeling comes from *Star Trek*—as do many of my favorite life-explaining quotes. In the movie *Star Trek II: The Wrath of Khan*, the villain and title character, Khan, is obsessively driven to find and kill Admiral Kirk. He is so obsessed that when his followers beg him to take what they have stolen from Kirk and get on with their lives, he paraphrases *Moby Dick*: "[Kirk] tasks me. He tasks me and I shall have him. I'll chase him 'round the Moons of Nibia and 'round the Antares Maelstrom and 'round Perdition's flames before I give him up!" Khan's obliviousness to everything but his need for revenge allows Kirk to bait him into a trap, and Khan dies while cursing Kirk's name. Like Khan, when I am manic, incomplete work tasks me to the point of self-destruction. Even so, my mania was often an asset when it came to completing my dissertation.

There are also downsides, of course. My spinning thoughts can run through my mind so fast that I am unable to communicate them with anyone, let alone do anything with them. And beyond that, there is the fidgeting and anxiety. There is the agitation and irritability. There are the panic attacks that make me convinced that I can't breathe or that the world is shattering around me. And there is the paranoia: I imagine that other people's motives are impure or, even worse, that they are plotting against me. This is unpleasant for myself, and for them.

Finally, with the mania comes a combination of horrifying nightmares and a terrifying, nagging feeling that the world is not real. In some cases, something feels off about where I am or what is happening, so I begin to worry that I am in fact asleep and dreaming. This propensity is not at all helped by the fact that I often "wake up" repeatedly in my dreams only to discover that I am still asleep. It is also not helped by the fact that I seem to remember my dreams far more than most people; I remember them basically every day. So many of my memories are of dreams rather than of real events. All of this adds to a nagging feeling that nothing is truly real. The amount of doubt that I have about the reality around me varies widely. But, to this day, I always have some doubt. Even now.

Clashing Paradigms: My Mental Illness Meets My Intellectual Self

My first year of graduate school, things got really bad. I was in such a deep bout of depression that I finally told my husband how much pain I was in.

I don't really remember what got me to that point or all the details of what happened next. I have found that my memory from times of high levels of mania or depression is very poor. The events, the things people said, and my thoughts are all hazy. The feelings, though, I remember with intense clarity. And I remember very well what it felt like to want to die.

I couldn't let it get to that point. I couldn't do that to my husband. And so I asked for his help before it got worse. As always, he took care of me. He called the psychiatric department at the university hospital and got them to see me that day. I begrudgingly agreed to take more pills—or maybe it was different pills—and to start seeing the doctor regularly. I had been off and on different medications for depression and bipolar disorder since I was an undergraduate student. At that point, I hadn't stumbled on a mix that was right for me, so my medications only partially helped to alleviate my symptoms.

During this time, I was also exploring the exciting and, to me, very novel notion that disabilities are social constructs; they are problems located not in disabled people's bodies but in the attitudes of everyone else. I'm not sure what the experiencing of stumbling onto this line of thinking is like for others, but for me it was exhilarating. Douglas Baynton's 2001 article "Disability and the Justification of Inequality in American History" was especially mind-blowing. The connection Baynton drew between oppression of disabled people and the oppression of other identity groups made me view the concept of disability as central to the concept of identity itself. Immersed in works like this, it felt like a renaissance was going on in my own mind.

At the intellectual forefront of this concept in my mind is the social construction of deafness as a disability, because I did my master's paper and my Ph.D. dissertation on American Sign Language (ASL). While researching ASL, I read countless books and articles by and about Deaf people, in which the authors argued that, for the Deaf, Deafness is their identity and their culture, and they had no desire to be "fixed." Nora Ellen Groce's (1985) ethnohistory of Martha's Vineyard provides a particularly striking example. Groce demonstrates, through oral history about the island's sign language, that when everyone in a community knows how to sign with deaf people, deafness is not a barrier to social life. In a more modern example, Carol Padden and Tom Humphries (2005) cite anthropologist Clifford Geertz's explanation of human culture, that "one of the most significant facts about us may be that we all begin with the natural equipment to live a thousand kinds of life but end in the end having lived only one" (as cited in Padden and Humphries 2005, 4), and connect this with the Deaf experience. To Padden and Humphries, Deafness has less to do with "equipment" (that is, hearing) and more to do with a Deaf life that results from a particular history. The Deaf people I interviewed for my dissertation echoed this view of Deafness, with one ASL teacher telling me that if his students were to remember only one thing, he hoped they remembered that Deaf people do not want to be fixed.

The trouble with my immersion in the world of disability studies is that at first I viewed it very simplistically. Before, disability had been to me what it was and is to many people: a problem. Now, disability was (and still is) a part of a large spectrum of human existence. If Deafness is only a problem when people don't know sign language (Groce 1985), then surely being bipolar might be a problem with the world and not with me.

I supported this conclusion with an array of research. For example, cross-cultural examinations of depression reveal a remarkable amount of variability in the symptoms, interpretations, and understandings of depression (Kleinman and Good 1985). Fieldwork among Shiite Muslims in Iran, for example, revealed an understanding of depression that differed greatly from the dominant Western perspective. Informants associated sadness with personal depth and thoughtfulness, and signs of depression included anger and mistrust (Good, DelVecchio Good, and Moradi 1985). Similarly, Joshua Wolf Shenk (2005) argues that not only was Abraham Lincoln clinically depressed, but his greatness was in fact fueled by his depression. I was drawn further to Shenk's description of a 1979 study by Abramson and Alloy, which suggests that, contrary to our belief that depression distorts reality, it is in fact depressed people who perceive things more objectively, while nondepressed people are overly optimistic. This study was on my mind when a psychiatrist I didn't like very much asked me why I was feeling depressed. I responded by pointing out that the world was full of sexism, racism, homophobia, rape, murder, and generalized exploitation, and so a better question would be *why wasn't he* depressed? He upped the levels on my mood stabilizer, which, in my mind, solidified the notion that the rest of the world was the problem; they just couldn't see as clearly as I could.

The ultimate result of my simplistic view of the social construction of disability was a strong resistance to taking my medication. I felt like the problem was not in me, it was with everyone else. Why should I have to take pills because everyone else couldn't see things clearly? So sometimes I wouldn't take them. Sometimes my husband practically had to beg me to take them. I resisted therapy because I felt there was nothing to talk about and they wouldn't understand anyway. I hated the medication, I hated the psychiatrist, and I hated the world.

Complexity and Freedom

My ultimate salvation was the clarity that came with a more complex and nuanced understanding of disability as a social construction. I can see three possible reasons for my overly simplistic view. The most obvious one is that I was a young scholar freshly exposed to a novel concept. First, I had to wrap my head around the notion that disability was socially constructed. I couldn't get into the nuances until I did that. Another possible explanation is the tendency of people with bipolar disorder to view the world in black-and-white terms (Deckersbach et al. 2014). The third possibility, the one that I favor, is a combination of both.

Several personal and intellectual experiences helped me gain a more complex view of disability and, through that process, a more complex view of my own mental health. The first emerged from a personal conversation with a professor. After hearing me describe my extreme version of the social construction of disability, she responded quite simply, "Yes, but what about people in physical pain?" It seems silly, retrospectively, that someone had to point out to me that many disabilities are physically painful and that understanding social construction would never do anything to make that pain go away. At the time, however, it was a revelation.

The second experience was via an article I wrote analyzing the role of social class in memoirs by parents of disabled children (Calton 2010). My article examined how all the memoirs I analyzed were written by parents who did extraordinary things for their disabled children with the resources available to them as members of the upper middle class. Of the memoirs I read, I was most personally moved by the memoir of Fern Kupfer (1982). Kupfer describes the anguishing guilt she felt as she attempted (and failed, in her eyes) to be the idealized heroic mother of a disabled child. Kupfer ended up institutionalizing her son, albeit with hesitation and guilt. Though I thought, and still do think, that deinstitutionalization of people with disabilities is overall a positive movement, I also found myself sympathizing with Kupfer because she lacked the resources to care for her disabled child. Deinstitutionalization is not as black and white as I had thought.

Finally, and most importantly, I read *An Unquiet Mind* by Kay Redfield Jamison (1995). I was attracted to the book because "unquiet mind" seemed like such an apt description of my own experience. I have never finished her book, as too much of it hits too close to home. I have, however, read her epilogue many times and gained much clarity from it. When she addresses the question of whether she would choose to have manic depression if given the choice, she says, "If lithium were not available to me, or didn't work for me, the answer would be a simple no—and it would be an answer laced with terror. But lithium does work for me, and therefore I suppose I can afford to pose the question. Strangely enough I think I would choose to have it. It's complicated" (Jamison 1995, 217). That one quote changed my life. Medication is available to me, medication that takes the edge off deep depression and extreme mania. However, as I argued earlier, my depression and my mania are part of who I am. My experiences with depression have given me a gift of empathy for people in pain that no other life experience could have. My "concrastination" lets me have bouts of productivity and creativity. I just wrote this entire chapter in one day. However, I could never benefit from either of those things if medication was not available to curb the harshest effects.

Concluding Thoughts

Coming to a complicated view of disability as a social construction may very well have saved my life. It allowed me to embrace my difference while simultaneously taking care of myself. My personal experiences taught me that we need to have a nuanced view of the social construction of disability not only to move forward intellectually as a discipline but also to make people feel welcome, regardless of what, if any, treatment they seek for their disability. As I said before, I say this not to suggest that disability studies scholars view things in the simplistic way I described in my younger self. For example, Tavian Robinson's (2010) examination of the ableist rhetoric about Deaf people in 1880–1920 U.S. publications calls into question the divide between Deaf studies and disability studies. Similarly, Khadijat Rashid (2010) argues that Deafness as a culture and deafness as a disability need not be mutually exclusive; cultural Deafness occurs in addition to auditory deafness. What I am suggesting is that a simplistic view was for me a burden, and a complex view was salvation.

REFERENCES

Baynton, D. C. 2001. "Disability and the Justification of Inequality in American History." In *The New Disability History: American Perspectives*, edited by P. Longmore and L. Umansky, 3–57. New York: New York University Press.

Calton, C. 2010. "The Obscuring of Class in Memoirs of Parents of Children with Disabilities." *Disability and Society* 25 (7): 849–860.

Deckersbach, T., B. Hölzel, L. Eisner, S. W. Lazar, and A. A. Nierenberg. 2014. *Mindfulness-based Cognitive Therapy for Bipolar Disorder*. New York: Guilford.

Good, B., M. DelVecchio Good, and R. Moradi. 1985. "The Interpretation of Iranian Depressive Illness and Dysphoric Affect." In *Culture and Depression: Studies in the Cross-cultural Psychiatry of Affect and Disorder*, edited by A. Kleinman and B. Good, 369–428. Berkeley: University of California Press.

Groce, N. E. 1985. *Everyone Here Spoke Sign Language: Hereditary Deafness on Martha's Vineyard*. Cambridge, MA: Harvard University Press.

Jamison, K. R. 1995. *An Unquiet Mind*. New York: A. A. Knopf.

Kleinman, A., and B. Good. 1985. "Introduction: Culture and Depression." In *Culture and Depression: Studies in the Cross-cultural Psychiatry of Affect and Disorder*, edited by A. Kleinman and B. Good, 1–33. Berkeley: University of California Press.

Kupfer, F. 1982. *Before and after Zachariah: A Family Story about a Different Kind of Courage*. New York: Delacorte.

Padden, C., and T. Humphries. 2005. *Inside Deaf Culture*. Cambridge, MA: Harvard University Press.

Rashid, K. 2010. "Intersecting Reflections." In *Deaf and Disability Studies: Interdisciplinary Perspectives*, edited by S. Burch and A. Kafer, 22–30. Washington, DC: Gallaudet University Press.

Robinson, T. 2010. "We Are of a Different Class: Ableist Rhetoric in Deaf America, 1880–1920." In *Deaf and Disability Studies: Interdisciplinary Perspectives*, edited by S. Burch and A. Kafer, 5–21. Washington, DC: Gallaudet University Press.

Shenk, J. W. 2005. *Lincoln's Melancholy: How Depression Challenged a President and Fueled His Greatness*. New York: Mariner.

VI.3

Flourishing with Polio

A Spiritual, Transformational, and
Disability Studies Perspective

RODNEY B. HUME-DAWSON

G one are the days when the focus of telling one's disability story was about overcoming one's challenge. For me and many others whose work I have been privileged to read, our focus is not so much on the triumphant aspects of our lives but on telling the story from a social perspective. Simply, I want to narrate a story that looks at disability in relation to society and the African context. I want to tell a story that captures how I was treated and viewed and how that affected and shaped my life. Perhaps the following questions are worth asking: How was disability situated in Freetown, Sierra Leone, where I was born, and how were attitudes connected with some traditional African views of disability? How did people respond to physical disability? Was their response a nurturing one or a stigmatizing one?

I contracted poliomyelitis when I was eighteen months old. So I was told. In all honesty, I had no clue that I was different or that something was

Rodney B. Hume-Dawson is a scholar in education and disability studies and a certified English educator in Los Angeles, California. He is currently a lecturer in the Department of Liberal Studies at the College of Education at California State Polytechnic University in Pomona, California. He holds a bachelor's degree in English and philosophy and a master's degree in teaching and curriculum. In 2016, he received his Ph.D. in education, with an emphasis in disability studies, from Chapman University. His dissertation is a phenomenological inquiry on the resilience of people with poliomyelitis. His book chapter, "A Spiritual and Transformative Perspective on Disability," appears in *Emerging Perspectives on Disability Studies* (2013).

wrong with me until I was about four or five. For the most part, I crawled all over the place. I had become accustomed to that way of life. I was fast and versatile at crawling. As a child, I had learned my surroundings so well that I knew where to hide from my siblings, parents, and grandmother. I played hide-and-seek all the time with some of the children who lived in the same building.

I can only imagine the persistent symptoms, my inability to stand up and walk, and the response from my parents. Did they scream, cry, blame themselves and others? How did they react? Was it too much for them to handle? What sort of advice did they receive from friends, relatives, and neighbors? What about the professionals who treated me? How were they able to make the diagnosis? How much wailing and screaming did I do? As a baby, was I in constant pain? Was I uncontrollable? Did they try to calm me down? I can only imagine.

The truth is that, as a child, I never really reflected on my difference. I did not have a reason to. I never went to preschool, so for the most part I did not encounter peers who would have questioned my difference. I stayed home all day with my grandmother, who took care of me. She also was responsible for escorting me to my numerous visits to the hospital, to the physical therapy department, and to the Limb Fitting and Orthopedic Center in the heart of the city. Most of the children with whom I played were warm and welcoming. They were my contemporaries, so my difference never really mattered to them (at least that was the impression I was given). I was able to play with them, and that was what mattered. Because my peers were so nonjudgmental, my early years were one of the best periods in my life.

I also had a mother who was intensely spiritual and religious. She had a faith that never wavered. In many ways, she was like Abraham. She chose her path lovingly and without question. She never asked, "Why me?" Instead, she was always communicating with God to find solutions to her numerous challenges. She had the belief that in spite of my disability, I had something to offer. She believed that God had a purpose for my life. She loved holding me on her lap as she read Bible stories. However, the most incredible thing my mother said to me when I was a toddler was that I may not be able to walk, but with faith, I could do anything with God's help. Those words have stayed with me all my life. Whenever people whom I love and trust say negative things about my disability, even if I get disappointed, I always search deep within me for those comforting and reassuring words.

In addition to my positive memories of my mother and grandmother, I do remember that I was constantly in and out of the hospital. In fact, I became so accustomed to hospitals that I never feared going there. I have made numerous reflections on my fascination with doctors. I was so often in the hospital that I felt the only profession that mattered was medicine.

I wanted to be a medical doctor because I thought that doctors never died. They were responsible for fixing people when they were sick. They were going to fix me, cure me, rehabilitate me, and, if possible, make me walk again. I was so obsessed with this idea, not because I felt that way, but because others hoped for that. Most of the people who loved me wanted me to walk the "normal" way. For some of them, the implications of what that meant did not matter. As long as I walked like them, that was what was important. They loved me, and, naturally, they thought that walking the normal way was the only way to walk.

At two years old, I was scheduled to have an operation at Connaught Hospital, which was one of the largest hospitals in the country. It was located in the heart of the city, surrounded by businesses and government offices. It was the first hospital in West Africa that emulated Western values. At the time of my diagnosis, Sierra Leone was a relatively new nation. It had just gained independence from the British about fifteen years earlier. The country had enjoyed its best of days soon after independence. However, things were beginning to fall apart. There were sporadic blackouts in the city of Freetown, which affected the smooth operation of the hospital.

At first, everything went as planned. I had been formally admitted to the hospital for the operation. My clothes had been removed. I was wearing a hospital gown and had been pushed to the surgical room. Dr. Tom Lewis, the leading orthopedic surgeon, had assembled his team. They were ready to begin when suddenly, out of the blue, the lights went out. They waited. They hoped, but no lights came on. I was taken to the children's ward to wait until the next day. What a disappointment for my parents and grandmother. Did this affect my dad and mom's plans? Did they take time off from work? We were lucky to have my grandmother there, but I can only imagine the frustration and the pain going through her mind. She had been there since my illness started, running around for the family, and now, the one day she had hoped would bring some joy was not going well.

The next day, I was back in the surgical room. Again, I was undressed and was encouraged to put on the hospital gown. I had to go through another set of anesthetics, another set of preparations for surgery. Was it fair for a two-year-old? This time we had light. The surgical team was there, but then the doctor came up, looked at me, and was not comfortable. He was not ready to operate. He listened to his instinct. His small voice had warned him not to operate.

In retrospect, was the doctor's decision not to operate a good thing? Perhaps, to some of my loved ones, it was a disappointment. However, I had several discussions with the lead surgeon before he passed away. I inquired why he had chosen not to operate, and he mentioned that he was concerned about my life. He conceded that the surgery was a difficult one for a two-year-old.

I respected his decision. In my quiet moments, I have thought about other things that might have gone wrong on that day: electrical problems, surgical procedures, and doctors' last-minute decisions. What if other complications had emerged? What if I had died?

I am grateful for the doctor's decision because I now realize the importance of having people with disabilities in societies. That is not to say that I do not respect the need for medical alterations or procedures to make life better for people with disabilities. I do believe in that wholeheartedly; my life is more functional because of the braces and crutches that I use. However, people with disabilities are human beings. Our difference matters. It teaches us humility and makes us ponder the triviality of the things we tend to focus on. Disability helps us create a better society that is organized to serve all people, not just some.

Disability is also significant because it teaches us about the politics of the human body. People are sometimes valued just because of how they look, not for who they are as a person, spiritually or emotionally. I have never seen myself as a problem, but others have because of their learned biases or traditional beliefs about disability. Sadly, the social model says a lot about the psychological damage that our societies have done to many people.

When I learned about the social model of disability, I realized that social exclusion of people with disabilities thrived in Sierra Leone. For one, people with disabilities were hidden from mainstream society. The few who were out in the public sphere there did not talk much about disability. They tried to pass as nondisabled as much as they could. The few organizations that existed for people with disabilities were not operated or organized by people with disabilities. Buildings were not accessible. There were no laws protecting the rights of people with disabilities.

Disability in Africa had its own connotations. For instance, there were some people who felt that my disability was a curse. They believed that I, or my parents, must have done something wrong. A few felt that I *was* my disability. They never tried to separate the two—my disability and my actual personhood. When they spoke about me, they did so with authority because they had interacted with me in the past or had spent a few occasions with me. Sadly, they focused more on my impairment than on my heart and soul or my personhood. Some of these individuals misconstrued what living a meaningful and active life meant. They felt that such a life was only for certain individuals who are considered normal. In this culture, the person with a disability who attempts to live the same kind of life is labeled as stubborn and given other stigmatizing attributes.

Others told me that I ought to be angry with my parents for not making sure I was given the polio vaccine as a baby. Another response that dominated our community was the idea that I had to be healed. I was constantly taken in and out of religious rituals from the time I was a baby. Everyone thought they were doing us a huge favor by extending an invitation to us whenever there was a national Christian healing crusade. I went to so many that I can't even count them all. On numerous occasions, I was led to the front where the prayers where held at the national stadium. Sometimes, I tried so hard to get healed. It never worked. I was judged as someone without any deep faith. I was also told that perhaps I liked my condition because I wanted people to feel sorry for me. It was confusing: What did they mean about my lack of faith? Did they really understand what it meant to live daily on crutches? Did they really know what faith was all about? Wasn't my life on crutches and a brace a demonstration of faith?

Even as a child, I always felt uncomfortable with that kind of spirituality. It affected me emotionally and psychologically. Every time I was invited to those crusades, I wept internally. I never wanted to go because I felt that I was a spectacle for others to watch. If God wanted to heal me, why did He not do it quietly? Was God about a show? Did I have to get in front of the entire nation for God to heal me? Those were questions that often ran through my mind.

As an ardent Christian, I have pondered reflectively on the issues of faith, healing, and disability. Essentially, I believe that faith is not just about dropping one's crutches and walking the traditional way for all to see. Rather, it is far more than that. It is using the gifts that you have to succeed. It is about getting up in the morning and going to school. It is accepting and loving yourself when others have issues with you. It is doing many of the things that no one expects you to do. For me, healing is more about one's perception and one's spiritual, emotional, and psychological health. It is more about how one feels or looks inside than about trivial outer appearances.

However, social stigma and the rejection of disability existed when I was a child, and it created problems for my parents and me. They had challenges getting me into a couple of private schools they wanted me to attend. The headmistress at one of the schools was concerned about my ability to go to and from the restrooms when I needed to. She wondered whether there was a need to hire someone to be with me in school. She was clueless about my physical challenges, and, sadly, she was not prepared to invest in me, or in others with disabilities.

Eventually, when I was accepted into an elementary school, it was not one of the best schools in town. However, my parents welcomed the admission, as it was the only one we received. Although my parents were not highly educated or affluent, they did have the social capital that enabled me to gain access to a "regular" school. My uncle, a civil engineer, was trained in Great Britain. He was a voracious reader. He had read about people who had physical disabilities and had gone to school. He also came to our home regularly and interacted with me daily. He advocated strongly that I had the intelligence to do well in school. As far as he was concerned, I should be in school.

Later, my maternal grand-aunt was also influential in securing me a place at another school, which I moved to because it was closer to our home. The staff at this school also had concerns. However, as a transfer student, overcoming these concerns was much easier. I had been accepted in a school before, and I had reports to show for it. I was also blessed because my grand-aunt was a board member of the school at that time. She lived next door to a teacher from the school, and two of my cousins were also enrolled there. With these relationships and family connections, my grand-aunt was able to convince the headmistress that I was going to be fine. All the aforementioned parties were strong advocates for my enrollment at Roosevelt Elementary School, where I ultimately received my primary education.

Schooling in Sierra Leone was based on the British system. Roosevelt Elementary had some qualified teachers, but a few had no formal teacher training. None of them had any training in special education or had taken courses on disability issues or educating children with disabilities. Considering the situation they found themselves in, my teachers did their best to accommodate a child with a disability. The school was not accessible, but, thankfully, my classrooms were on the first level. There were no sensitization workshops or disability trainings for parents, teachers, and students. Many of the students welcomed me with open arms, but there were those outside my school community who teased me and called me names. In fact, within a few days of my arrival at Roosevelt, I was pushed by some kids into a gutter. I broke my arm and had to be in a cast for six weeks, which devastated me because I had to stay home from school during that time. I had already stayed home until my sixth birthday, and now, I was in the first grade and missing more days of school.

Throughout the early years of my academic journey, I ambulated with some very heavy elbow crutches and metal braces. I also had a metal corset all the way to my stomach, and my knees were slightly bent. It was painstakingly difficult to move around. It took forever to get to my destination. I developed calluses on my hands and feet. My feet were also very uncomfortable in my braces. Numerous times, I felt like ripping them apart and freeing myself from the pain. I also detested getting new braces, because it took me awhile to adjust to them.

Walking with crutches or a cane in Sierra Leone can be laborious because of the inaccessible sidewalks, streets, and buildings. The weather patterns and dirt roads also did not help. As a result of these obstacles in the environment, I fell very frequently. In fact, falls were almost a daily part of my life. Once, I fell in the middle of the road while trying to cross the street, and I had to drag myself over to the other side before a car sped by. As I look back on that incident, I am immensely grateful to God for guiding me through that ordeal. Other memories of my early life are more positive. Secondary school turned out to be the most fruitful time in my life. It was a family tradition for all the male children in my father's family to attend the Sierra Leone Grammar School (it was an all-boys school). My older siblings were already at the school by the time I got there. I had seen them attend formal functions, and I loved the school's ceremonial attire and its annual celebrations. When it was time for me to make a decision to attend a secondary school, I had no problem choosing the family's alma mater.

After surmounting several medical and social obstacles to complete elementary school, I worked very hard during my first year of secondary school, and I was first in my class. I believed that my performance that year changed my teachers' and friends' perception of me. They recognized that I was as capable as anybody else. I had so many admirers and developed a relationship with many of my teachers. One of those was my English teacher, a remarkable man who opened his home to me. He encouraged me, loved me, and cared deeply for me as if I were his own child. Like my mother, he never saw a difference when he looked at me. They both saw a human being, a child with the potential to flourish if given the chance.

Nevertheless, several years ago, although I had developed a rock-solid faith that was carrying me through life's difficulties, I still had concerns about the negative meanings people attributed to my disability. Some people had imagined a less-promising life for me. I never did have such a life, but I did worry about their perceptions. I lost my mother in the summer of 1993, and I have lived without her now for more than twenty years. I have lived independently and have gone through so much in life; I am a new person. I fundamentally view life differently now, and I do not let negative perceptions affect me anymore. The field of disability studies has helped shape my life and my views about disability. It is amazing how theory, disability scholarship, and spirituality have given me the words that I never before had to articulate my genuine feelings about disability. First, I have always felt that all human beings have their own imperfections. As a teenager, I argued that all human beings had a disability. Today, as a student in a doctoral program in education with an emphasis in disability studies, I do not believe that all human beings have disabilities but, rather, that we all have our imperfections and that normalcy does not exist.

In fact, the problem that normalcy creates is the belief that if you do have a disability, you have a problem, or that if you are a person without a disability, you are capable or "normal." This notion affects what we perceive or fail to perceive about people with disabilities. Instead of focusing on whether or not people with disabilities are normal, we should be welcoming of their differences and seek ways to learn from them and support them to become more productive and self-fulfilled human beings.

As I take a retrospective view of my life, I am grateful for my disability. I do not harbor any grudges against those who have misunderstood, labeled, or tried to harm me or cause me any pain. Rather, my disability has given me a different perspective about life; I am able to appreciate, empathize with, and sympathize with others who have disabilities because I know what it feels like to live with a disability. I have also lived to understand that perfection is a myth. All of us are aging and will likely face a disability sooner or later. Today, I am flourishing with polio because I now appreciate my talents and gifts. I do not focus so much on what I cannot do; rather, I focus on my strengths. I realize the importance of political involvement in ensuring a socially just world for all human beings.

VI.4

Learning to See Myself in the Mirror

ADAM P. NEWMAN

In June 2009, after completing an arduous sophomore year at Vassar College in Poughkeepsie, New York, I was informed that my childhood brain tumor had recurred. Eight years prior, at the age of thirteen, I had been diagnosed with a cerebellar astrocytoma, for which I required immediate surgery. Though I did not need radiation or chemotherapy after the surgery, the months that followed were very difficult nonetheless. Long before they found my tumor, I was diagnosed with fibromyalgia, a chronic health condition that causes a variety of symptoms; the ones that were and continue to be most prominent for me are chronic joint pain, headaches, and fatigue. In the wake of my surgery, the pain and fatigue that the trauma of the surgery had produced were piled on top of my usual fibromyalgia-related symptoms. Unsurprisingly, I ended up missing even more school after my surgery than the considerable amount I usually missed because of the fibromyalgia, but thanks to the very understanding people at my middle school, I was able

---

Adam P. Newman is a graduate of Vassar College and is currently completing a Ph.D. in English at Emory University. His dissertation examines the intersections of issues of disability, race, and dependency in representations of interracial caregiving in nineteenth-century American literature and culture. While at Emory, alongside his research, he has continued his community-building work through the university's Transforming Community Project and Disability Studies Initiative.

to do my work from home, attend for half days when that was all I could manage, and ultimately stay on grade level.

The five years that followed were far from easy. Not only did my fibromyalgia continue to affect me throughout high school, but being at a small school meant that my health status, particularly my brain tumor, were common knowledge to all and in large part defined my on-campus identity; I was known as "the sick kid," and even by some malicious and ignorant classmates as the "brain tumor boy," who could be contagious. When you add to all this the fact that I had been seeing a behavioral therapist, since my original diagnosis of fibromyalgia, for chronic depression, it might suffice to say that high school was no walk in the park for me, though, admittedly, it is difficult for most teenagers. What ultimately made my experience different from that of the average misunderstood teen, however, was the singular role my health problems played in my burgeoning attempts at self-definition. If our teenage years are when we begin to exercise independence and cultivate independent identities, what are we to do when such independence is simply not possible? As I struggled to embody even a limited amount of independence, it seemed to me more and more that I was being defined and could only define myself by what I couldn't do, rather than what I could.

When I finally began college, I dedicated myself to leaving that stigmatized identity of my childhood and adolescence behind and instead strove to pass as "normal" and "healthy." At the urging of my mother, I did my due diligence and registered with the office of disability services, so I would not be penalized for those unavoidable absences or missed deadlines as a result of my health, but I rarely told my professors about the nature of my disabilities that necessitated such accommodations and all but hid such accommodations as best as possible from my fellow students. For the first two years, I succeeded in "passing" to a large extent. Very few people knew of my chronic illness, brain tumor, or mental health issues, and those who had some knowledge of these matters did not know the extent of my health issues or the effects they had had on me.

The recurrence of my childhood brain tumor changed all that. My mental state deteriorated noticeably. The emotional toll of my attempts at continuing to "pass" at my summer job as a camp counselor became increasingly unbearable. Long days were spent trying to mask my ever-present anxieties until I returned to my room for a night filled with uncontrollable tears. By the time I returned to Vassar for my junior year, still unsure of when, precisely, I would even have surgery and what might happen during or after it, I had completely given up trying to "pass." It had just become too much work. Finally, I made my tenuous position clear to the administration, told my friends, and informed my colleagues and teachers. Admittedly, most people reacted much better than my classmates in middle school had, but nonetheless, few really knew how to respond to such news or even talk to me after finding out. Awkward about broaching the issue, many simply avoided me. Yet again, I felt the increasing pain of isolation, and my depression continued to worsen as I awaited my surgery.

But then something happened. The prior spring, while attending a conference on critical race theory with my professor—and now friend—Tyrone R. Simpson II, I had been intrigued by the lack of any mention of disability or health in the rich and multifaceted discussions of intersecting identities that had touched on seemingly every other type of identity: race, ethnicity, nationality, gender, sexuality, class, and so on. When I queried Professor Simpson about this absence, he informed me that he himself knew little about the issue of disability, but he was able to recommend the work of a few scholars. That fall, withdrawn and isolated as I awaited my impending surgery, I began reading the works he had mentioned, beginning with Tobin Siebers's *Disability Theory* (2008) and Rosemarie Garland-Thomson's *Extraordinary Bodies* (1997). Enraptured by both texts, I began following their references to more works in the field that I came to know as disability studies. While other students pre-gamed and partied, I continued to read, devouring Irving Zola's *Missing Pieces* (1982), Simi Linton's *Claiming Disability* (1998), and Lennard Davis's *Enforcing Normalcy* (1995), among many other texts.

In reading those works, I began to see my own education, particularly in the humanities and social sciences (as an English major with a minor in cultural anthropology), in a startlingly new way. But more importantly, I began to see myself in a new way. Describing her own experience as a lesbian in college well before the acceptance and embrace of LGBTQ communities, Adrienne Rich writes in her essay "Invisibility in Academe" that "when someone with the authority of a teacher, say, describes the world and you are not in it, there is a moment of psychic disequilibrium, as if you looked into a mirror and saw nothing" (Rich 2011, 218). As I read works in the field of disability studies, especially those that dealt with representations of disability in literature and culture, my primary area of study, I began to realize how little I had ever seen or heard spoken about experiences similar to my own in the classroom. Further, I realized that I had never before been exposed to the idea that my disabilities could be thought of as anything more than impairments that prevented me from being a fully functioning human being—as "problems" to be courageously faced and overcome. I certainly never thought of them as the material for an identity, except in a highly stigmatizing way, nor did I think of them as sources for critical insights.

All that changed when I found disability studies. I began to see myself in the mirror. I didn't have to be a lone "sick kid" trapped in his room; I could be a member of a community—a community of those who had been excluded and overlooked because of their various physical and mental disabilities but who still had something important to contribute to the world. While various scholars have recently debated the academic merits and pitfalls of disability studies as a form of "identity studies,"[1] my personal experience testifies to the continued relevance and necessity of the field for the identity (re)construction of students with disabilities.

I know for a fact that my own experience as a student with a disability, marked by isolation and the inability to see myself in the mirror of academe, is hardly unique. Shortly after my return to campus following surgery, I began to realize that, in addition to those books and articles, I needed something else, something more visceral—I needed a physical community of people with disabilities. Such a community need not be composed of people with the exact same disability; rather, it needs only to be bound together by a common understanding of what it means to live outside the "norm" because one's body or mind has been designated "different." As I soon realized, however, while there were groups for students of color, LGBTQ students, and so on, no such organized community of or for students with disabilities existed or had seemingly ever existed at Vassar College. Vassar is hardly unique in that regard. Few colleges have student organizations for people with disabilities. For the most part, institutions of higher education seem to be satisfied with having an office of disability services that provide such students with accommodations. Colleges remain hesitant to recognize students with disabilities as an actual constituency and group, rather than just a collection of "broken" individuals that they are legally mandated to accommodate.[2]

Newly equipped to recognize this lack through disability theory, I decided that if I couldn't find my place at Vassar, I would make a space for myself. Thus, I turned my limited energy toward finding other students with disabilities on campus and creating the community I believed that we all so desperately needed. It was slow going at first. Thanks to an experimental therapy group explicitly for students with chronic health conditions, organized by the student counseling center, I began to meet a few other people with disabilities who had experienced similar struggles at Vassar. From there, I began to advertise for group meetings and talk to everyone I could about the idea.

That spring, after I returned perhaps too soon from my surgery, the group finally began to hold regular meetings and go about attracting new members. After some very tense, though illuminating, meetings about how we each chose to identify and how the group could be most inclusive for those who identify differently (whether as disabled students or students with disabilities[3]), we finally decided to call ourselves Access, which we felt expressed the goal that we were all ultimately striving toward. In those early days, we had no budget and, in fact, were not even officially recognized as a student organization, but we had each other, and that was a huge step for all of us. Like my experience learning to see myself through disability studies, we all learned to better see and accept ourselves through each other. Our shared stories and mutual understandings affirmed those identities we had all been hiding, or hiding from. Some of our disabilities—including my own—were invisible, and thus we had been able to hide the very fact that we were disabled at all from those around us. But even those others whose disabilities were far too visible to be literally hidden shared that they, too, had been hiding from identifying with their disabilities.

The next year, we continued to meet and began to think about how we could reach out to more students, as well as what we could do for students beyond merely meet for fellowship. Ultimately, we decided to take advantage of our institution's proclivity for academically mediated discussions, and in collaboration with Vassar's office of disability services, we managed to bring Tobin Siebers, the noted disability studies scholar, to campus to publicly discuss disability from an academic perspective. The academic and critical nature of Siebers's lecture on the visual stereotyping of women with psychosocial disabilities proved particularly useful for Access, as the discussions that ensued among students, faculty, and administrators not only raised the profile and legitimacy of disability as a subject for conversation on campus but also suggested the need for conversations to move beyond the facile stereotypes so often used to talk about disability, some of which Siebers had directly dismantled.

While it was disability studies that helped me to first see myself as a person with disabilities, and to see myself as such in a positive light, it was ultimately the disability community, which those scholarly insights had given me the ability to imagine and the confidence to create, that helped me to see myself as a potential scholar of disability studies. Outside of Siebers's lecture, I found myself repeatedly sharing the vocabularies and frameworks I had learned from disability studies in personal conversations, Access meetings, and classrooms. Most often, what I shared was related to the foundational insight of disability studies—namely, that there is no necessary correspondence between the lived experience of disability and the social meaning that is assigned to disability and people with disabilities. Over and over again, I found that illuminating this distinction—between what some theorists have called "impairment," the literal embodied experience of a nonnormative body or mind, and "disability," the socially determined identity imposed on those with such impairments—freed people with disabilities to finally fully recognize and articulate the gross inequality of their treatment (Oliver 1990). Further, this approach then allowed them to begin divesting some of the negative feelings they had internalized about themselves and their worth and to form supportive relationships and communities that, through mutually supportive relationships, would allow them to advocate for fairer treatment of students with disabilities and greater accessibility. The palpable power that these encounters produced, which so closely mirrored my own earlier encounter with disability studies texts, made it increasingly clear that teaching and continuing to foster such moments was my purpose.

With all this in mind in my senior year, I applied to graduate programs in English with a particular emphasis on disability studies, with the hope that I might use my existing literary and cultural analysis skills to better understand precisely how disability has been represented in American literature and culture and what the consequences of those representations have been. Luckily, I ended up at Emory University, where there is a profusion of disability studies scholars to work with and learn from, including Benjamin Reiss, Sander Gilman, and the author of one of the first disability studies books I ever read, Rosemarie Garland-Thomson. But while Emory has and will continue to provide me with a wealth of opportunities and support for development as a scholar of American Literature and disability studies, it will always be those first experiences at Vassar, of reading *Extraordinary Bodies* and *Disability Theory* in bed and meeting with fellow students with disabilities in the Jade Parlor, that shaped the rest of my personal and professional life as a student and scholar with disabilities. It was then and there that I began to see the world, and myself, in a radically new way: for the first time, I saw that I was not alone, and no one with a disability was alone; we needed only to find each other and make those communities that we didn't find ready-made for us.

NOTES

1. See, in particular, Davis 2002, Mollow 2004, and Siebers 2008.

2. And schools only make such accommodations when those students can show extensive (and, I will say, sometimes absurd) documentation of their disability.

3. For an in-depth discussion of such debates, see the voluminous literature arguing for and against "person-first" language in disability studies and by disability activists and advocates. For a notable recent intervention countering the long-standing uncritical dominance of person-first language, see Brown 2011. For a more general overview of the debate, see Dunn and Andrews 2015.

REFERENCES

Brown, L. 2011. "The Significance of Semantics: Person-First Language; Why It Matters." *Autistic Hoya* (blog), August 4. Available at http://www.autistichoya.com/2011/08/significance-of-semantics-person-first.html.

Davis, L. 2002. *Bending Over Backwards: Disability, Dismodernism, and Other Difficult Positions*. New York: New York University Press.

Dunn, D. S., and E. E. Andrews. 2015. "Person-First and Identity-First Language: Developing Psychologists' Cultural Competence Using Disability Language." *American Psychologist* 70 (3): 255–264.

Garland-Thomson, R. 1997. *Extraordinary Bodies: Figuring Physical Disability in American Culture and Literature*. New York: Columbia University Press.

Mollow, A. 2004. "Identity Politics and Disability Studies: A Critique of Recent Theory." *Michigan Quarterly Review* 43 (2): 269–296.

Oliver, M. 1990. *The Politics of Disablement*. London: Macmillan.

Rich, A. 2011. "Invisibility in Academe." In *The Broadview Anthology of Expository Prose*, edited by L. Buzzard, D. LePan, M. Moser, and T. Roberts, 217–220. Peterborough, Canada: Broadview.

Siebers, T. 2008. *Disability Theory*. Ann Arbor: University of Michigan Press.

VI.5

Writing Myself into Madness
and Disability Studies

REBEKAH MORAS

T here is a feminist idea that scholars should sincerely and transparently write themselves in to all their work. This means that rather than claiming objectivity and neutrality, we should purposefully disclose our social and personal identities, allowing others to judge our claims within the context of who we are. I seek to "write myself in" here, as an aspiring academic in disability and gender studies. I am from a lower-middle-class, white, European American family. My psychiatric disability (a.k.a. "madness") is unapparent to most people most of the time, so I do not typically deal with ableism directed at me personally. However, I am usually a fat woman, and this comes with some overt experiences of discrimination. I am cisgendered, queerly heterosexual, and sex positive. I am not a primary caregiver, so I put a lot of my resources into my own mental health

Rebekah Moras obtained her disability studies Ph.D. in August 2015. Her dissertation was a feminist mixed-methods evaluation of the Illinois Imagines curriculum. While at the University of Illinois at Chicago, she was a community educator in the Sexuality and Disability Consortium, worked in a graduate research position at the Great Lakes Americans with Disabilities Act Center, and had teaching assistantships in the psychology and gender and women's studies departments. Currently, she works in a research and evaluation position for the Center for Human Development at the University of Alaska Anchorage. Ultimately, her dream is to become a disability studies professor in a critical cultural studies department, braiding intersectional thinking into the national Association of University Centers on Disabilities network.

supports. I have been able to manage my impairments in part because of my minimal experience of interlocking oppressions. I believe I am both lucky and responsible for my life situations, but probably not in equal measure. I openly disclose all of this here in order to position myself, to acknowledge my unearned privileges, and to not risk minimizing the barriers to mental health that exist for other people with disabilities.

Going Mad

Growing up and going to high school in Alaska, I went from being a quiet, studious, conscientious young woman obsessed with "health" to binge drinking, smoking, and dropping out my sophomore year. The change in my character was so profound that I was unrecognizable to family and friends who had known me my whole life. I attributed my hopeless emptiness and anger to external factors, like my family life, and structural inequalities of violence, sexism, religion, and the pressures of "society" to be "normal." In so many ways, my hopelessness with these systems was not unfounded. I think that hopelessness can be an expected reaction to social injustice, disparities of access, and environmental destruction; however, I almost could not survive my despair. I have often wondered if the difference between people deeply and personally affected by our world's injustices and people who are not is one of the foundational differences between mad and non-mad people.

Those closest to me explained the changes in my personality in various ways. For my distant father, I was simply being a teenager. For some of my extended WASP (White Anglo-Saxon Protestant) family, I needed more discipline and to be more productive and less selfish. I was commonly told that I was not sincere enough in praying for alleviation of my suffering, or else that I was being taught a spiritual lesson. (There were some supportive people in my religious circles, although they were outnumbered.) Only from my mother, after she reached out to many other parents, did I hear the words, "mental illness." I denied everyone's attempt to "help" me and especially resented those who got in the way of my most destructive behaviors, which were, ironically, the life-saving coping mechanisms that best assuaged my despair.

As my white, middle-class privilege dictated, I had always dreamed of both traveling and going to college. After leaving high school early, I chose travel first because I thought getting away from it all would alleviate my unrelenting melancholy. Yet, as I traveled, I continued to be just as reckless, hopeless, and desperate as before. I remember one particularly beautiful day on a train in Switzerland, staring out over a serene and picturesque landscape of Alpine foothills, replete with bell-hung dairy cows and crisp, clean air, and feeling nothing. No joy, no wonderment, no gratitude. I was devoid of all emotion, too empty even to cry; nothing that used to comfort me brought any relief. I could not remember ever feeling happiness, contentment, or even just neutrality, and I could not imagine I would ever feel them again.

The worst part was the sense that I was to blame for my incessant emptiness, that my ingratitude, self-absorption, and lack of willpower were my fault, that my own laziness was the reason it was hard to get up, shower, dress, eat, and move through the world doing the most basic and unremarkable things. I returned home and got my GED, but since I wasn't "productive" enough to go out of state to a private university, as many of my peers did, I enrolled at the local state university instead.[1] I had intense difficulty passing my classes the first semester, and I barely kept it together. The "cloud," as my mother called my shadowy moods, as unpredictable and varied as the weather, still lingered heavily on me, and I couldn't understand how my dream of college was failing as miserably as travel had.

Throughout all of this, my mother continued to insist that something was "wrong" and that perhaps I should seek professional help. I refused to heed her until I almost failed a second semester. I finally admitted that both my lifetime dreams, of travel and college, were crumbling, and I was just too out of it to care. My first semester was in 2001, and I went to class on September 11. Watching TV at my house, I saw the planes fly into the Twin Towers, and then I drove to my human sexuality class. People in my class were crying, and all the students in the military had been called back to base, on high alert. We talked for a while about our fear and confusion, sharing what we knew, and then the teacher dismissed us to go and "be with our families." While I am mystified and aghast to admit it now, I felt even less on that day than I had during my travels. It was not that I didn't understand the horror and agony of it all; it was just that I didn't feel it—I couldn't feel it. I wondered at how I felt so little when those around me seemed totally overwhelmed.

Writing from a disability studies perspective, Margaret Price (2011) cites a story by Geneen Roth about being in Guatemala after a major earthquake that left many in the community experiencing post-traumatic stress disorder. I resonate with how Roth felt somehow at home in the chaos, fear, and grief. As a person with anxious, intruding thoughts that she attributes to post-traumatic stress disorder, the result of childhood physical and sexual abuse, Roth felt at ease in an environment where everyone was experiencing the kind of mental distress she felt on a regular basis: "It was so familiar to me, this irrationality, this insistent need to protect myself from the possibility of disaster at any moment" (Price 2011, 51).

I connect with this passage because it explains a lot about how I experienced my own bodymind on and around September 11: the familiarity of heightened anxiety, depression, and offbeat affect reflects my emotional landscape as a person who is often mentally unwell. As Price writes about

Roth's experience, "While the sense of horror is, well, horrible, there may also be a feeling of relief at finally no longer being the only person around who shakes unpredictably, loses words, can't sleep, can't get it together" (2011, 51). I now attribute part of my lack of emotion during crises like September 11 to my madness: I often do not feel things when I am "supposed" to; I have delayed emotional reactions to events of joy, disappointment, and horror, sometimes experiencing my own feelings days, weeks, and even months after the incident. I am often deeply sad for no apparent reason.

I finally made a counseling appointment at the university, as so many did during that time, with the excuse that it was to appease my mother but actually with the hope that someone could "fix" me. I sat down in a tiny office across from a slight woman with glasses and a gentle voice. I folded my hands on my lap and was suddenly overwhelmed with emotion. When I tried to speak, I was unable to, and I cried for most of the hour instead. Her brow was furrowed with concern as she said something like, "Sweetheart, let me take you over to the student health center across the hall, because this is academic advising."

That was the beginning of my ongoing work with a team of psychological and psychiatric professionals, and it has now been over a decade since that day in academic advising. At the beginning, I was strongly against taking medication, and only after a year of therapy did I agree to try. To my relief and dismay, when I began taking medication, I did start to notice welcome changes in my moods and a reduction in symptoms like panic attacks, un-relenting anxious rumination, and insomnia. I did not want to take medica-tion, and I still resent it sometimes. I believe medication is not for everyone and that it usually works best in conjunction with trauma-informed thera-pies, developing political consciousness, critical education and community, movement, healthier boundaries, stress management, adequate sleep, experimental nutrition, physical connection, and controlled substance use, among other measures. Such changes can be intensive commitments, and even then they are usually frustratingly slow and comprehensive processes that take place over time.

In my first year of therapy without medication, I was able to reduce my binge drinking somewhat, which helped me complete my classes but did little for dismantling the chronic and unpredictable hopelessness of experi-encing the cloud. The necessity, for me, of developing a critical cultural stud-ies consciousness in conjunction with my use of medication and therapies exemplifies the complexity of disabilities as both social constructions and impairments; I got what I needed through both sociopolitical and medical interventions. The next section explores my experience with intersectional disability studies in fostering access and living with my mental unwellness in healing ways.

Disability Studies: Connection and Politicization

After beginning treatment, I was able to complete my undergraduate degree in psychology and German. During this time, I discovered the disability rights movement by accident during a paid internship at the Center for Human Development, the University Center for Excellence in Developmental Disabilities in Education, Research, and Service (UCEDD) for the state of Alaska.[2] It was through this work that I knew I wanted to pursue disability studies, but I needed something to improve my résumé in order to get into a program. After quite a few rejections, I was awarded a Fulbright Teaching Assistantship to northern Germany, with the incredible support of my German professor at the University of Alaska Anchorage.[3] From Germany, I applied for the disability studies program at the University of Illinois at Chicago (the UCEDD for the state of Illinois) and began the program in 2008.

During my graduate studies, I wanted to bridge what I perceived to be the divide between disability studies and madness by working with the organization Erasing the Distance, a theater company that turns interviews with people who have mental illness into performance monologues, with the aim of reducing stigma. Even though the company, at the time of my graduate study, did not make an explicit identification of mental illness as disability or connect to broader disability art and culture communities, it was still a cathartic experience for me when my personal story was turned into a performance piece in which I was easily recognizable. Rather than wait to be publically outed by the piece, I chose to officially disclose my status to the Sexuality and Disability Consortium (SDC), a group I worked with on our campus. The SDC was a safe space for me, and the group actually applauded me for my disclosure, which I was tickled by. Bolstered by the experience, I disclosed to another student in the program when we saw each other unexpectedly in a psychiatry office. While I was elated and excited about the possibility of finally claiming a madness identity with others, the colleague I had run into was less than enthused. Aghast, she looked at me and replied in a hushed tone, "Oh, no! I'm not disabled. I'm not ready to go there yet."

I was a little shocked and disappointed by her disclaimer, but I realized that I can disclose or not disclose my own psychiatric disability whether or not others do, and, regardless, I continue to feel welcome and accepted in disability studies and in crip communities of Disabled people. I use a capital D to indicate politicized disability communities, spaces where disability art and culture flourish and where the social model is central, even as impairments are accounted for. Through Disability art, culture, and disability studies, I have found community and have been able to give myself permission to make the most of medical interventions, even as I am critical of them. Through disability studies, I am accepted and nurtured, as much in times of active madness as in those of relative balance. I continue managing my psychiatric disability largely within medical and rehabilitative frameworks outside of disability studies. Yet I have been able to work with feminist and disability-positive practitioners who have supported me in framing my experiences within social and institutional contexts and who have not solely individualized my madness.[4]

In October 2015, after many years of her own shaking unpredictably, losing words, not sleeping, and not being able to get it together, my little sister took her own life. As I move with grief, and contemplate yet again our experiential and biological history as a family, I believe all the more fervently that disability studies has saved my life. In disability studies spaces, as well as in spaces within the UCEDD network, the accommodations I need are seamlessly built into my worlds. I have the flexibility and health insurance I need to go to medical and therapeutic appointments; I can do self-care while I work; I can rest, lie down, stretch, publically cry and tremble, request fragrance-free meetings, work from home, and be open about my madness. While suicide is not an inevitable outcome of madness, I feel terror in knowing that my sister and I struggled in many similar ways. A member of my chosen family reminds me that everyone has been young, but not all of us will know what it is to be old. My disability studies life has made possible my survival into my thirties, not within a framework of "supercrip" passing, isolation, and shame, but in one of complex discovery, critical interdependence, and intermittent healing. I am hopeful to experience getting older, and I believe that disability studies will continue to create space for that possibility.

NOTES

1. Thinking back on my dream of a private, Ivy League education, I recognize the unexamined classism there, and I am grateful to have stayed home.

2. Since 1963, the UCEDDs have provided research, services, and information dissemination related to developmental disabilities. Each state and territory has at least one UCEDD, with a total of sixty-seven throughout the country; refer to the Association of University Centers on Disabilities (AUCD) website, at http://www.aucd.org/template/index.cfm.

3. Liebe Natasa: Du bist für immer und ewig meine allerliebste Professorin und Freundin, und ich liebe dich sehr (Dear Natasa: You are forever and always my beloved professor and friend, and I love you very much).

4. These practitioners include C. Montgomery, J. Simon, P. Smith, M. Serrato, and Brock. I thank them for helping me survive.

REFERENCE

Price, M. 2011. *Mad at School: Rhetorics of Mental Disability and Academic Life*. Ann Arbor: University of Michigan Press.

VI.6

Autism Isn't Speaking

Autistic Subversion in Media and Public Policy

LYDIA X. Z. BROWN

Who Speaks for Autism?

A round seven in the morning on a cold November Wednesday, I hurried as fast as I could over the red brick sidewalks in Foggy Bottom, one gloved hand gripped firmly around the handle of a large black crate filled with flyers and posters painted with bright colors. One of my best friends followed, his arms wrapped around larger posters on thick stock

Lydia X. Z. Brown (Autistic Hoya) is a genderqueer and transracially/transnationally adopted east asian autistic activist, writer, and speaker whose work has largely focused on violence, especially in institutionalization, incarceration, and policing, against multiply marginalized disabled people. Brown is chairperson of the Massachusetts Developmental Disabilities Council and serves on the board of the Autism Women's Network. Brown is lead editor of *All the Weight of Our Dreams*, the first-ever anthology by autistic people of color, and has been honored by the White House, the Washington Peace Center, the National Council on Independent Living, the Disability Policy Consortium of Massachusetts, Pacific Standard, and Mic. Brown's work has been featured in various anthologies, including *Criptiques, Torture in Healthcare Settings, Feminist Perspectives on Orange Is the New Black*, and *QDA: A Queer Disability Anthology*, and periodicals, including *Tikkun, Sojourners, Disability Intersections, Black Girl Dangerous*, the *Establishment, Hardboiled Magazine, POOR Magazine*, and the *Washington Post*.

Acknowledgment: I am grateful for support and comments from Shain M. Neumeier and Corey Sauer in preparing this chapter, as well as comments from my editors, Alison, Michelle, and Leila.

featuring hand-painted slogans such as "Civil Rights, Not a Cure," "Autistic People Deserve Better," and "Nothing About Us Without Us." Once we had everything ready, five of us took up position on the corner of Twenty-First and H Streets, where we would stay for the next four hours. Ultimately, our numbers would swell to about fifteen. We spent our time chanting, speaking to passersby who paused on the sidewalk beside our protest, and chatting amicably among ourselves between reinvigorating cups of hot chocolate. Most of the passersby who looked curiously at our signs or paused to ask why we were demonstrating outside George Washington University's School of Public Affairs were students who knew little about the event going on inside. Less than twenty feet away, on the other side of the walls, the national organization Autism Speaks was hosting its first-ever National Policy and Action Summit. And much to the surprise of most who passed by, but likely without any surprise to the Autism Speaks executives who were used to protesters at their events across the country, we were protesting both the summit and the organization hosting it. As many of our signs suggested, our group was primarily made up of autistic people, joined by a few allies to our cause.[1]

In the relatively short history of the autistic rights and neurodiversity movements, the discourse propagated by Autism Speaks, as well as the social and political capital of the organization as an entity, have become prime sites of contention over the core question of *who represents autism*. The spokespersons for disability in general and autism in particular have historically been either the professionals—the researchers, clinicians, educators, and professors, who themselves are presumed to be nondisabled—or the nondisabled parents of disabled children. The dominance of abled people in reifying, defining, and categorizing disability has created the cultural conditions necessary to claim that disability, or, more specifically, autism, can speak or act as an amorphous, disembodied entity. Since such modes of disability advocacy rely on the presumed objectivity and social capital prescribed to so-called scientific accounts of disability rather than on lived experience, this discourse creates and maintains the erasure of the very existence of *the autistic*. Instead, as suggested in the infamous 2006 Ransom Notes campaign, I am merely a "normal" person whose mental faculties have been kidnapped and held hostage by the condition named autism. The answers that have been posited in much public discourse in response to questions of who represents autism, who is autistic, and how the autistic exists in relation to the neurotypical are steeped in the contours of ableism and compulsory ablenormativity.

In this chapter, I argue that autism itself does not speak, as suggested by Autism Speaks' name, though autistics do. Autistics speak and type and sign and flap and rock and echolale. Our collective voice and loud hands, simply by existing, work to resist and subvert the dominant narratives of autism and disability that inform much of autism representation in media and public policy. We are neither monolithic nor homogeneous, our communities and spaces neither universal nor united. The publication of Temple Grandin's 1986 memoir *Emergence: Labeled Autistic* (coauthored with Margaret M. Scariano), in which Grandin became one of the first to publicly challenge the prevailing ableist notion that autistics are incapable of either meaningful communication or self-awareness, laid the groundwork for the development of an autistic movement. Jim Sinclair's 1993 revolutionary address, "Don't Mourn For Us," at the International Conference on Autism in Toronto, in which an autistic first offered a new paradigm of autism as diversity in direct opposition to the dominant narrative of autism as tragedy, marked the beginning of the development of an autistic consciousness and an autistic movement. Followed by the seminal work of autistic activists like Cal Montgomery, Laura Tisoncik, Judy Singer, Mel Baggs (formerly known as Amanda), and Kassiane A. Sibley, and later by the rise of autistic-led organizations, the autistic community has come to develop its own history, cultural norms, iconic moments, and sites of resistance to the co-optation of autism and autistics (see, e.g., Baggs 2007; Baggs et al. 2006; Montgomery 2001). In seeking to subvert the demands of compulsory ablenormativity on autistics, we continue to develop new modes of resistance and resilience. In the context of a profoundly ableist society, even the existence of this (rather aesthetically autistic) chapter is a point of resistance, albeit one of many proliferated in academic, policy, and activist contexts where autistics have staked a claim in our collective fate.

What Do We Want to Say? Representing Autism without Autistic Representation

I'm standing at the front of a contemporary college classroom, the Power-Point slides with my presentation projected onto the screen behind me. I pause before I ask the attendees to raise their hands if they've ever heard of the organization Autism Speaks. Nearly all of the hands immediately shoot into the air. I tell them to keep their hand in the air if they've ever heard of the Autistic Self Advocacy Network. There are two remaining. I've posed the same question in many other presentations. The results rarely change.

Autism Speaks, which bills itself as the world's largest science and advocacy organization, first came into existence in February 2005, when millions of dollars from wealthy and white cofounders Bob and Suzanne Wright and their celebrity cronies created a mammoth nearly overnight. In contrast, the Autistic Self Advocacy Network, which is the largest organization run by and for autistic people, was founded in November 2006 and rose to prominence for its successful, highly publicized organizing against the New York University Child Study Center's Ransom Notes ad campaign. The readily apparent differences in how frequently recognized these organizations are among the public are evidence of the power differentials in discourse on disability in general and on autism in particular. While Autism Speaks excludes autistic people from its leadership and has no meaningful representation of autistic people among its several advisory boards, autistic people comprise the vast majority of the leadership of the Autistic Self Advocacy Network. Until more than ten years after its founding, there had never been a single openly autistic person on Autism Speaks' board of directors, and there are still none in its executive leadership. The presence of only a handful of openly autistic people in any even peripherally leadership role constitutes tokenism at best and brazen mockery at worst.

When I ask whether you, well-meaning stranger trying to raise money for autism to help autistic people, want to actually talk to autistic people, I want to say, "Wait. Stop. Listen." But then you glare and crumple the flyer I've handed you before striding away into the sea of people walking for Autism Speaks. I'm left with wanting to say anything to make you stop and come back but not saying anything at all because—because—because none of you will even so much as look at me with anything other than pity or contempt or anger. Those words don't come, but the scripted words printed on a handy cheat sheet—those do. This is autism.

Autism Speaks relies on ableist rhetoric and fundraising tactics that promote fear-mongering and pity about autistic people rather than genuine understanding or acceptance. Only two days in advance of our protest in the national capital, Autism Speaks cofounder Suzanne Wright (2013) suggested that the existence of autistic people is comparable to the mass disappearance of three million children overnight. As if to underscore the idea that autism is terrifying and tragic, former Autism Speaks board member Harry Slatkin, whose wife, Laura, continues to serve on the board of directors, said that sometimes he hoped their autistic son, David, would drown in the backyard pond rather than "suffer like this all his life" (quoted in Guernsey 2006).

Evoking similar themes of violence, in the 2006 propaganda film *Autism Every Day*, Alison Tepper Singer, the Autism Speaks vice president at the time, says on camera that she considered putting her autistic daughter in the car and driving off a bridge.

I remember that was a very scary moment for me, when I realized I had sat in the car for about fifteen minutes and actually contemplated putting Jodie in the car and driving off the George Washington Bridge. And that would be preferable to having to put her in one of these schools. And it's only because of Lauren, the fact that I have another [nonautistic] child, that I probably didn't do it.

Jodie was in the room as her mother was talking about possibly killing her, on camera. Yet since the release of *Autism Every Day*, neither Autism Speaks nor Singer have ever retracted those statements or apologized for the violence embedded in them. In fact, the producer later admitted that they had intentionally staged the film to depict negative images (Liss 2006). The only way in which the film engaged autistics was to turn autistic lives into spectacle for public commodification and consumption. From this perspective, autistics are nonpersons, so why should they need apologies? It is no accident that those whose views on autism are lent the most credence and presumed authority are anyone *but* autistic people ourselves.

They do not need autistic people to represent autism when they have the tools of fear on their side, driving forward with relentless terror. In the Autism Speaks 2009 public-service advertisement "I Am Autism," an ominous voice-over identifying itself as autism threatens to destroy marriages, finances, and dreams (see Wallis 2009). In another 2009 announcement by Autism Speaks, "Neighbors," the narrator implies that autistic children cannot have friends until their parents subject them to compliance-based behavioral interventions to suppress natural movements. After all, within a narrative dependent on compulsory ablenormativity, the outward appearance of autistic signifiers matters far more than the bodily integrity and autonomy of autistic people. As if to further underscore their disregard for us, in 2013 Autism Speaks released the film *I Want to Say*, which ostensibly gives space for nonspeaking autistic people who use augmentative and alternative communication. After its release, the film received scathing criticism by Amy Sequenzia (2013), a prominent nonspeaking autistic activist, for its failure to meaningfully include or represent the perspectives of actually autistic people who communicate by typing.

Autism Speaks draws its power from its commitment to the ultimate elimination of autistic people through preventing or potentially curing autism. Suzanne Wright (2008) has stated that the organization's goal is to "eradicate autism for the sake of future generations." Autistic people are disproportionately targeted for abuse in homes and schools, rape, and other violent crimes, yet Autism Speaks does nothing to combat these appalling crimes. Instead, it chooses to funnel the vast majority of its research dollars and political clout into cure-oriented research in the hopes of eliminating autism. Yet the root cause of these problems is not autism but ableism. The solution to the problems that afflict autistic people hinges on deconstructing ableist hegemony while promoting research and policies to improve access to and quality of support services, eliminate legal barriers to equal access and opportunity, and challenge attitudinal barriers to full participation and inclusion in society. These are not goals that Autism Speaks supports or funds, yet Autism Speaks remains the most dominant voice in the conversation.

I Am Autism: Mediating Autistic Experience through Mass Media

In 2007, the New York University Child Study Center released a new publicity campaign with enormous billboard advertisements depicting messages in the style of ransom notes sent by different disabilities claiming to hold children captive. The newly formed Autistic Self Advocacy Network (ASAN) fought back furiously with a medium relatively new at the time, drawn from mostly uncharted territory. ASAN circulated an online petition demanding the removal of the advertisements and an apology for the offensive and dehumanizing language; it drew 1,200 signatures and coverage in the *New York Times* (Kaufman 2007). The New York University Child Study Center defended the campaign vigorously before finally conceding. With the withdrawal of the advertisements, autistic resilience moved from the subaltern to the revolutionary.

"Autistic" is a way of life more than it is merely a diagnostic label assigned to those who meet certain criteria printed in a psychiatrist's manual. To "live life the autly way"—as described in the tagline for Autreat, the first autistic-run autism conference—demands the deliberate rejection of mandatorily neurotypical modes of *being* in the world as much as it requires acceptance of autistic as a way of being, as a type of human existence, as a mode of knowledge production. Some terrifying monster, as implied in the Ransom Notes ad campaign, did not kidnap autistic people. We are not hostages to our own neurology. To suggest that behind the autism lies a "normal" (read: nonautistic) person is to suggest that autism is something separate from the person or incompatible with personhood. Yet such tropes litter popular literature, film, and television, as well as the spades of ostensibly journalistic articles in which autism figures as subject.

Mass media is rampant with representations of autism but so rarely represents autistics. Ask most people what they imagine when they think of autism, and two of the most common responses will be Temple Grandin (a wealthy white woman) and the 1988 film *Rain Man*. Grandin's life story has been largely mediated through the *overcomer* trope, or that of inspiration porn, while Dustin Hoffman's performance as Raymond Babbitt is largely exotified spectacle of the caricatured autistic savant. Elsewise, the public feeds on such representations as in *Simple Simon* (the 1996 novel, by Ryne Douglas Pearson, adapted into the 1998 film *Mercury Rising*) or, more recently, the Fox television show *Touch*, in which the magical autistic's convenient savant-like ability serves a plot device. In contrast, autistic people have found solace in finding television character representations that speak to autistic experiences, ranging from the BBC's Sherlock Holmes to Suzanne "Crazy Eyes" Warren on the Netflix series *Orange Is the New Black*, or from

Abed Nadir of the television series *Community* to the dragons in the novel *Seraphina*.

There is much sound and fury around the idea of autism as something to terrify or amaze or inspire, because acknowledging the realities of autistics as *ordinary* is necessarily dangerous in the context of an ableist world.

Sounding the Alarm: Politicizing Autistic Oppression in Public Policy

In 2009, President Barack Obama appointed Autistic Self Advocacy Network cofounder Ari Ne'eman to the National Council on Disability, an independent federal agency tasked with advising Congress and the administration on disability policy. Upon his confirmation by the Senate in 2010 following an anonymous hold, Ne'eman became the first openly autistic presidential appointee (Baker 2011, 1). Yet in November 2012, the U.S. House Committee on Oversight and Government Reform convened a hearing on autism with several witnesses—and not one was autistic (Autistic Self Advocacy Network 2012). This second event in our history is much more typical of the (lack of) autistic representation in policy making. And while, after public pressure, the committee ultimately invited both Ne'eman and another autistic leader—both white men—to testify, it is obvious that we face a crisis of representation in public policy (Williams 2012).

In 2011, I served on the Adult Services Subcommittee to the Massachusetts Special Commission Relative to Autism. During one of our monthly meetings, I had the gall to suggest that self-advocacy is an important goal. No sooner had I said "self-advocacy" than the nonautistic parent of an autistic adult interrupted to snap, "Don't exclude nonverbal people with autism!"

Baffled, I replied, "Excuse me, I didn't say anything about excluding nonverbal people."

"Not one nonverbal person is in this room," she retorted.

"But they are welcome to come," I said.

She nodded triumphantly. "They are welcome to come," she said, implying *in theory*, "but you won't see any of them here. They're not represented here."

She was operating on the presumption that self-advocacy—the radical act of naming for ourselves our own needs and desires, in whatever form we can or wish—is something limited to those considered "high-functioning" or "mildly disabled." She argued that discussing self-advocacy was necessarily exclusionary to people with significant impairments, especially those who do not use speech, and that the absence of nonspeaking autistics was evidence of this. The privilege assigned to those who use speech—myself included—creates an additional barrier to autistics who do not speak.

Thus, her argument essentially used the immediate absence of nonspeaking autistic people, a result of systematic exclusion, as the reason for shutting down any discussion of self-advocacy, which itself is necessary for including disabled people, including those who do not speak.

In March 2013, the Autistic Self Advocacy Network published a report documenting widespread discrimination against disabled people in need of life-saving organ transplants. Cases like those of Mia Rivera, who was initially denied a kidney transplant in January 2012 because she has an intellectual disability, and Paul Corby, who was, in a decision that was never reversed, denied a heart transplant in August 2012 because he is autistic, exemplify organ-transplant discrimination against disabled people (Ne'eman, Kapp, and Narby 2013, 4). In the same month as the report, the United Kingdom released the final report of a three-year study on medical discrimination that resulted in premature and preventable deaths of people with mental disabilities (Bingham 2013). Their investigative team uncovered over 1,200 cases where doctors made more rapid life-and-death decisions for patients with mental disabilities or issued do-not-resuscitate orders solely on the basis of disability status (Heslop et al. 2013).

In 2006, doctors at the University of Wisconsin Hospital and Clinics murdered a thirteen-year-old with multiple disabilities by withholding routine, life-saving treatment for pneumonia and rescinding artificial nutrition and hydration. Staff at his institution had been treating him successfully with standard antibiotics, but on the recommendation of bioethicist physician Dr. Norman Fost, the parents and attending doctor transferred him to the university hospital to discontinue treatment and end his life (*Disability Rights Wisconsin v. University of Wisconsin Hospital and Clinics*, 2009). The rationale was the assumption that he would have poor quality of life simply for living while disabled.[2]

The connection among lack of autistic representation in policy making, the comments that parents made during our committee meeting, and the pattern of often-fatal medical discrimination against autistics and other disabled people is clear. When we are excluded from the policy-making process, those in positions of authority enact policies that both reinforce existing discriminatory and violent practices and engender new ones. If that were not enough, those responsible for perpetuating these harms further their work through producing knowledge about autism and autistics that at once seeks to justify their violence and silence any proposed challenge to it. This pattern of rhetorical practice says that autistics who speak have no right to speak because their speech somehow excludes nonspeaking autistics, but people who don't speak must have nothing to say anyway. It argues, why bother saving the life of someone who is already dead—or worse than dead—from the moment they exited the womb?

We, Neighbors: Deconstructing Empathy, Reconstructing Empathy

I'm sitting in a hard-backed chair at a round table inside an administrator's office. The walls are painted a deep blue. It's tenth grade, and I've been at my new school for less than two months. "Is there something you want to talk to me about?" He looks directly at me, as if waiting for me to give a confession. I can feel my heart rate increase. I'm wondering if I failed a test already. So I tell him no, I don't think so. Then, staring right at me, he asks, "Are you planning a school shooting?"

There is a lot of background laying the groundwork for what happened that day, drawing from both my own history and the continuous pattern of criminalizing divergence and policing disability in particular. We have long contended with the profoundly ableist notions that it is better to be dead than to be disabled, that a disabled life is not worth living, that when we are killed, it is an act of mercy. In 1927, the U.S. Supreme Court ruled in *Buck v. Bell* that there was no rights violation when a woman with an intellectual disability was involuntarily sterilized. To prevent disabled reproduction or any reproduction deemed perverse, the court ruled that the involuntary procedure was not merely constitutionally acceptable but in the public interest. The exercise of such surveillance and control over nonnormative sexuality evidences the threat that disabled sexuality, as part of disabled existence, poses to ableist hegemony. If those who are sterilized are those whom ablenormative society does not wish to exist any longer, then there is no outrage—there is no empathy for the victims of ableist injustice.

On May 13, 2006, Karen McCarron murdered her three-year-old autistic daughter, Katie, by smothering her with a garbage bag. McCarron stated that she murdered Katie because her "autism had not been improving," and that she thought killing Katie would make her "complete" in heaven (*People v. Frank-McCarron*, 2010); the murder occurred four days after the release of Autism Speaks' *Autism Every Day* video. In the years since Katie's death, our community has marked the names of hundreds more who were likewise murdered by family members and other caregivers.

On March 8, 2012, on the same evening of the first vigil organized by autistic activist Zoe Gross to remember disabled people murdered by caregivers, Robert Latimer appeared on television to defend himself for murdering his disabled daughter, Tracy, in 1993 (Gross 2012, 238).

On March 30, 2012, our community hosted vigils across the United States. On March 31, 2012, four-year-old autistic Daniel Corby was murdered by his mother, who told police that she believed he would have no life or future without her (Littlefield 2012).

Our collective trauma has become the basis for another site of resistance—in mourning our dead, we affirm our shared experiences and our shared loss. Yet with each passing year, the lists we keep of those among us who were murdered grows longer, and the train of ableist violence trudges onward with no signs of stopping.

One of the most common myths about autistic people is that we are incapable of experiencing empathy. You can find language like "deficits in empathy" and "mindblind" (a doubly ableist term) in psychology and special education textbooks currently in use. The claim that we autistics cannot empathize is not merely ironic but profoundly disturbing when considering the lack of empathy for us when we become victims of murder. The effect is heightened when the perpetrators are the people who are supposed to love and care for us. Rather than having empathy for the victims of violence, the dominant narratives of disability urge empathy for the perpetrators. When parents face accusations of murdering their nondisabled children, the media present narratives of promising lives cut short at the hands of a monster. When the victims are disabled, the narrative changes—our lives, rather than our deaths, were the tragedies.

Atrocities like those committed by the reportedly autistic Adam Lanza, who murdered twenty-six people in an elementary school, and Elliot Rodger, who murdered six people in a rampage fueled by misogynistic rage and toxic masculinity, become tools to emphasize our supposed lack of empathy. Policy makers and journalists alike are consistent in labeling perpetrators of mass killings as mentally ill or autistic or both—as the mentally ill and autistic must, by neuronormative definition, lack empathy. This creates the environment of fear in which people like me and my friends face false accusations and insinuations solely on the basis of our neurologies. For black and brown autistic people whose experiences of ableism inevitably intersect with racism and white supremacy, opposition to fear-based policy proposals is ever more urgent in the face of increased state surveillance and the attendant danger of potentially deadly police violence.

The violent ironies of the clinical presumption that autistics are incapable of empathy manifest in other, less dramatic, but equally traumatizing patterns. Autistics are subjected to compliance training from an early age on the presumption that it is we who suffer from deficits in social development and interaction, and that our natural ways of moving and communicating are symptoms of autism that should be mitigated or eliminated. There is no pause to consider that perhaps the clinicians lack empathy for autistic experiences.

In Massachusetts, there is a residential institution where the prevailing philosophy of treatment is based on the use of painful punishment for behavioral modification. The prized machine of the Judge Rotenberg Educational

Center (JRC) is a device that administers painful electric shock at the push of a button for offenses as mild as closing your eyes to block the overwhelming fluorescent lights, covering your ears to shield them from loud sounds, or reaching to hold a staff member's hand to show that you care about them (Neumeier 2012, 211–212; Msumba 2015).[3] For over four decades, the JRC has successfully defended its practices before state courts and regulatory agencies as necessary medical treatment (Neumeier 2012, 206, 209). And while the JRC may be an outlier, the behaviorist model of psychology that underlies its work also informs the most common "evidence-based" autism intervention—applied behavior analysis, a treatment model that relies on compliance training for behavioral modification to meet the impossible goal of indistinguishability. (Ole Ivar Lovaas, who pioneered applied behavior analysis as well as contingent electric-shock aversive treatment, first used these treatment models in attempts to coerce boys displaying stereotypically feminine behavior to become more masculine in order to prevent them from "becoming" gay. One of his first subjects, touted as a shining example of success, ultimately committed suicide as an adult.)

The common thread among these cases is the use of ideas fabricated from ableism about the value, worth, or nature of autistic lives—ideas that simultaneously dehumanize autistic people through ascribing to us a lack of empathy and a propensity for violence while justifying the violence of torture and murder enacted against autistic bodies. There are peer-reviewed studies demonstrating that both autistics and those with psychiatric disabilities have lower rates of violence when compared to the general population. There are also numerous peer-reviewed studies demonstrating that we are significantly more likely to become victims of violence and abuse— findings substantiated in the lives and deaths of those like Mohammad Usman Chaudhry, Melissa Stoddard, Lexie Agyepong-Glover, and Jaelen Edge. Yet ableist hegemony makes it possible to ignore the stark realities of the ableism embedded in the assumption that autism is somehow a predictor of future violent acts. Ironically, policy makers and school administrators use the very same assumption that autistics are likely to perpetrate mass shootings to justify their own violence against us.

It is not so much that autistics necessarily lack the ability to empathize but that our society automatically assumes that those in positions of power have experiences that demand empathy, while those marginalized to the status of other do not and cannot.

Autistic Every Day: Embodiment, Performance, Aesthetic

I sit in a small, softly lit office buried deep within a building perplexingly known as the Car Barn. It's a running joke among Georgetown University students. It was never a barn, and it never had cars, and for the most part, no one really knows how the building got its name.[4] I'm meeting with the study-abroad adviser responsible for my region. I watch her pale-skinned fingers as she types something into her computer before turning to look at me, really look at me. She sits facing the wall, the door to her right. I'm sitting between her and the exit, my back to the door, unable to see the way out. There's probably less than three feet, less than a full meter, of space between us.

"I think you should tell your professors right away." She's talking about disclosing the fact that I'm autistic.

I shake my head and give her a pointed look. "Why do you say so?"

"Well . . . ." She grimaces a little, and I can almost see her squirming behind her eyes, behind the mask of professionalism. "Well, it's very obvious, when you're in a classroom, you know, that you're just . . . different."

I stiffen, staring directly at her, feeling my pulse quicken and tension spread throughout my body. "Excuse me? What exactly do you mean by that?"

I don't remember her excuse. She tells me that if I don't tell professors that I'm autistic, they will attribute my strange behavior to some other, more negative source. Open defiance? Utter disrespect? Total lack of interest? She tells me that I stand out in a classroom, leaving *and not for good reasons* unspoken but hanging just as heavily in the air as if she'd swung the words into my face.

"And when, exactly, have you ever been in a classroom at the same time as me, ever?" I throw the question right back at her, fighting to keep from shouting, because I know, I know, I know, that the slightest hint of aggression and I'll become the angry autistic, the bad mental cripple. And then, she hesitates. Because she knows as well as I do that she's never once been in a classroom at the same time as me.

But still, she insists. "But I was there during the orientation session." I asked too many specific questions. I was too precise. I made the wrong jokes. Everything I had said, everything I had done, she reduced it down to evidence of pathology, symptoms of autism—anything other than me simply being a twenty-year-old nervous about leaving the country for the first time in my memory.

What strikes me most, in retrospect, is the impossible choice she gave me and the social conditions that created the framework for that choice. I could choose to deny, suppress, or hide any outward signs of autism, any behavior or speech or movement whatsoever that marks me as autistic, and in so doing claim the right to humanity and dignity while sacrificing my own dignity and self-worth. Or else, I could choose to fight years of acculturation to profound internalized ableism and accept that I don't pass as well or as

often as I had secretly prided myself on doing for so long; I could choose to
be openly, unapologetically, proudly autistic in defiance of the inevitable
repercussions. Though in no way diminishing the very real impact of her
extreme condescension, the conversation forced me to admit to myself that I
did not feel merely patronized but also deeply uncomfortable with the notion
that I, in whatever way, marked myself as autistic without intending to do
so. Bodies with visible markers of disability are long nails, and there is no
shortage of hammers to crush them into submission and compliance. Yet for
all the hammers in the hands of policy makers, service providers, doctors,
and teachers, we too carry heavy, strong hammers forged from shame. We
are taught from a young age to hate ourselves, to hate how we speak and
move and think and feel. We are taught to imitate abled people in the hopes
that we can become so indistinguishable that no one will notice that we are
disabled anymore.

"I would have never guessed." It's supposed to be a compliment. But there
is an enormous amount of violence wrapped into those words—the violence
of indistinguishability philosophy, compliance training, and compulsory
ablenormativity, all of it coalescing into the violence inflicted on autistics
by special education teachers and institutional staff and medical professionals and police and abusers disguised as loving caregivers and partners. It
is extremely difficult to begin to unpack such deeply internalized ableism.
And for all my work in advancing radical disability justice and anti-ableism
theory and organizing, I still find myself in those odd paradoxes of realizing
that I have not, in fact, discarded all of my ableist social conditioning. I
found myself ashamed to be pegged as autistic when I was not intentionally
trying to broadcast autistic, and I found myself ashamed that I still carry the
weight of this stigma with me. How many years of anti-ableism work does it
take to eradicate the ableism inside yourself?

When I was growing up, I didn't flap or rock. The lack of such typified
"stereotyped movements," as defined so impersonally in the *Diagnostic and
Statistical Manual of Mental Disorders*, probably contributed to my late identification. These days, I flap and rock and jump and spin—especially in public
spaces. Performing autistic is a way of staking a claim in autistic identity,
community, culture, and pride. It is a way of communicating solidarity with
fellow autistics, marking myself as a member of the autistic community, and
expressing my pride in my neurological expression. Stimming—short for
"self-stimulatory behavior"—is primarily an instinctual, intuitive way for
autistic people to self-regulate overstimulation. Many autistics also stim to
express other internal states—anxiety, anger, fear, happiness, excitement. But
the stereotypical hand-flapping is now a symbol for autistic pride, used in
place of clapping to respect a common autistic experience of auditory hy-
persensitivity. With this gesture, we have initiated the process of producing

cultural artifacts to demarcate autistic culture as a specific, if indefinable, domain.

For autistics to flap or rock in public, knowing that flapping and rocking mark our bodies as autistic, this is a revolutionary act. Compulsory ablenormativity demands that we strive to the impossible, asymptotic standard of indistinguishability. Failure to conform is construed as laziness and personal failing—*if only you tried harder!* Deliberate refusal to comply with these arbitrarily defined standards of human normality is dangerous and subversive, because such refusal necessarily challenges the legitimacy of the system that demands compliance in the first place. The pathology paradigm of disability rests on a moral obligation to emulate its imagined template for normative, and therefore ideal, human existence. Any deviation from this imagined ablenormativity is evidence of deficiency, defect, or disorder. This pathology paradigm comingles with the capitalist compulsion to quantify human worth by the deeply oppressive standard of productivity. Disabled bodies exist under constant surveillance both by external systems enforcing compulsory ablenormativity and by internalized conditioning to hold ourselves to the same imagined standards. We are not permitted to speak, for even naming our existence is threatening. Disabled movement and communication are dangerous. They must be fought and overcome, both in the arena of rhetoric and in the battleground of our own bodies.

The question becomes not whether autism can speak to name itself and demand its own demise by challenging ablenormativity through its own existence (it cannot) but rather whether we, autistics, can. And autistics are indeed speaking, in voices and signs and movement, loudly and persistently amid the noise of ableist modes of knowledge production. When we create hubs of autistic culture on e-mail lists and Internet forums, we are speaking. When we flap and jump and spin in our homes and in the streets, we are speaking. When we realize, one at a time, that we can unlearn the litany that we are unworthy, damaged, and broken, that in fact, we are *okay*, we are speaking. When we stand beside Autism Speaks walk events with posters and flyers laying claim to the legitimacy of our existence, we are speaking. When we spend long nights sharing excitement and feelings over our passions—passions so often pathologized as perseverative, repetitive interests—we are speaking. When we recognize and celebrate autistics who think in pictures and autistics who think in concepts and autistics whose entire mode of thought is nonverbal and nonlinguistic, we are speaking. When we write essays deconstructing media representation, we are speaking. When we gather in defiance of the presumption that autistics, by definition, cannot socialize, we are speaking. When we build culture and community centered on the simultaneously common and diverse experiences of being autistic, we are speaking.

When we continually survive and resist in the face of overwhelming vio-
lence and pressure to succumb, we, autistics, are speaking—and our speech,
little by little, works to subvert the structural violence of ableism.

NOTES

1. I intentionally reject person-first language (i.e., "person with autism") in favor of identity-first language (i.e., "autistic person" or "autistic") in respect of the widespread preference of those for whom autistic is a politicized identity, including myself.

2. In 2014, Norman Fost sat on an advisory panel to the Food and Drug Administration that convened a hearing to discuss the use of painful electric shock as punishment on disabled people. His comments consisted of repeated justifications for the abusive practices in the name of ameliorating disability. I was personally in attendance along with several other autistic people. The hearing of the FDA's Neurological Devices Panel of the Medical Devices Advisory Committee was convened on April 24, 2014, in Gaithersburg, Maryland, pursuant to docket number FDA-2014-N-0238.

3. See, for example, writings by Jennifer Msumba, a biracial autistic woman who survived seven years of treatment at the JRC, for first-person accounts of the institution's extremist behaviorism and other abusive practices. Msumba blogs at *The REAL Judge Rotenberg Center* (http://jrcabuse.tumblr.com) and authored an exclusive four-part series about her experiences at the JRC for the Autistic Self Advocacy Network (see Msumba 2014a, 2014b, 2014c, 2014d).

4. From its construction in 1895 until 1962, this building served as a depot for cable-powered streetcars. It was originally intended to be Union Station, though today, of course, Union Station in D.C. is the building close to Capitol Hill and not this building in the corner of Georgetown on M Street. (Of course, my notes pander to the autistic.)

REFERENCES

Autism Speaks. 2009. "Neighbors." *YouTube*, July 7. Available at http://www.youtube .com/watch?v=7rVX_nSLFtg&feature=channel_page.
———. 2013. *I Want to Say. YouTube*, February 26. Available at https://www.youtube .com/watch?v=Iu3c8fqBQcA.
Autistic Self Advocacy Network. 2012. "ASAN Statement on Upcoming House Autism Hearing." November 21. Available at http://autisticadvocacy.org/2012/11/ asan-statement-on-upcoming-house-autism-hearing.
Baggs, A. 2007. "In My Language." *YouTube*, January 14. Available at https://www.you tube.com/watch?v=JnylM1hI2jc.
Baggs, A. M., P. Schwarz, J. Smith, and L. Tisoncik. 2006. "Who Can Call Themselves Autistic?" *Autistics.org Autism Information Library*. Available at http://web.archive .org/web/20150429093051/http://archive.autistics.org/library/whoisautistic.html.
Baker, D. L. 2011. *The Politics of Neurodiversity: Why Public Policy Matters*. Boulder, CO: Lynne Rienner.
Bingham, J. 2013. "Doctors Put Lower Value on Lives of the Disabled, Study Finds." *The Telegraph*, March 19. Available at http://www.telegraph.co.uk/health/health news/9940870/Doctors-put-lower-value-on-lives-of-the-disabled-study-finds.html.

Buck v. Bell, 274 U.S. 200 (1927).

Disability Rights Wisconsin v. University of Wisconsin Hospital and Clinics, No. 09-CV-2340 (Dane Cnty. Cir. Ct., Wis., May 14, 2009).

Grandin, T., and M. Scariano. 1986. *Emergence: Labeled Autistic*. Novata, CA: Arena.

Gross, Z. 2012. "Killing Words." In *Loud Hands: Autistic People, Speaking*, edited by J. Bascom, 238–240. Washington, DC: Autistic Press.

Guernsey, D. 2006. "Autism's Angels." *Town and Country*, August, pp. 90–101, 131. Available at http://www.autismspeaks.org/docs/Town_and_Country.pdf.

Heslop, P., P. Blair, P. Fleming, M. Hoghton, A. Marriott, and L. Russ. 2013. "Confidential Inquiry into Premature Deaths of People with Learning Disabilities (CIPOLD): Final Report." Available at http://www.bristol.ac.uk/media-library/sites/cipold/migrated/documents/fullfinalreport.pdf.

Kaufman, J. 2007. "Ransom-Note Ads about Children's Health Are Canceled." *New York Times*, December 20. Available at http://www.nytimes.com/2007/12/20/business/media/20child.html.

Liss, J. 2006. "Autism: The Art of Compassionate Living." *AlterNet*, July 10. Available at http://www.alternet.org/story/38631/autism%3A_the_art_of_compassionate_living.

Littlefield, D. 2012. "Mother Admitted Killing Son to Police." *San Diego Union-Tribune*, April 4. Available at http://www.utsandiego.com/news/2012/Apr/04/mother-pleads-not-guilty-killing-son.

Montgomery, C. 2001. "Critic of the Dawn." *Ragged Edge*, no. 2. Available at http://www.raggededgemagazine.com/0501/0501cov.htm.

Msumba, J. 2014a. "JRC Survivor Speaks Out (Part 1)." Autistic Self Advocacy Network, November 17. Available at http://autisticadvocacy.org/2014/11/jrc-survivor-speaks-out-part-1.

———. 2014b. "JRC Survivor Speaks Out (Part 2)." Autistic Self Advocacy Network, November 19. Available at http://autisticadvocacy.org/2014/11/jrc-survivor-speaks-out-part-2.

———. 2014c. "JRC Survivor Speaks Out (Part 3)." Autistic Self Advocacy Network, November 21. Available at http://autisticadvocacy.org/2014/11/jrc-survivor-speaks-out-part-3.

———. 2014d. "JRC Survivor Speaks Out (Part 4)." Autistic Self Advocacy Network, November 24. Available at http://autisticadvocacy.org/2014/11/jrc-survivor-speaks-out-part-4.

———. 2015. Post of behavior sheet. *The REAL Judge Rotenberg Center* (blog), June 14. Available at http://jrcabuse.tumblr.com/post/121539723101/this-was-my-behavior-sheet-from-a-later-time-at.

Ne'eman, A., S. Kapp, and C. Narby. 2013. "Organ Transplantation and People with I/DD: A Review of Research, Policy, and Next Steps." *Autistic Self Advocacy Network Policy Brief*, March. Available at http://autisticadvocacy.org/wp-content/uploads/2013/03/ASAN-Organ-Transplantation-Policy-Brief_3.18.13.pdf.

Neumeier, S. 2012. "Inhumane Beyond All Reason: The Torture of Autistics and Other People with Disabilities at the Judge Rotenberg Center." In *Loud Hands: Autistic People, Speaking*, edited by J. Bascom, 204–219. Washington, DC: Autistic Press.

People v. Frank-McCarron, 934 NE 2d 76 (Ill. App. Ct., 3d Dist. 2010).

Sequenzia, A. 2013. "Autism Speaks, I Want to Say." *Autism Women's Network* (blog), March 28. Available at http://autismwomensnetwork.org/autism-speaks-i-want-to-say.

Sinclair, J. 1993. "Don't Mourn for Us." *Our Voice* 1 (3). Available at http://www.autreat
.com/dont_mourn.html.

Wallis, C. 2009. "'I Am Autism': An Advocacy Video Sparks Protest." *Time*, November 6.
Available at http://www.time.com/time/health/article/0,8599,1935959,00.html.

Williams, M. 2012. "Adults with Autism Tell Congress More Funds Needed for Services."
Washington Post, November 30. Available at http://www.washingtonpost.com/
blogs/on-parenting/post/adults-with-autism-tell-congress-more-funds-needed-for
-services/2012/11/30/f07f1aa2-3a78-11e2-a263-f0ebffed2f15_blog.html.

Wright, S. 2008. "Autism Changes Everything." *Parade*, January 27. Available at
http://web.archive.org/web/20110407083057/http://www.parade.com/articles/
editions/2008/edition_01-27-2008/Autism_Changes_Everything.

———. 2013. "Autism Speaks to Washington: A Call for Action." *Autism Speaks Point
of View*, November 11. Available at http://www.autismspeaks.org/news/news-item/
autism-speaks-washington-call-action.

Afterword

Negotiating the Future

LEILA MONAGHAN

W here now? We hope you have found some resonances in the narratives of this book, by people who have shared a disability, a circumstance, or an outlook, and that these varied accounts have provided a sense of both the challenges of disability and the possibilities that disability may open up. A theme we have returned to again and again is *belonging*, the idea that everyone can have meaningful relationships with family and friends and that some of these strong positive ties can be intimately related to disability in a variety of ways. Disabilities can also open relationships and affinities across a wide variety of differences.

When I started the process of editing this book years ago, I did not consider myself disabled. I was an ally who worked with Deaf communities. But able-bodied is a temporary state. Last year I was diagnosed with and treated for ovarian cancer. First, I was mysteriously ill, losing weight and throwing up in reaction to dust or cat hair; finally, I was diagnosed and swept into surgery and then eighteen weeks of chemotherapy. Chemo was hard. On a few bad days, it was physically difficult to get out of my chair. Other days, I leaned on a cane and walked so slowly that elderly women made way for me. I took great comfort, however, in my knowledge of disability communities, in the right to be among people but also to be different.

My first public appearance after losing most of my hair was at an American Anthropological Association conference in Denver. I wore fabulous hats to make up for my unfabulous hair, and my guise slipped seriously only once. At the end of a session, as I made to leave, my turban slid off my head in front of Devva Kasnitz, doyenne of disability studies within anthropology. My reaction was to instantly know that Devva understood what my balding head meant and that she accepted me as I was. I stuck my turban back on, and she calmly asked for my e-mail address so she could make sure I was on the Anthropology Disability Research Network list. This moment was also a perfect indirect acceptance into the vibrant community of anthropologists with disabilities.

Relationships and commonalities open up a new way of considering disabilities outside traditional models such as the moral, medical, or social models. The work of Devva Kasnitz, the authors of this book, and many other scholars shows how we need to move away from seeing disability through static models and instead focus on a sociocultural approach, a process of perceiving and experiencing the world rather than applying a schema. This approach, in turn, can help us overcome some of the gaps in traditional theories. As an anthropologist who comes to disability studies from Deaf studies, I have long been struck by how much of the literature on disability has focused either on individual experiences or on issues with society at large. The many memoirs in the field reflect individual engagement with a wide range of disabilities. The highlighting of disability rights activists' impact on large-scale social reform, including the creation and enforcement of laws and regulations such as the Americans with Disabilities Act, reflects a larger societal model. In anthropology and Deaf studies, however, the focus is on intermediate groups between the person and institutions or governments. There, we look at people in communities, such as fellow graduates of a Deaf school, and try to understand the importance of these relationships.

The essays presented in *Barriers and Belonging* reflect both the tradition of memoirs and wide-scale social activism, but they also show how the recognition of disability as a unique way to experience the world is a crucial part of creating communities and making "affirming spaces." The authors write about both the challenges they have faced from the institutions they inhabit and the strength they have received from family, friends, and new disability-oriented institutions. As the chapters make clear, genuine acceptance is a precious thing. Even in the most private relationships, such as within a family, the authors find that intimacy can be a source of great strength and, conversely, the setting of their first experiences of stigmatization because of their disabilities.

Part of a sociocultural approach involves understanding that disabilities are often about communication. To understand any set of relationships, we need to look not only at the relationships themselves but at the information that flows through these ties. Just as families live within a larger social structure and the connected normative expectations, so do any relationships and the communication they produce. One step to opening up this issue is understanding that not only are there differences between disabled and nondisabled people, but there is variation among disabled people as well. Authors also discuss negotiating between stereotypes and expectations, on the one hand, and their own realities, often including an embrace of disability as a normal and powerful way to be in the world, on the other. The pieces in the final sections point the way toward a more inviting, inclusive social fabric, in which the strengths of people with disabilities become essential building blocks for identity, community, and grounded theory, even in the face of challenges such as stigma, rejection, and sometimes abuse so severe it becomes murder.

So what can you take away from all the lessons and insights of these chapters? First, the stories of ordinary people coping with the complications of disabilities are powerful ways to learn about disabilities. Individual stories convey nuances that broad summaries of experience just cannot convey. Second, complexity is at the heart of understanding disabilities. Recognizing that disability adds complicated layers to life, and that these complexities can be positive rather than negative, allows us to see disabilities as gateways to new, interesting, and fulfilling lives not often imagined within narrow able-bodied and able-minded perspectives. Third, a concentration on relationships is closely connected to a call to come together for social and political reasons. Disability rights activism is an essential part of tearing down barriers and creating new opportunities. Finally, everyone has experiences with disability, whether from firsthand experiences through close relationships or through observations of a world often not built for people with disabilities. This means that everyone has powerful insights to add to this conversation. This book's strength is its diversity and multiple perspectives, and it adds to a growing, rich tapestry of disability narratives that must be taken into account as we imagine and reorient our collective future. For me, these multiple perspectives helped me negotiate pain, medical visits, and hair as unruly as that of the children's book character Eloise. While I am back to considering myself temporarily able-bodied, I am deeply grateful for ongoing disability communities.

Index